Friends & Memories

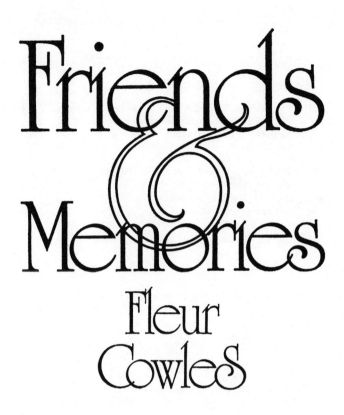

Friends & Memories

Fleur Cowles

REYNAL & COMPANY
in association with
WILLIAM MORROW AND COMPANY, INC.
NEW YORK   1978

Originally published in Great Britain by
Jonathan Cape Ltd. in 1975.

Printed in the United States of America.

1   2   3   4   5   6   7   8   9   10

Library of Congress Cataloging in Publication Data

Cowles, Fleur.
    Friends & memories.

    Includes index.
    1. Cowles, Fleur.   2. United States—Biography
3. England—Biography.   I. Title.
CT275.C8553A34   1978   909.82 [B]   77-83826
ISBN 0-688-61200-8

To Tom

To love is nothing

To be loved is something

To love and be loved

Is everything

> found scratched on the door of a
> deserted chapel in Galaxidi
> in Greece

Contents

Introduction   11

White House Occupants   15

Introduction   17
The White House: post-war   19
Herbert Hoover: Depression President   27
The Other Roosevelt   29
The Johnson Family   32

In Publishing   41

Introduction   43
Look Magazine Years   47
About *Flair* Magazine   51
Early Watergate: Senator Joseph McCarthy   57
Panmunjon: a visit to the Korean war front   61

Painting Section   67

Introduction   69
I Began to Paint   72
Georges Braque: the secret 'vice' in his life   77
Graham Sutherland: we discuss his 'lost' portrait of Sir
    Winston Churchill   80
Camille Bombois: a great painter 'repays a debt' to me   89
Rufino Tamayo: the making of a portrait   92
Pablo Picasso: is he a giver?   95
Enrico Donati: a painter joins a union   97
Paul Dufau: the shy farmer   99
Salvador Dali: a respectable art hoax   105

The England I Know   109

Introduction   111
My Appointment as Ambassador to the Coronation of
   Queen Elizabeth II   113
Life in Albany: where I live   122
Sussex: living in the country   127
An Evening in 1948 on the House of Commons Terrace   130

Important Gentlemen   133

Introduction   135
Gamal Abdel Nasser: the man I knew   137
Bernard M. Baruch: a girl's best friend   143
Winston Churchill: this is the story that wasn't   151
Oswaldo Aranha: the 'Churchill' of Brazil   156
Assis de Chateaubriand: the eccentric modern Robin Hood   164

Big Little Women   171

Introduction   173
Evita Perón: female rabble-rouser   176
Margaret Thompson Biddle: Renaissance woman   181
Madame Chiang Kai-shek: 'the greatest man in Asia'   184
Marilyn Monroe: how she took London   188
Conchita Cintron: first lady of the bull-ring   197
Baroness Blixen: Isaak Dinesen, teller of tales   204

Camera Collection   211

Introduction   213

The Birth of a Hospital   233

Introduction   235
John Converse: how reconstructive facial surgery got its   236
   chance
Jacqueline Auriol: a new face for a brave woman   244

Anecdotal Carousel   249

Introduction   251
Salvador Dali: the hazards of visiting him   253

Why I wrote my Book about Juan and Evita Perón   256
Mr Wiseman and his Singing Dogs   265
Muscat: a sultan's decision   269
Royal Dinners: feasting a king and queen   275
Pope John: a surprise meeting   277
A Surrealist Welcome at Durham University   280
Rio de Janeiro: a pilot answers my plea   284

    Interesting Talk   287

Introduction   289
Nixon and Alger Hiss   291
Harold Macmillan and Charles de Gaulle   295
A London Banker: a classic in banking tales   297
The Duke of Windsor: a luncheon in the Bois   299

    Last Word   301
    Index   303

Camera Collection

pages 211-232

1   Fleur Cowles with her first plane
2   With President Eisenhower
3   With Bernard Baruch
4   With Sir Stafford and Dame Isobel Cripps
5   *Flair* magazine
6   Cartoons inspired by the publication of *Flair* magazine
7   In a printing plant choosing paper for the new magazine
8   With President Vargas and Oswaldo Aranha of Brazil
9   With President Magsaysay
10   With Cary Grant in Spain
11   With Perle Mesta
12   Waiting to appear on TV with Carl Sandburg
13   Mr Wiseman with two of his 'singing' dogs
14   With President Nasser in his villa near Cairo
15   At the Feast of Ramadhan
16   The Shah of Iran in 1952
17   The son of Prince Abdorreza (and nephew of the Shah) aged two
18   King Paul of Greece with his daughters
19   At the marriage of Juan Carlos, now King of Spain
20   Marilyn Monroe and Bertha Stafford Vester
21   With Mendès-France
22   Fleur Cowles at home, painting

Introduction

This is a book of anecdotes. I love telling stories. My friends have paid me the compliment of urging me to write them down rather than continue adding them to the verbal sounds already accumulating in the atmosphere.

There is a fascinating theory that we shall one day be able to push a button and listen in on a Cleopatra talking to Mark Antony, or a Hadrian to his lovers — that all conversations presumably float about bottled-up in space, waiting for a simple electronic device to make them audible. True or not, the printed word does have known advantages, especially in one's own life-time — so I've finally written the anecdotal carousel which follows.

The telling of anecdotes gives one an artful dodge away from the abused literary exercise called the autobiography, which, other than in exceptional instances, can turn into an attempt at making a fortune and losing friends. Many things are indeed better left unsaid, including all that is private and confidential. Since my life was once lived in a goldfish bowl, I have no intention of dredging up anything private.

Mine is a typical American success story of a career during and just after the last war. It was easy then, and it still is now, for a woman to rise to the top in the United States. I've had an uncommon life (full of good luck) as a reporter, editor, magazine-creator, author and 'unofficial diplomat' (that American anomaly). In 1959 I added painting to my activities. I have always been an irrepressible traveller, totting up precious friendships *en route*. My present life is divided between three homes in two countries.

Altogether, these things have led to a mental trunkful of stories, a highly personal collection.

This book is written entirely from memory. I used to have total recall and, though I could cry now for that once magical asset, flashes of the old skill remain. I have never kept a diary or made notes but have mentally filed away the things that meant most to me. Others have passed like sand through the network of my brain.

I once taught myself a technique for 'storing' conversations: first I'd tuck away the whole visual situation, making a mental photograph of all persons involved in the conversation; most important, I had to 'stow' the first words spoken. Once done, I could count on the whole experience flowing out on command. I used to report to President Eisenhower in this fashion, sitting before him in the White House after a trip made at his request. What I wore, where I sat (who said *what* first) had to be called to mind. Once done, everything else came rushing into focus and I could repeat conversations verbatim.

Many early personal letters from important people whom I might have wanted to quote here are lost, having dropped out of sight when shipped from my *Look* offices in New York City to the London home where I came to live after marrying Tom Montague Meyer in 1955.

Everything I describe here happened after I became an adult. And this is as good a place as any to admit that I started my career at such a tender age I had to add six years to my real one in order to be accepted professionally. I have been officially toting these extra years around ever since I was seventeen.

Though I've had some highly interesting White House assignments, I've written only of personal experiences, without describing any confidential chores involved. I hope I've controlled any urge to take revenge on the few who've been unkind to me, with the result that this book should entirely lack the malice which so often seasons an autobiography. Making this decision may be one of my best human achievements to date.

The text is divided into nine separate sections, each with its own introduction. Since the 'professional' overlapped the 'private' during one period of my life, I've included a brief reference to my marriage to Gardner ('Mike') Cowles and how it led to my marriage to *Look* magazine; also my own version of the birth and death of the controversial but prideful *Flair* magazine, which I created and edited for its short and colourful span of life. These facts, I decided, were better left *said*.

I once received a letter from Christina Foyle, director of Foyle's Booksellers, the remarkable person who presides over London's important Literary Luncheons. I had sent her a cutting from an American newspaper with Alan Pryce-Jones's witty but somewhat acerbic review of an autobiography of her most recent Luncheon guest of honour. She wrote back: 'What a very funny review of the Gulbenkian book ... It is quite dangerous to venture into print.'

It's an awesome thought.

London   FLEUR COWLES
1974

Friends & Memories

White House Occupants

I GOT my first White House assignment immediately after Harry S. Truman became President. Like most good things in my life, a White House assignment fell into my lap without my trying, due to friends. I was one of the volunteers writing speeches for the War Production Board and other war agencies. Though very young, I was sharp-witted enough to wangle a permit to fly to Europe after VE Day, to be referred to thereafter as the first civilian American woman to get into Europe after the fighting stopped.

This label gave me the status which helped me into the White House as Special Consultant to the Famine Emergency Committee, as the only full-time member of the group assisting Herbert Hoover, its chairman.

Since these thrilling days, I have come to know the White House and many of the occupants well, some while in office and others after they left. I went back to the White House under many other circumstances, mainly as a journalist, but often on White House assignments for President Eisenhower, including many in connection with the Cyprus question.

Whatever time I spent in the White House is still so sharply etched on my consciousness that I can't help relating one fact to Watergate. In my time, I never knew anyone who didn't want whatever he did to be brought to the President's attention — whether of consequence or ridiculous. 'Apple-polishing' got a slice of everyone's time. You 'told the President', or saw to it that someone else 'told it to him'. A pat on the back or a thumbs-up sign from 'the Boss' was manna from heaven to every member of the overworked staff (and at every level).

Of the Presidents I've encountered, I knew best of all Dwight D. Eisenhower, but I most enjoyed my time with Harry Truman, whom I really got to know after he left the White House.

Although I served the austere ex-President Herbert Hoover on the 'Famine' Committee, I knew him not at all until he moved to New York City. He must have developed a warm spot in his heart for me after that—which I was fortunate enough to tap eventually. I also got to know Eleanor Roosevelt in post White House days, when she, too, came to New York to live after F.D.R.'s death. Lyndon Baines Johnson was a long-time acquaintance who (with his family) became a good friend after he had left Washington.

President Eisenhower was most generous and kind to me. That fabled smile may have evoked Bernard Baruch's remark that 'behind Ike's grin was a man of iron', but like millions of others all over the world, I couldn't resist it.

The extraordinary Dr Kissinger, the first man to combine the jobs of Presidential Adviser and the special envoy who carried out his own advice both in the White House and as Secretary of State, I knew first in 1954 at Harvard University, when invited by him to speak there.

The stories, anecdotes and opinions that follow are of mixed length, differing in form and content, as did my contacts with the persons involved.

The White House: post-war

I owe so much to Dwight D. Eisenhower for the fascinating experiences he made possible for me while he was President. He appointed me Ambassador to the Coronation of Queen Elizabeth II; he sent me (as that American phenomenon, a presidential agent) to Greece and England on the Cyprus issue, spanning a year and a half of effort; I went on fascinating assignments for him to Gamal Abdel Nasser, President of Egypt, also to Getulio Vargas, President of Brazil, where doors were always opened so splendidly for me by that great Brazilian, Oswaldo Aranha. Many of these experiences are written about elsewhere. I've been decorated for three of them.

Everything Dwight Eisenhower tried in his lifetime (soldiering, electioneering, writing, even investing) was touched by luck. He always won, even at poker. The man who was a major for sixteen years, promoted by seniority, actually won his four stars through someone's death.

Many people feel, however, that he lost one of his most prized victories, the glory of his great reputation as a peacemaker and a leader, by accepting a second term as President of the United States. If he'd refused (and he did originally yearn to do so), his record as a great American President would be untarnished.

His predecessor, Harry Truman, will probably be regarded as on a par with Lincoln in future accounts of his era. He was a very different figure when he first came to the White House; I was there and saw his insecurity – and then I saw it evaporate, saw his nervousness turn to firm control (occasionally larded with arrogance) in very few months. At Truman's first visit to Congress, he was so unsure of himself, he started to talk immediately. 'Wait!'

admonished Speaker of the House Sam Rayburn. 'Wait, Harry, I have to introduce you first!' Another time, he was so troubled in the troubled world, he told one of his first visitors to the White House, 'The world has fallen on me.'

However he acted and whatever he said, occasionally unquotable, he will remain for me one of the century's greatest figures.

In many ways, Truman's presidency marked the beginning of the end of the non-violent era in which I grew up. Those were the days when danger of assassination didn't accompany the honour of being President—as it automatically does today. There had been one attempt by an insane man to kill Truman, but that never stopped the taciturn President from taking his 'constitutional daily' on the streets of Washington, D.C., or from strolling, at a neat clip, up Park Avenue whenever in New York City for United Nations business. Only one lone detective trailed behind. Truman was the last to know such luxury.

I have a feeling of unreality about my days in Washington in the late 'forties.

In the early winter of 1946, the Famine Emergency Committee was formed by President Truman as one of his first acts in office, on the advice of the Advertising Council in Washington. The Secretary of Agriculture, Clinton Anderson (now an ageing senator from Arizona), had pointed out to the Council that the U.S.A. had not met its commitments to the United Nations Relief Association in providing food for the starving people of Europe.

Eugene Meyer, then publisher of the *Washington Post* (and father of its present publisher, Kay Graham), took the matter immediately to President Truman and the Famine Emergency Committee was created, with Herbert Hoover as Honorary Chairman. Hoover had not set foot in the White House since he stopped being President sixteen years before, but Mr Meyer got him to take the Chair, and I became a working part of that committee as Special Consultant.

Mr Hoover went abroad to see for himself which wheats and fats were needed so desperately. Having just returned myself, I was asked by Drew Dudley, of the Advertising Council, to help. I was not only willing but eager, having left Europe with an overwhelming sense of guilt. When invited to serve the Famine Emergency Committee, I accepted instantly and in a few days moved into the White House as the only full-time member of the group assisting Herbert Hoover.

It was a fascinating job which involved propaganda, marshalling top journalists and top broadcasters to awaken national conscience. And there was a good deal of lobbying to be done to get wheat-growers to give us wheat at the *source*. Through the Commissioner of Education, I organized an event that was a difficult feat (in those days): every schoolchild in the United States listened to a special broadcast in which I asked each one to get his parents to 'set an extra place at their tables and to feed an extra child' – donating the food they didn't actually eat to Europe.

I remember cornering the Secretary of Agriculture, in a White House lift, making him promise to vote in favour (against his strong wish) of an unpopular issue on the agenda at the Famine Emergency Committee's first meeting. I used to go back exhausted to my hotel apartment after fourteen-hour days. The results were worth it; millions of tons of wheat were shipped almost immediately to Europe. They were enormously exciting days, not only for me but for my two colleagues, Drew Dudley and Charles Jackson.

Recently I looked at a clipping of an interview I gave to the *Washington Post*, dated August 7th, 1946. When asked by Martha Ellyn why I worked so hard, I had replied, 'To get back my peace of mind.'

In Europe, I had tried to find missing friends who had fled into hiding. After three months in England, France, Holland and Belgium, I was so distressed by the unspeakable bomb-destruction, the haunted faces and so many indescribable stories, I simply had to do something. The memory of terribly exhausted people with grey faces, children with blue-ringed eyes, was impossible to erase. I was the lucky stranger who could go away from it all; none of them could escape. I realized that food was an urgent peace-time need. Being thin for *fashionable* reasons seemed shameful.

In the White House days I saw President Truman mainly at

meetings. But when I think of him now, an exquisite little conversation I had with the ex-President in 1966 in a New York restaurant, crowds out the other impressions.

To tell it I must return to the visit Mr Truman paid to England in June 1956, to receive an honorary degree at Oxford. All Americans, regardless of politics, were aware of his presence.

The university gave him their total attention and a crowded welcome. Mr Truman was in the vivid robe of his new doctorate. Wearing the famous, floppy velvet cap, he looked a very odd and very modest little man, peering at his admirers through those unchanging silver-rimmed, old-fashioned glasses. A large car, flying the stars and stripes, took him everywhere. It was his first and last trip to England. London papers were friendly; people were friendly. As an American, newly arrived in England, I was proud.

So it was quite normal that, sitting beside him at the small luncheon given by Victor and Helen Weybright at the Pavillon Restaurant ten years later, I should ask him why he never returned to London.

'Why should I do that?' he retorted.

'Because people love you there,' I replied. 'Have you any idea what an impact you made during the Oxford visit?'

'No, I haven't. You don't mean to say I'm really popular in England?'

'Just come back and find out. It would make your heart feel good,' I insisted with a broad smile.

'Are you *sure*?' he demanded seriously.

'Of course I am,' I said firmly.

'Do me a favour, will you?' Mr Truman asked, pressing his hand firmly on mine. 'Do me a great favour.'

'Of course, Mr President. Anything! What would you like me to do?'

'Go and tell Bess,' he beseeched.

And I did. I walked around the table of six and changed places for a few minutes with my husband, to talk to his wife. I left Mrs Truman beaming.

The next time I saw Harry Truman was when we were both in Athens for the funeral of King Paul of Greece. He and Lady Bird

Johnson were there to represent President Johnson and the American people.

The funeral proceedings were exhausting, and particularly for the elderly. We had assembled at an early hour in the lovely Orthodox church lying at the foot of Athens. After the long ritualistic mass, the King's coffin was raised from the altar to be carried on the shoulders of his devoted friends, who walked slowly from the church steps to the top of Athens. All of it was *uphill*, amid huge crowds.

Guests moved on foot behind the coffin on the arduous journey. Representatives of much of the world's remaining royalty were in the procession, as well as heads of state and government representatives. Leading it, and holding a heavy, sacred icon high, was the stalwart Archbishop of Greece, over ninety years of age.

At the apex of the hill, just outside the Hilton Hotel, a catafalque took the coffin. Guests were driven to Tatoi, the royal family's country home, which nestles in the hills outside Athens. Following the army vehicle, the elegant procession made its way to the house, a journey which normally, driving fast, took forty minutes. Luncheon was served when the guests were fully assembled, but it was very late in the day.

The next morning, I asked if I could pay my respects to Mr Truman, who was installed at the Hilton Hotel. He hardly knew me. I was shocked by the change and how he'd aged, but he was his usual bluff, direct self after I made it clear who the 'Fleur' calling on him happened to be.

'I was distressed to think of you on that long, hard climb through Athens on those packed streets, up those hills.'

'Who was tired? Not me. *Who walked?* I sat in my comfortable limousine, just behind everyone!' he announced.

'Oh, that's very good news. I'm delighted someone thought that one out. But what about *food*? You must have starved before you ate again after such an early breakfast?'

'Who *starved*? Not me! I had my own bag of chicken sandwiches!'

Some years later, Eve and Henry Labouisse and my husband and I reminisced about that visit. We were in Greece on a holiday, dining at a resort hotel overlooking the sea outside Athens. Mr Labouisse (now head of UNICEF) had been American Ambassador to Greece when the King died, and he and Mrs Labouisse had been at the airport to meet the American delegation.

The Labouisses took Mr Truman in their car. Knowing how exhausted he must have been, they explained that it was a quick trip to the hotel. 'Hell, no!' Mr Truman answered, 'I want to go to the Acropolis first!'

'But it's a steep climb and it's such a hot day! We don't recommend it,' Mrs Labouisse pointed out.

'Never mind! I've been waiting a long time for this visit. I want to go *now*!' he insisted.

Up they went, and fast – Harry Truman like a mountain goat, full of energy and excitement. He knew all about the history of the Acropolis as well as its architectural details. That isn't surprising: actually he was a very fine historian. Dean Acheson once said that Harry Truman knew more history than Roosevelt and Churchill together.

He didn't seem at all tired when he was finally deposited at his hotel rooms in Athens, despite the climb after the wearying flight from the U.S.A.

I once asked Mr Truman what *he* considered was the most important single act he made as President. Without hesitation, he replied, 'My decision to go into Korea.' The move was his retort to the first major thrust of the Soviets: 'Because we had not included South Korea in the written list of Asian areas we would defend. So the North Koreans moved in. We had to get them out!'

Truman needed courage to declare war, but he preferred to do it through the United Nations and in this way, wittingly or otherwise, prevented a Vietnam. He lived to see a truce in his time.

After he had called all his advisers together to discuss Korea, he listened, blinking his eyes and saying nothing eloquent for hours. Then he announced, 'The League of Nations collapsed when there was no support for Abyssinia. If you're going to keep the U.N. alive, we're going into South Korea – *tomorrow*!'

I often think of his enemies (and they are legion) and ask myself what justification they have. Generally, it is because of his controversial decision to use the A-Bombs – and to drop not one, but two, on two different cities. Even those who accept the claim that only the A-Bomb could end the war still ask themselves (as I do) *why two bombs? Why two cities?* Wouldn't capitulation have followed after one city had been destroyed?

The decision, which this small, lonely man made in a vast War Room where the real control of the war existed, was as momentous as any a president has ever had to take. Despite the continuing debate (and the distress of many who still feel an uninvolved but personal guilt), Truman himself quickly wrote Hiroshima and Nagasaki off: to him, it was *an essential artillery tactic,* done to save the lives of 100,000 American men who would otherwise have been mown down as they waded through the lapping waters of Japanese beach-heads.

'I have no qualms. Never lost any sleep over it since,' the President tersely maintained. Once he made a decision, he always sent it on a 'one-way' journey in his own mind.

Harry S. Truman died just after Christmas in 1972, aged 88. *The Times* obituary described him as a 'President of great decisions and little failures' — a remarkable seven-word appraisal of a man remembered just as much for his foibles as for his unexpected acts of courage and vision.[1]

His death brought to light the touching and little-known letter he wrote to his mother, Martha Truman, on April 12th, 1945, when Roosevelt died. 'Dear Mama, It was the only time in my life, I think, that I ever felt as if I'd had a real shock. I hurried to the White House to see the President, and when I arrived I found I was the President. No one in the history of our country ever had it happen to him in just that way.'

Oh yes, I think Harry Truman was a wonderful man. If I were to write his obituary, it wouldn't be long:

This man, before the war was over, organized the group to help produce wheat for the hungry Allies. I was part of this effort. I shall be forever grateful to him for this experience.

He ordered the go-ahead for the United Nations;

[1] In 1973, Senator Barry Goldwater, himself once a Republican candidate for the Presidency, said of Democrat Truman that 'he will probably go down in history as the best president of the century'.

He went to the U.N. to protect South Korea, preventing the war from becoming a solo United States action;

He stopped Tito from moving into Trieste;

He inaugurated the Marshall Plan (and who can deny that this saved Europe after the fighting ended?);

He sent the Mediterranean fleet into the Persian Gulf and headed off a Soviet thrust into Iran;

He concluded the NATO Treaty (and nothing better has yet superseded it in Europe);

He gave the 'go-ahead' to the Berlin Airlift – 'to prove to the Commies we aren't fooling about our rights in Central Europe';

He fired General MacArthur;

He was an old-fashioned family man;

And the Presidency didn't go to his head.

Herbert Hoover: Depression President

The unsmiling Mr Hoover, known by his enemies as the 'Depression President' (Roosevelt inherited America's great financial crash after succeeding him), was a far more complex figure than his dour public image revealed.[1] Considered humourless and arid, his wit must, in fact, have been biting. I like to quote his remark when he was asked his opinion of Senator Taft, once a candidate for the American presidency. Hoover promptly replied: 'He has the most brilliant mind in Congress – until he makes it up.' That remark still serves me over dinner-tables, putting new faces and names to it.

People thought the ex-President was awesomely remote; unless you knew him (and that was difficult to do) he had a fairly off-putting personality. Time showed he was warm enough to concern himself inexplicably over a modest need of mine.

Once, when we were dining with him at his Waldorf Towers Hotel suite, he turned from a piece of history he was recounting in praise of Nixon, to question me about my work.

When I explained that I was running several homes, working at *Look* and *Flair* magazine from nine till seven daily, entertaining constantly and travelling equally often, he seemed quite flabbergasted. 'I can only assume you have a remarkable secretary,' he responded.

'No, Mr President. The problem is that though I have two secretaries, one of them isn't worth her desk-space!'

'But that's not good enough,' he answered. 'I must see if I can help.' About three weeks later, a letter was delivered by hand.

---

[1] Whoever said that 'no one on earth really liked Herbert Hoover except, possibly, Mrs Hoover', overlooked Harry Truman who was his warm friend until Hoover's death in 1964.

27

Dear Mrs Mike,
　　I have found you a secretary.
　　　　　　Sincerely,

　　　　　　　　　HERBERT R. HOOVER

The woman he provided had, indeed, superior qualities. He took the time to interview her personally after other candidates had been weeded out by his own secretary. She proved to be a remarkable right hand for one precious year until marriage took her from New York. She was followed by two remarkable women, both still good friends, Gertrude Chase and Aina Townsend.

The Other Roosevelt

When I finally met Eleanor Roosevelt she was a busy woman, crowding her days with merciless activity at an uncheckable pace. She was one of this century's unique women, the person who made Franklin D. Roosevelt tick. Without this earnest wife, F.D.R.'s natural love of the good things of life might have interfered with his eagerness to change the face of America. Some people say Eleanor Roosevelt sacrificed being a good mother to her five children to do so — but if she did, she exchanged a handful of her own children for millions belonging to others in a troubled world.

It is impossible to forget the first story I ever heard about Eleanor Roosevelt, which came rushing to mind the very first time we met (at least twenty years after the event). It had been told to me as a wide-eyed teenager by a lady journalist whom I used to regard with unwarranted idolatry. She described a State Democratic gathering for Eleanor Roosevelt after F.D.R. was elected Governor of New York State.

The reporter made her way to the friendly lady (who, we now know from her own written account, was actually desperately nervous and shy). 'What', the reporter asked her somewhat sarcastically, 'are *you* planning for your husband now that he has become Governor?'

'To make him President of the United States,' Eleanor Roosevelt instantly replied, with a toothy smile.

As one grew to know more about Eleanor Roosevelt, such a retort was not only to be expected but to be respected for its simple candour: you asked a question, you got a direct answer, and an accurate one, as this proved. Few doubt that her efforts, combined with Louis McHenry Howe (F.D.R.'s gnome-like political adviser), played a major role in delivering the presidency to Franklin D. Roosevelt. Louis McHenry weighed less than eight stone: he was a tiny wrinkled man with fascinating power in the Roosevelt inner circle. The two were a formidable pair.

America has produced many remarkable ladies, but never one so prodigious as Eleanor Roosevelt. She was not unlike two other famous Roosevelts: one was her own husband, Franklin D. Roosevelt (who was her fifth cousin), and the other was her imposing Uncle Theodore who boldly stole the show from the stars when he attended her wedding.

Even today few people are indifferent to Eleanor Roosevelt. I still feel the reverberations when talking about her. Amid the smiles of approval there are, just as frequently, the snorts of contempt, mainly from men who can hardly, twenty-five years later, shrug off their hate for the name Roosevelt.

The governor's lady made good her early claim to the journalist! Not only did her husband become President, but he was America's first crippled, paralysed President, and he had four terms, more than any other President. He died after becoming mentally (and even more physically) disabled by strokes. During nearly sixteen years of office, beginning with America's financial collapse in 1929 and ending with the Second World War, his wife's activities and views were always germane to his programme.

Her genuine compassion for the have-nots certainly helped mould the master-plan for F.D.R.'s historic New Deal. She got the credit she deserved — but paid for it in equal doses of hatred. Boos followed her as well as applause. Fortunately, she made her reputation before violence was introduced into heckling.

She also became a symbol of America's matriarchal society (which earned the name of 'The Generation of Vipers' after an acerbic book by Philip Wylie). It is odd that such a reputation came to a woman so totally devoid of beauty, but it did. Nevertheless, the shy girl (already known as an ugly duckling) did marry the handsomest catch in her own family — the man who probably invented the word 'charisma' in politics — and became the leading woman in the U.S.A., if not the world, in her lifetime.

After F.D.R.'s death, her activities were so much more exhausting that White House days must have seemed calm in retrospect: she became a member of the U.S. delegation to the United Nations, the Chairman of the Human Rights Commission, a post that carried great prestige; she was a regular radio broadcaster, wrote a daily syndicated newspaper column, 'My Day' (into which she poured a mixture of superficial thoughts and keen journalism), and even found time in 1951 to write a book called *On My Own*.

It was in the years after she'd left the White House that I got to know her, seeing her as she darted in and out of New York City. I found her far from the 'egghead' she was often dubbed in derision. In fact, she describes her lack of erudition in her book: 'Only a third-year college student could ever understand Walter Lippmann, anyone who had gone through fifth grade in school could understand my column.' Such an admission wasn't odd; Eleanor Roosevelt simply didn't care what people thought or said about her.

She loved words, and had a way of learning new ones, which she explained to me in detail. 'Do as I do,' she urged. 'Open your dictionary blindly the last thing every evening. Let your finger rest on a word. If it is a word you already know, close the book and start again. If it is new to you, study it, absorb its meaning, go to sleep with it (your brain will work on it during the night) and be sure to use it in a sentence during the following day. Once you've used the word, it remains a part of your vocabulary.'

I followed her example and for years used my dictionary in her way, putting countless new words to use. I cannot open a dictionary without thinking of her; *this* is not a bad way to remember an ex-President's widow.

The Johnson Family

I saw Lyndon B. Johnson close to the time of his death; in October of 1971 I went to stay on the L.B.J. ranch. It was the first time I had visited the President since shaking his hand briefly and having an impertinent little stolen conversation with him whilst moving slowly in a receiving line in the White House in 1967. I had flown over from London, one of three guests from England (Lord and Lady Bessborough were the other two), to attend Lynda Bird's wedding in the White House.

In the receiving line, I whispered to President Johnson:

'May I have five minutes tomorrow with you before I fly back to England?'

The weary President, who was perspiring over his make-up, still under TV cameras, replied with a grin, 'Hell, no! Tomorrow's Sunday, I'm going to Texas for a rest. Ask me what you want now.'

'*Now?*' I asked. 'O.K., why don't we stop spending so much on bombing Vietnam and put the money into housing instead?'

'Because Congress won't vote for it,' he whispered as I moved on my way.

I saw Mrs Johnson a year or so later, first, when she came to England with her daughter Luci to launch *White House Story*, and when she visited us in Spain. Everyone who met them when I entertained for them was immensely impressed, first of all by Mrs Johnson's good looks, which let her down in most photographs. Then for her directness, her curiosity, and her well-informed views. The far from shy Luci bowled one over by her frankness, particularly on politics. (Her sister, Lynda Bird Robb, has the same appeal.) This amusing young woman, whose personal independence led her to change religion while her father was still in the White House, had equally independent and quite passionate views on the American political scene, which she revealed without hesitation. Very much like her father.

My trip to the L.B.J. ranch a year later followed a journey that Princess Grace, Prince Rainier and I took to Texas, for the Nieman-Marcus 'Fêtes des Fleurs' in Dallas (in which my paintings were featured), officially opened by the royal pair.

After the festivities, we parted for very different destinations; Princess Grace and Prince Rainier to Iran for the Shah's 2,000th anniversary celebration at Persopolis, and I, in a beautiful little jet lent by Eugene McDermott, to fly to Austin in Texas to visit the Johnsons.

A few days of Dallas wall-to-wall wealth had been a splendid foil for the relative simplicity I found at L.B.J.'s plain, white-washed clapboard house on a ranch on the Padernales River, fifty miles from the Texas capital. Not a Renoir in sight.

Mrs Johnson was waiting on the tarmac at Austin airport full of welcome despite my late arrival (we had had trouble locating the private plane-port). 'Lunch is ready for us at the club,' she announced as we were whisked off in her car with a half-apology for the haste, which was, after all, my fault. 'I hope you'll enjoy the club. It is one of our show places. And I have interesting people waiting to meet you there.'

Among them was the former White House adviser to L.B.J., a relaxed and tanned Walt Rostow. The famed Vietnam-hawk, now teaching at the L.B.J. School of Public Affairs in the University of Texas, explained that being an educator gives a man time 'to write books about his political theories – and that's just what I'm doing.'

At the end of the meal, by some invisible signal to which I soon grew accustomed, word came through to clue Lady Bird in to the President's whereabouts in Austin. We were to meet him and fly together to the ranch in the afternoon; everything in between had been precisely organized. From lunch we went to visit the L.B.J. Library, our time so allotted that we could go through it at leisure and still be at the airport to meet the President at his plane.

The great L.B.J. Library, which someone once described as the

Pyramid of Texas, rises high above its landscape, six floors of cream-coloured travertine boldly set on a knoll of terraced green grass and trees. It cost nineteen million dollars to build, the most expensive and impressive of the five presidential libraries in existence. Since most of the expense has been paid by the University of Texas, there is no admission charge and it is open seven days a week. It is always crowded.

Until his death, the President himself was the Library's chief magnet. Everyone who visited there had a very real chance of meeting him, shaking his hand and 'chatting things up'. The President liked to come and go to his office on the top floor without notice, and since his unexpected arrivals became well known, people tended to look over their shoulders to see if he was coming along instead of looking straight ahead.

The main architectural feature of the Library is its display of the collection of presidential papers, on five floors behind a glass wall. Forty-three thousand huge, red buckram boxes (each with its impressive gold presidential seal) contain the letters, documents, minutes of meetings, notes, reports from the advisers and all records of conversations with L.B.J. Thirty-one million papers.

Lady Bird and I stood at the bottom of the magnificent stairway and looked five floors up at the backs of these forty-three thousand boxes. This enormous mound of décor, I thought, is *history*. 'Packaged history' inside bright red covers in stacks which, though never open to the public, are made available in part to scholars and researchers; by 1975, all that is non-classified will be theirs to see.

I felt that those rows and rows of boxes were too abstract; they evoked no quickening of the heart. I longed to give them 'life', to spoil their flawless symmetry with a sweep of my hand. 'Couldn't one volume be blown up to giant proportions, its contents enlarged, so the public would understand what was inside the other 42,999 red backs?' I asked. 'Otherwise they seem to me to be pure visual decoration.' Both agreed, and the suggestion may well be taken up.

The rest of the Library is homelier, full of gaily presented (even 'talking') displays. The President's White House office and private family room are reproduced. So are life-size models of Lynda

34

Bird and Luci in their wedding-gowns. The biggest attraction of all is the reproduction of the White House Oval Office (rimmed in bullet-proof glass). A similar replica is in the Truman Library in Independence, Missouri.

'It didn't take long for this building to become the most visited of all Presidential Libraries. In its first month of existence, more than 300,000 visitors have poured in,' Lady Bird explained to us as we went on our way to her own office on the top floor, near L.B.J.'s. The room has her stamp: it is feminine, efficient, welcoming, all her personal characteristics.

Nothing could have been better timed than my husband's telephone call from London (which had been chasing me from place to place in Texas). When finally tracked down in Lady Bird's office, I sat behind her desk trying to convey to him some of this special corner of Texas.

Just after I hung up, a signal was flashed. 'The President is on his way to the airport.' We left immediately and soon all met at the front of his private plane. With a grip which my hand will always recall, L.B.J. gave me an all-embracing greeting. 'Come on in, we're heading for home!' he announced with a broad grin as he helped me leap up the plane's stairs.

Lady Bird motioned me to a single seat with its back to the pilot. The President sat down opposite me; his secretary sat across the aisle with Mrs Johnson. A table came down between L.B.J. and me and in those twenty precious minutes before we landed, a huge pile of mail was examined and sorted.

Mail obviously poured in. When I returned to London I remembered those two dividing the stacks into 'urgent', 'not so urgent' and 'not at all important'. I gulped every time I got an immediate reply to a letter. The attractive secretary, Mrs Dale Malechek (wife of the late President's ranch-manager), must have had a hard time competing for the President's attention to deal with the mountainous pile.

One of L.B.J.'s fleet of cars was waiting on the tarmac. They included a 1910 model 'T' Ford, which he loved. Ours was air-conditioned, long and sleek. L.B.J. took the wheel for the short distance from the landing strip (called Johnson City) to the door.

The cosy white house (sitting well amid its 330 acres) is

dominated by a red oak tree which is three centuries old. After Dallas's tales of multi-thousand acres, this was small.

Early in December 1972, the house and more than two hundred acres (as well as a four-mile stretch along the Padernales River) were donated to the National Park Service. Meanwhile, Mrs Johnson continues to live on the ranch, tours being limited to the exterior of most buildings. Tourists in buses often get a wave from her as she comes and goes.

Though the L.B.J. home was vaguely like an armed camp, few signs of protection were obvious.[1] The ranch looked and acted like any modestly successful farm in the centre of a small county. Delicious, wholesome food came from the kitchen; chintzes and comfortable chairs were everywhere in a home which reeked of family life. Everything was dominated by the Big Man's personality and his presence.

Its visitors, in fact, did set it just as much apart as its owners and their guards. When the President was alive, the caller might be South Vietnam's Nguyen Cao Ky, or the Columbia Broadcasting television gentlemen and their crew, or, another day, Henry Kissinger. Interestingly enough, he used to fly regularly between the White House and the ex-President, bringing him the sort of White House briefing which was instigated by John Kennedy after taking over from Eisenhower. 'I insist on brief reports from Kissinger. I don't want to wade through too many words,' Mr Johnson told me.

The traffic in big names was high but it didn't alter the scene. The President seemed to be living out the final chapter of his life in a merry way; behaving as if he'd turned off the past (without noticeable change in personality).

Behind him were forty years in Washington in differing seats of power, many of them in the dead centre of it. Yet, as the most active of ex-Presidents, he managed to fill the hours in changed but satisfying ways, in a very different white house.

I assume I got the same turns round the ranch which were given all visitors, but it was pleasant to have it in the privacy of the President's company, getting his own pithy (often earthy)

---

[1] Mrs Johnson as a president's widow must, by law, still have armed protection which follows her wherever she goes. Several F.B.I. men came with her when she visited us in 1973.

descriptions about livestock and the land. The ranch table was a favourite of his – not only to preside over but to grow the food for it! The black-eyed peas, potatoes, onions, squash and corn and beans; the fillings for ranch pies, the 'cow-butter' and the 'cow beef'. Mealtimes were great occasions. L.B.J. lovingly absorbed the scene as he surveyed his table, his food and his guests.

Before the farewell dinner given for me by the Johnsons, the sky was full of little planes. Distances are so vast, the private plane is commonplace. The guests leave early to fly very far to their homes. Mr Johnson's toast to me at the end of that meal was heart-warming; after the guests left, he was in no mood to turn off the talk. 'To sleep? Out of the question!' L.B.J. announced. 'The evening's just begun. If you insist on leaving in the morning' (I was headed for a day at the NASA space centre in Houston), 'don't think of rushing off too soon tonight!'

We stayed up quite a long time, Lady Bird and I on a couch facing the restless talker. Confidences oozed and I felt relaxed enough to ask a few questions.

At the time when the Warren Report on President Kennedy's assassination was being prepared, I had flown to Washington to see Chief Justice Earl Warren. There, in those august chambers at the Supreme Court, I'd tried to persuade my old friend to take into account a list I had brought from London. 'These are the questions the Europeans are asking,' I explained. Would the Chief Justice consider them in his report?

Earl Warren (who was also a member of our U.S. delegation to the Coronation of Queen Elizabeth) had been solicitous but dubious. He clearly thought I was overstating people's suspicions; perhaps I was. In any case, he'd explained, my trip was too late. The Report had already been written and was at that moment being printed.

With the memory of that Washington visit, I suddenly turned to L.B.J. and asked, 'May I be impertinent and ask you what your brief was to Earl Warren? Was it to do a "Sherlock Holmes" on the murder of John Kennedy or was it to produce a statement whose principal aim would be to pacify a public which was hysterical at the time of the assassination?'

'Now that's one question, little lady, I won't answer,' L.B.J.

promptly responded. I still wonder if, in fact, he hadn't given me the reply.

One other question concerned a journey he'd intended to make – but didn't – with Clark Clifford before the elections in 1968.[1] The totally unexpected invasion of Czechoslovakia put paid to that possibility. Was its purpose, I asked, to try to settle the Vietnam issue before the elections? And if the trip had been successful (unlikely as that may have been), would it not have elected the man Lyndon Baines Johnson scarcely lifted a finger to help, Hubert Humphrey? Peace in Vietnam would have scotched all complaints about the war and kept the Democrats in office.

'Yes, indeed,' he admitted with a wry smile.

For me, Lyndon B. Johnson will always be remembered for the social legislation which he was able to pass – despite the attempts and failures of his predecessor. Johnson tackled and dealt with America's terrible race problem. His tough fight not only shifted public opinion but the nation's laws as well.

That L.B.J. was a complex animal all who knew him have already testified, but one of the best comments was written by a man who scrutinized him for years, both as a journalist and as a friend: Hugh Sidey, Washington Bureau chief of *Time* magazine. After L.B.J.'s book *The Vantage Point* (1972) was published, Sidey summarized him in this way:

> Lyndon Johnson has seen and heard more of the important affairs of this nation's world than any other living American. He is like Mount Rushmore, a sort of elemental part of the land, shaped by man and events, but enduring.

Lyndon B. Johnson died on January 23rd, 1973, and everyone who knew anything about the companionship of this man and his wife felt very sad for Lady Bird Johnson.

After recently spending some days alone with her in Texas on my second visit to the L.B.J. ranch, I can only marvel at her spirit and character. To me, she is one of the most admirable women alive today.

[1] The theory is that the men in the Kremlin weren't aware of the armys' plans or they wouldn't have let the American President plan a trip to Moscow at that precise moment.

She was anxious that I should know 'the other Texas'; the artistic and creative Texas – the Texas of so much unexpected ethnic variety. In pioneer times, the restless, the oppressed and the adventurous of much of the world left countless impressions on the state (the new Texas having welcomed more nationalities than most other states). The result is a fascinatingly mixed cultural pattern – which only the hale and hearty visitor can take in, since the state covers an area larger than most countries.

I was delighted to taste a good slice of the cake. To do this, in October 1974, we did a certain amount of fast-stepping – by private plane, by car and on foot. At the end of these five action-packed days, I felt refreshed by an incredible variety of beauty – from original 'homestead houses' and simple village museums (with the tools and clothes and tenderly gathered memorabilia of the pioneer past) to one of the best romanesque collections in private hands anywhere in the world, belonging to Gilbert Denman in San Antonio.

We listened to Mexican and German music and dancing on the Padernales River, then, two days later, we heard an opera performed by the students of the university in Austin, and left stunned by one or two beautiful young voices. We spent one night in the home of Mrs Johnson's friends, Mr and Mrs Marshall Steves, who have re-created in San Antonio, with lavish gaiety and skill, an early Spanish Colonial masterpiece of a home. And took in too many other sights to mention ...

More than anything else, I was refreshed by Lady Bird's tireless mind and curiosity – and her control. She never loses it, whatever the situation; one can only imagine what that meant in the life of an American President who was, himself, often under pressure and attack. 'She is my strength,' Lyndon B. Johnson once admitted publicly. She was always there, always part of his political scene.

In
Publishing

WHEN, just after the war, I married the publisher of *Look* magazine, Gardner ('Mike') Cowles, I had no intention of working. I was ready for the life of ease which this marriage promised. But it didn't take long before he developed a flattering habit of carrying notes of my advice in his pocket as he left for the magazine each morning. From writing those notes to an occasional visit to his offices – and, finally, to full-time partnership of effort – took a very short time, a few months.

I didn't wish to marry Mike Cowles unless he agreed to move to New York City from Des Moines, Iowa (from which he was then operating), to take over the personal editorship of his magazine, which had become by then the subject of derision. He had started *Look* before the war began; it was making money ('a million a year' was the gossip) but it never gained respectability. Categorized as 'barber-shop' reading, it was rejected by the serious advertising community.

This rejection was quite understandable to me. In fact, advertising brought Mike Cowles and me together. We met when he called on me to solicit advertising for *Look*. My remarks, quite unprintable, must have made an impact. Little more than a year later, I married the man whose creation I had insulted so convincingly. I continued to criticize it, this time constructively, after I became his wife. An account of that marriage, to a man and his magazine, follows.

Even my departure in late 1955 was done with such discretion that it couldn't mar the record of a long partnership. The divorce was the subject of a leader on the editorial page of New York's *Daily News* – surprised that two such public figures could act so civilized over the dissolution of their marriage.

During the time I was a lady editor, I became such a public figure that I soon developed a mythical reputation.

A myth is easy enough to create. My own world, publishing, has its ready-made apparatus, a built-in nemesis of the famous and infamous, called The Morgue. Few things have been more aptly named, for inside it lie the reputations (not necessarily true) of the well known. Unless one is 'buried' in it, the idea is hard to comprehend. Unlike the real thing, the publishing morgue functions even while the body is warm – although it can turn blood cold.

The Morgue exists on every magazine or newspaper in the Western world. In form it is notably unpretentious, usually just a series of dog-eared manila folders or envelopes, each with a celebrity's name on it, slipped into the drawer of a file in the research department. Inside each is a hit-and-miss *mélange* of clippings, with a Scissors Executive in charge. One has to rate being called a 'public figure' to get into it. To any person who shrinks at the thought of being buried away impersonally with the wrong image, it is known as The Enemy. To the publicity-mad, it is The Friend. Every day of the week someone is scissoring what's in print about the famous (not only their own columns but all others are being combed). Every quotation and misquotation, every phrase out of context, every slip of the tongue (which only a robot can avoid) is cut out and tucked away. The most awful mistakes (the most *regretted* remarks) are those which have most permanence. Anyone who has had any kind of public life knows the trauma of having one's personality misrepresented, even by the well intentioned. Career women are fair game, sitting ducks.

If you get into a goldfish bowl by design (if, in fact, your chances of remaining a public figure depend on public attention) then all those faces looking into the bowl could be a welcome sight and you could count yourself a success. Those faces mean money in the pocket. But what if you got there by chance – and didn't want to be inside? A myth can be established without your consent or even your awareness.

I dare say envelopes still contain certain dusty clippings about me. But one 'quotation' which used to snap at my heels seems finally to have been laid to rest: Mike Cowles and I had been asked to meet another publication's chief editorial staff at the time *Flair* magazine was launched. Something I said to one of the luncheon participants in a completely relaxed way when he rode back with us on the short car journey from their offices to ours

44

found its way into the magazine's next issue, although we were not being interviewed.

The young man noticed a ring I was wearing. Why had I left it unpolished? he asked. 'Oh, it's like me,' I answered, 'uncut,' suggesting a preference for the natural rather than the embellished (it was too large to embellish). 'Big, uncut me' went into print—a quotation which was promptly cut out and filed into many brown envelopes.

So, also, was one phrase unkindly attributed to me when I attended the Coronation of Queen Elizabeth, as American Ambassador. I was so incensed, I cabled the publisher to ask if his magazine had gone in for fiction. A letter of apology followed but not before the offending remark had filled morgues everywhere. I had worn a Valentina-designed voluminous dark-grey taffeta coat over a beige dress to Westminster Abbey for the ceremony. It was published that I said (which I never did—I wasn't even asked about it) that I wore this 'underplayed colour-scheme' so as 'not to compete with the Queen', a statement so patently ridiculous and so unlikely that everyone I knew laughed it off. But not I.

A libel suit or insistence on the apology in a publication which misquotes a person would have been fair in retribution, but I accepted the private apology instead (it wasn't 'cricket' for one publisher to sue another). The letters-column is one place a hard-pressed publisher sometimes prints letters to soften the damage done in previous issues, but I think this is the short end of the stick for anyone feeling bruised.

Once I had a short-lived victory—but an ironic one. I'd been asked to dine with one of the executives of the London *Evening Star*. The host took his guests to the newspaper as a pleasant public-relations exercise. Although I knew perfectly well how a newspaper is written, put to bed and printed, I nevertheless went along with him; I wanted to get into The Morgue, to look up the Fleur Cowles file!

When it was turned over to me, I paled at the thickness of the envelope. I particularly winced over phrases which needed the sound of my voice to be able to judge (otherwise how else to know if I was joking—or where the emphasis was originally placed?). Just stop and think of things you've said in jest. Without a mocking tone of voice might not even an *opposite* meaning be given if it is written down?

After looking into those files with so much drivel so carefully preserved, I silently tore all the contents of the file to shreds and dropped it all back into the manila envelope before returning it to the unsuspecting librarian. The paper suspended publication soon after; my elation was short-lived.

Today, I am pleased to have dropped out of the limelight. I think life in the goldfish bowl (which leads to The Morgue I've described) has very few compensations, except for those to whom publicity is bread.

Like all journalists, I have always been plagued by questions about on-the-spot reporting. How can one surmise so much in so little time, is the most often asked; few people realize the value of sharpened instincts or the capacity to ask the right questions. Nor to understand that one can risk a lot if one foot is in an airport.

The very best response I ever heard to the question of 'quick-knowledge' came from the American writer, the late John Gunther, who made a world-wide reputation by his on-the-spot reporting and his 'Inside' books.[1] He used to write as he travelled – and this quick journalistic feat bothered people who thought ideas should brew before being written into books. This never bothered Gunther, whose 'Inside' books are still basic research for the areas he reported.

One day, when he was in South Africa, he was approached by an irate settler. The white farmer thoroughly disapproved of his 'instant expertise'. 'How can a man like you come over from America and tell us all about ourselves after staying here a week or two?' he shouted at Gunther.

Calm and smiling, Gunther gently replied, 'My good man – I've only seen you for two minutes and I can sum *you* up quite accurately now!'

---

[1] *Inside Europe, Inside U.S.A., Inside Africa, Inside South America* (Hamish Hamilton).

Look Magazine Years

Look magazine is now dead. The burial took place in 1972, but when the shutters closed I was as unhappy to see it go as anyone on the staff, although I'd severed connections with it in 1955. *Look* ink still flows in my blood. It is impossible to shrug off the death of a property to which I've given many years of affectionate effort.

When I married Mike Cowles in 1946, the magazine's high profit was due to a low-operating budget. The contents were printed on paper which wasn't much better than newspaper and its readers at that time were all male.

The magazine was 'running itself' since Mike Cowles's appointment as Domestic Chief of the Office of War Information, which required him to live in Washington. Whilst in that wartime job, as a close personal friend of Wendell L. Willkie, he went with the defeated Republican candidate for the Presidency on his famous 'One World' global flight. He had been commuting to Iowa as well, to manage his two successful middle-western newspapers, the *Des Moines Register* and *Des Moines Tribune*. *Look*, of necessity, took its place alongside many other activities, and was run by absentee-management, in an inelegant though fascinating and financially agreeable groove.

I was unabashedly ashamed of *Look*. I urged Mike (who had actually invented a magazine which used *pictures* to tell stories) to make the changes that would nudge it slowly into the world of women, without giving up the male circulation – this because important advertisers simply did not make big appropriations in magazines which reached male readers only. Women readers were essential to tempt the big advertisers.

47

In 1946, food, medicaments, cosmetics and fashion products were advertised solely to women buyers; even expensive capital-purchases like motor cars, homes and holidays, were never made without a woman's acquiescence. It was foolhardy to print a magazine which ignored women readers. Those were the golden days of women's magazines.

My work began by half-days at *Look*; gradually the time increased until I finally set up a large separate department for Women's Features and became its editor. Soon, I added the role of Associate Editor of the magazine (Mike being Editor-in-Chief) and my dream of a dual-content publication – with features of interest to women as well as to men – became a reality. It was not accomplished without constant bickering. Though equal space was eventually given to features of primary appeal to women (and as many as possible of interest to men *and* women), there were many bruised male egos on the staff to contend with. That's a story I'd like to forget.

My own contribution to the magazine's changing image is on record, written by outside journalists, but I can with objectivity make a few claims. When I left for England in 1955 after my divorce, the magazine's image, personality and size hadn't any resemblance to the *Look* I married. In the best part of ten years I was there I had helped to influence three vital changes:

1. Circulation had mounted to nearly 4½ million; the original tawdry male readership of 1 million had been replaced – in advertising terms – by desirable families. The magazine was edited in such a way that all members of the family could enjoy it.
2. More than half the circulation was composed of women; advertisers reacted by spending more than $25,000,000 in *Look* the year I left. The figures climbed to $90,000,000 by 1965.
3. The appearance of *Look* had changed; cheap paper stock and printing had given way to fine coated stock, and the magazine was printed on the best presses available. It was respected, and that respect continued to grow for years to come.

Look's transformation meant a climbing circulation, which rose to nearly 8 million readers by 1972. This, in fact, helped lead to its downfall. Advertisers simply weren't willing to pay a colossal price for more circulation than they could afford (or wanted). Advertising revenue began to fall.

The issue of October 19th, 1972 was *Look*'s last. Like any death, it deeply saddened everyone who was in any way connected with it, including millions of its readers.

According to Mike Cowles's own valedictory statement, the last nail in the magazine's coffin (after rising paper and printing costs) had been the cost of postage. To reach the readers, many of whom paid almost nothing to subscribe to the magazine, four million dollars had been spent in the twelve months before its demise. Readers had been sought at any cost to help *Look* fulfil circulation claims.

Look's death recalled my years as the Associate Editor with vivid clarity. The life I led while in my editor's chair at *Look* had always been exciting, although sometimes delicate. Whenever I poached on men's territory, male hackles went up. Being constantly in the public eye as a famous lady editor was not without its attendant difficulties; I would get the attention, the press, the kudos. Envy and other psychological reactions grew up around me.

When I first began to influence *Look* into new directions a few heads had to fall, mainly the men incapable of contributing to the 'family-image' needed. I got credit for every person fired. Over the years few things ever hurt me more than being referred to by these men as 'the hatchet woman at *Look*'. Even after I moved from America, the phrase continued to haunt me. Finally, in one nation-wide opportunity in 1960, I found a way to kill the phrase during a television programme seen by millions of Americans. Mike Wallace, then conducting an interview show, telephoned me in London from New York, inviting me to discuss my newly published book, *The Case of Salvador Dali*.

Warnings flashed before me: 'Don't do it … Don't do it … Anyone who goes on with Mike Wallace is absurdly brave,' I'd heard a friend say after appearing on his programme.

In the end, vanity took over and I said yes, succumbing to the flattery of the New York call. I still wonder why a telephone conversation from overseas can make any matter *seem* urgent, even exciting ...

When I was sitting in the studio make-up room, being done up to face Mike Wallace and television cameras, my nerves crumbled. 'Why had I fallen into the trap?' My courage, never at best before facing a TV camera, vanished.

In a moment of panic, I decided to walk out! I actually planned my escape: I could turn right (to end up on the street) instead of going left (to end up in the studio). I did turn right, but to my horror (with a few minutes left to go before I went on the air) I found myself inside the studio, being helped on to a high stool. Though I didn't know it, time had been working for me. I had got so frightened I simply hit rock bottom and at the crisis-moment the secret weapon we all carry around with us, called the adrenalin, came to my rescue. Suddenly I felt calm and 'levelled off'. I was in control.

Nothing Mike Wallace said could upset me. Smiling coolly, I replied with great courtesy to all his questions. When he finally came to the most sensitive one of all, I was somehow (and for the first time) ready with the only answer it deserved. 'Is it true that you were the "Hatchet Woman" at *Look*, Fleur?'

'You can't really be serious, Mike, asking me that tired old question?'

'Yes,' he replied, 'I am.'

'Well, isn't that question terribly unfair to *Mike Cowles*? After all, wasn't *he* supposed to be running *Look*?'

With that, I put the old canard to rest.

About *Flair* Magazine

There are certain facts about *Flair* magazine (which I created and edited in the United States in 1950 while still Associate Editor of *Look*) which, in my view, had better be left *said*.

Flair magazine was the most expensive and exciting gift Mike Cowles ever gave me; unlike most wives who choose yachts, horses, jewels (which I never wanted), I preferred the costly luxury of creating a magazine – and he let me do so, although not entirely out of altruism. For over a million dollars, Mike Cowles became the proud publisher of *Flair*, which had an unintentionally short life of thirteen issues and was followed by a hardcover book a year after the original magazine died. Whatever *Flair* lacked in longevity it made up for in publishing immortality.

It was not meant to be a pastime. I had already been Associate Editor of *Look* for four years and Mike Cowles, born to a distinguished newspaper family, had created his revolutionary picture magazine more than twenty years before. Between us, we knew the publishing scene well enough to sense a readiness for a new kind of reading. Even more importantly, *Look* still needed upgrading – publishing an elegant magazine from 'the same shop' would help achieve that end.

Whatever else *Flair* accomplished, it became for me a lifetime passport; after *Flair* was born, Fleur and *Flair* were inextricably and permanently intertwined, and we have never been untied. It is twenty-three years since its demise but *Flair* and Fleur are still synonymous; wherever I travel, *Flair* is a calling card, with its own special identity whenever the name Fleur is noted. It still opens doors to writers, painters, designers, even to students who weren't born in *Flair*'s time but somehow now know it well. Copies have been bound, cared-for, read and re-read and passed down to succeeding generations two decades after the event.[1]

For the years between 1949 and 1952, creating and launching *Flair* gave me great happiness. On the day Mike Cowles suggested that it was wise to close it down (I believe the decision took ten terse minutes) I was too shocked to be vocal. A meeting was promptly called – it was on a Saturday morning – for which all the staff's business executives came to a Waldorf Astoria hotel suite to be given the news. Mike Cowles announced that *Flair* would cease publication at once. 'The Berlin air-lift had just begun ... a European war could be in the offing ... Korea was still being fought over ... paper prices were sky-rocketing.' These were the reasons given.

I sat on a couch on the sidelines, emotionally drained, tears unchecked, inarticulate. The experience was much more grim the following Monday morning when I called my staff together to tell them it was all over.

The same emotional canvas was repainted (according to a member of the staff who'd been on both *Flair*'s and *Look*'s teams) when *Look* closed its doors in 1972, after more than thirty years of publishing. The occasion was described in a letter to me: 'Even Mike Cowles had tears in his eyes as he went around personally to confirm a constant rumour.'

Flair had given jobs to many gifted, unknown Americans, to whom I had opened a door; it brought a new public to names that have since become literary legends. *Flair* organized new ways of saying things in print. It had both a dedicated staff and dedicated readers. It was, in fact, a phenomenon in American magazine publishing.

No publication ever caused the same stir or evoked more violent passions against it ('too odd, too daring, too different'). Nothing looked more menacing to its in-the-rut magazine competitors and never was such an imaginative battle mounted (than by them) against any other magazine. Some even stooped to

[1] Both *Flair* magazines and the *Flair* book are collectors' items today; I am constantly asked if I know where to find a copy (for which from $30 to $50 per copy is offered). Recently in the U.S., I saw a complete set tied in green velvet ribbon, occupying an antiquary's window on its own. The price was $500.

spreading gossip about me personally ('divorce rumours', which were then completely unfounded, were persistently planted in gossip columns, so were other items that suggested the magazine was 'temporary').

No publication ever aroused less understanding from its enemies or as much loyalty from its friends. Nothing so costly to produce was ever 'given away' so cheaply. *Flair* cost $1.65 for each issue; the price to the news-dealer who sold it was 33 cents, it was then sold to the public for 50 cents – *365,000 copies each month!*

The expected advertising revenue to make up the deficit didn't materialize. The magazine was too new in format to be judged by any but the trail-blazers; I made a plea to agencies that they create specially-designed advertisements in keeping with *Flair*'s content. In doing so, I chased off countless potential advertising agencies who saw no profit in creating something suitable only to one magazine.

No magazine was ever sold by such mistaken methods. *Flair* was, in hindsight, born to the right parents but reared by the wrong nannies! It deserved a selective direct-mail readership (and a much higher selling-price) but was sold instead just like its mass-market sister publication, *Look* – pushed by the hundreds of thousands by news-dealers. It needed reserve, not push. It should have built a selected circulation by mail order, yet it was put up for sale on the most popular-priced and competitive market-places of America, the news-stand.

This is not written in anger or ingratitude. I've had a very long time to dissect *Flair*'s short and emotionally-charged existence; it is now possible to make judgments without letting either personalities or arguments get in the way.

Apart from Mike Cowles's money and advice, *Flair* was made possible because of three men; first of all, Arnold Gingrich, the publishing genius who created the original *Esquire* magazine in the 'thirties (and now edits the current one). We flushed him out of the bitterness of his self-imposed retirement in Switzerland and he helped make the mechanically-impossible innovations found in *Flair*. Secondly, the pale, often paranoiac editorial genius, George Davis, late husband of Lotte Lenya, who fell on

Flair like a last drink of water and helped me, as my Managing Editor, to give it such an eclectic content. Lastly, that transplanted Italian-Hungarian aesthete, Count Federico Pallavacini de Berzeviczy, whom I brought to the U.S.A. after the war on a stateless person's passport (which was eventually changed for one of a United States citizen's). From his tiny, hopelessly cluttered studio in our offices, he brought the living germ of a Renaissance man to the artistic appearance of the magazine.

What *was Flair* magazine, you may well ask?

To describe the physical format, here are the questions I asked when creating it: If a feature would be better in dimension than on flat-pages, why not fold half-pages inside double-page spreads? If a feature was significant enough, why not bind it as 'a little book' into each issue of *Flair*, giving it a special focus? If a feature was better 'translated' on *textured* paper, why use shiny paper? Why not follow shiny paper with features in a matt finish? If a hand-fed offset printing or hand-fed gravure suited a photographic essay better than letterpress, why not use it?

If a painting was good enough to frame, why not print it on properly heavy stock? Why not bind little accordian-folders into each issue to give the feeling of something more personal to the content? In fact, why not create a magazine with an element of surprise in every issue?

It is difficult to sum up anything in words which was designed to tempt the visual as well as the mental appetite, but this is a condensed version:

I thought it made sense to publish one magazine, with pertinent coverage on each of the categories for which there is now a separate magazine, a beautiful new condensation of many magazines within the covers of one – the first honestly *general* magazine of all the arts.

I wanted a *new design* for this magazine. I felt it wasn't exciting to invade with old weapons in a country which has set the world's standard in packaging and design. I wanted a magazine with dual-reader appeal, male as well as female. And, in the framework of television's allure, I wanted a magazine of extraordinary *visual* excitement.

I wanted to 'repackage' my magazine as a new product; to free it from orthodox and accepted formulas for binding, for covers, for page-sizes, for paper stocks. It took nearly two years of pre-publication effort, wheedling, coaxing, and protesting to persuade machines to do jobs never before done except by hand in limited, expensive quantities. It took mule-ish effort (even financing) to make high-speed equipment do such painstaking work.

The public was alert and critical of even our most obscure errors; we were dissected with every degree of anxiety as well as affection. We made many mistakes but they were the implements of experimentation and they took courage.

A year after *Flair* magazine closed, as a form of consolation, I produced the *Flair* book. Unlike its predecessor, which had an immense staff, this book was the personal effort of myself and two assistants – Robert Offergeld, who wrote many of the features, and Federico Pallavacini, who designed the pages and contributed many drawings.

If a post-mortem was in order, it would probably read this way: The money *Flair* lost will probably never again be available on the same basis. It was put into my hands by Mike Cowles to prove that artistic effort *can* be commercial – which for good or bad reasons it wasn't, *and may never be*. I'm grateful to have had the opportunity to try to find out. I'm grateful this effort is part of my record. I would never want to try to do *Flair* again. Could one ever again find the fresh, untapped talents that filled the cubby-holes at *Flair*, or the enthusiasm and seven-day dedication? I doubt that this emulsion can be re-stirred.

I received a letter in 1970, which moves the memory of *Flair* from the abstract to human terms. It came from a total stranger, obviously still in his teens as he had just been drafted, who wrote before being shipped off to Vietnam. He hadn't been born when *Flair* was published.

'I hate this war,' he wrote, 'and I don't want to go. I'm pretty sure to get killed in action. Anyway, who'd want to survive?

'The only things I have of any value in this world are my twelve copies of *Flair*, which I've collected all over the place. I'm leaving them all to you. They will arrive by separate post. So long!'

The package arrived. It remains sealed, ready to be sent back to this young man to whom they meant so much — if he has survived. If I can find him.

Early Watergate: Senator Joseph McCarthy

The Watergate hearings had a dreadful precedent when Senator McCarthy conducted a very different set of Senate hearings in 1953. When I returned from a trip to Egypt after seeing Gamal Abdel Nasser, I was met at the airport by Mike Cowles: 'No matter what you intended, you are an editor and you must know what's going on in America. Go home and listen to the television.'

I changed my plans and stayed to watch the McCarthy hearings on television, instead of flying off at once to Washington. To see McCarthy in action was infuriating; his technique had distressed millions of other Americans before me. Sitting during the daytime before a television set was a new experience but I was riveted to the box for the next harrowing forty-eight hours. Like many other viewers, I sat with pad and paper in hand, making notes. Each time I heard the lies and contradictions of McCarthy's team, I silenced a scream. Each time a helpless victim was trapped and pilloried by vicious interrogation I vowed vengeance.

I decided I must get to the hearings, an idea which was greeted with a condescending pat on the back. 'Not an extra fly could wedge into the crowded courtroom,' it was explained.

I refused to be put off. Influence in Washington was quickly mustered and, a day later, I found myself in a chair which had hastily been placed behind Senator Stuart Symington at the counsel-table. There, no more than five feet away, I sat directly facing the dreadful Mr McCarthy. There was little between me and that curling upper lip every time the Senator launched an attack on his witnesses. Two smirking legal serfs, Messrs Cohen and Schine, sat on each side of him. There, also, was Senator Robert Kennedy,

57

close to McCarthy – part of the Senator's own 'prosecuting' team.[1]

One day at the hearing was all I could bear after seeing strong men reduced to mumbling incoherence through sheer brutality. In my view, the gentlemanly defence lawyer, Joseph Nye Welch, was no match for McCarthy. Lies flew past Mr Welch, darting about like missiles. Not an ounce of flak to shoot them down. *Darkness at Noon*, Koestler's book on the Moscow trials, and accounts of Nazi interrogations floated to mind.

I left the court sad and frustrated, unable to shake off a melancholia. How could a man like McCarthy go unchecked, openly smacking his lips over each battered victim? That he was 'saving us from Communism' was ridiculous.

All decent people who saw these so-called 'democratic' processes on television turned against the Establishment. Not long before he chose to become official 'Mr Anti-Communist', he was himself considered a 'Red'. His tactics, his speeches, all his politicking in his home state of Wisconsin were considered left-wing (and by some, even downright Communist). McCarthy's conversion to anti-communist ring-leader was far too rapid; here was another rabble-rousing, opportunist politician with enormous skill.

Not everyone hated him; McCarthy was extremely popular with isolationists and right-wingers, who urged him on with their dizzy acclaim. There was even a brief flurry to back him as a candidate for the Presidency.

Why doesn't someone kill this man, I wondered, while realizing that neither a potential nor a real victim could dare it. He had to be disposed of by someone who couldn't be accused of fearing him personally. *Who* should do this? I asked myself many times.

I was completely obsessed; in a neurotic moment of heroism I reasoned that I was the best possible person to do it; I could get the best legal counsel and it would be a trial of good against evil. It never entered my mind that I had never held a gun in my hand, that appearing only once in court, as a witness in a traffic case, had given me uncontrollable jitters, that the idea of murder on any level, for any reason whatsoever, had always been repugnant.

[1] Harry S. Truman has harsh words for Robert Kennedy in *Plain Thinking* by Merle Miller: 'I just don't like that boy. I never will. He worked for old Joe McCarthy, you know, and when old Joe was tearing up the Constitution of the country, that boy couldn't say enough for him.' About McCarthy, he was even more explicit; calling him a 'moral pigmy'.

I went back to New York and calmly explained my decision to Mike Cowles: 'After a great deal of thought, I'd decided to assassinate McCarthy myself.'

He didn't bat an eyelid or attempt to dissuade me. 'Of course. I understand,' was all he said, knowing that time was on his side, that arguing wouldn't be the right tactic. We flew to Des Moines the next morning for a regular four-day weekend. The assassination had to wait.

In Des Moines, it was our custom to meet members of the staff of the Cowles's *Des Moines Register* and *Des Moines Tribune* newspapers. This time, everyone had been briefed about my remarks. Everyone was ready for all possible outbursts on McCarthy; no one was to flap over any announcement I might make – including the possibility of murder.

'Don't cross swords. Just agree politely. Be understanding. The important thing is not to force her to take a stand,' they were instructed. In the meeting, I discussed my current activities, ranging from the recent visit to Nasser to my day at the McCarthy hearings. And when I announced quite calmly that I intended to kill the man, not a person demurred. Not a smile, not an argument. The statement was accepted without discussion.

Except for Editor-in-Chief Ken MacDonald's one very simple question: 'How do you intend to do this? With a gun across the counsel-table?'

'Oh no, I've never held a gun. I couldn't use one now,' I admitted.

'Then, with a knife, to stab him?' he pursued.

'Oh no, I couldn't possibly stab anyone to death,' I continued.

'Then, what weapon?' he persisted.

'I simply don't know. I just don't know,' I confessed. 'After all, I find it hard to kill a fly. I must find some bloodless way ... '

Mike Cowles had done his spadework well, and so had the others. No derision, no guffaws. A few days' time and quiet thinking and sanity returned. I never mentioned the gruesome idea again, and to Mike Cowles's credit, neither did he.

A year later, in Eisenhower's speech 'Mandate for a Change', the President said, '1954 began with McCarthy riding high – and ended with his being practically a political cipher.' That was putting it kindly. In November of the same year, McCarthy lost his Chairmanship of the Senate Internal Security Committee, a feat credited to the same Senator Sam Erwin who chaired the Watergate hearings twenty years after McCarthy. In December 1954, Joseph McCarthy was officially condemned in a Senate Resolution. Three years later, in July 1957, he died of natural causes, tarnished and demeaned.

There is an epilogue to the story of my 'assassination' scheme. In 1968, at a dinner in Washington given for me by Mr and Mrs John Alex McCone – he was then director of C.I.A. – I found myself seated at table next to Senator Stuart Symington, who had chaired the McCarthy hearings.

'I have a crazy story to tell you,' I said to him. I described the 'near murder' which might have been attempted from a chair directly behind him.

He roared with laughter. 'Gosh, Fleur, aren't you glad you didn't – *you'd have been the Jack Ruby of the McCarthy era!*'

Perfect disposal of a mad idea.

Panmunjon: a visit to the Korean war front

Journalism got me to many places but I'd like especially to tell of the Korean war front and of the Panmunjon Truce Conference. Few things I've seen in my life have been more ironically beautiful than the view of the site where men were attempting to establish peace between the North Koreans and the Allied Forces in Korea. The little place called Panmunjon buzzed with life. It became famous for the prolonged Communist guile which ruled for so long inside conference tents, baffling the best intentions of the Allied Command.

The Korean War had begun about 4 a.m. on June 25th, 1950 – when 150,000 Communist North Koreans, equipped with Soviet tanks and automatic weapons, suddenly crossed the 38th Parallel and ruthlessly invaded South Korea – a stunning surprise. No one – either in the Land of the Morning Calm or in Washington – expected it. Nor did General MacArthur, if John Gunther's account of the General's movements on that very night in Japan has validity. He had apparently accompanied the Gunthers when they went on his private train, on a visit to Kyoto and was deeply shocked, according to John Gunther (who was on an assignment to write 'Inside Japan' for *Look* magazine), to be told on the train that shooting had begun in Korea.

When I got there in the January of 1953, it was almost two years to the day since the peace-negotiations had begun. These started in Kaesong, but had to move to Panmunjon when the original site could no longer be protected from Communist fire. The weary scepticism at the opening of these talks finally led to a loud sigh of relief which was heard round the globe when the truce was eventually signed thirty long months later.

How did I get up to the front? President Eisenhower arranged for Mike Cowles and me to go. The request, made enthusiastically, lay heavily on my mind after the classified briefing given in Tokyo by General Matt Ridgeway's Command Headquarters, especially after being instructed on how to behave if captured. When I was finally fitted out in men's battledress (five layers) to cope with the weather out there my dislike of intense cold added to the jitters. I wanted, of course, to be intrepid – but I did once yearn (for a fleeting moment) for a terse order, rescinding the trip ...

General Ridgeway very generously lent us his own personal plane for the trip to Seoul, a bomber with a non-existent heating system. My teeth never stopped chattering. The little hotplate aboard was not working so we were given ice-cold cocoa ('to keep us warm') by a kind-hearted young airman.

The manner of the air force officer in charge of the plane was very different; to him, a woman was an idiot to ask to go up to the front and the General was an even bigger one for allowing it. You could sense his contempt. I felt as if a block of ice was strapped to me when he came back and thrust a parachute into my lap, barking out, 'Here. Put it on. You may need it!'

'I don't jump,' I explained meekly as I put it on the seat across the aisle. Mike Cowles's face was wreathed in a slightly nervous grin by then, but he didn't waste any time stepping into his.

'Do as I say. Put it on,' the captain snapped back. 'I'm in command here and you're under orders. If need be, we'll push you out!' he barked, brooking no nonsense.

So, without choice, I put the hideous object around me. The parachute, which doubled me up (adding cramp to coldness), was finally hooked on and I returned to my seat with my stomach turning over. The plane was constantly bombarded by pellets of ice flying off our wings. Each sharp rap, I was sure, was enemy fire (which, in point of fact, might not have been more dangerous than icing up). Below, the sight of the snow-capped jagged hills was Martian. As we flew over them, regret kept bubbling to the surface. That horrible terrain was hell for soldiers to fight over. It was hell to contemplate landing on it by parachute.

Bivouacking with the officers in Seoul was the next experience. Everyone slept on bunks in their dormitory; I was merely one new person, unrecognizably female. Toilet facilities then (and from then on) were a nightmare problem in a world where only men existed. Five layers of battledress were an added personal hazard.

Driving up to the peace talks at Panmunjon had been arranged by General Ridgeway. We were to go up with the men in the morning, so we rose early to clamber into the jeeps to ride up through the front. I was so disguised that only the most observant suspected a woman had arrived.

The horseshoe-shaped no-man's-land, almost encircled by Communist troops holding the famous 30th Parallel to the north (whose name Panmunjon meant Wooden Gate Inn), was once a trysting place for lovers, who will probably never use it this way again. When I went out there, all but a small gap to the south-east was held by Communist forces. Five decrepit huts still stood where the original hamlet was located, and women and tiny children still lived inside them, ignoring the war.

A huge area had been marked off in the low flat ground between two mountains. Inside it, men were safe from the action which continued to take place above and around the zone. On both sides, armies were entrenched in jagged, high hills, lobbing their heavy artillery through the skies above the talks. When there, beneath them, it took me a long time to accept that thought casually.

To get there, men from each side followed a daily ritual, from which no one deviated, not by a moment, not by a move. When I once put a foot outside the outlined truce area (by mistake) instant machine-gun fire from men whose placements I could actually see, warned me to hop back. I did, like a scared rabbit.

Each morning at nine sharp, a moratorium was declared for ten minutes. In this period, the flutter of action was like a ballet, and just as precise. Men in jeeps and in planes descended like bugs, lowering from both sides of the mountain, scurrying to the tents on the plain to take up their daily monotonous stations in the war of nerves across tables.

After ten minutes the shelling started again, but everyone who had scrambled through was safe until the time came to disband the conference. Again the ritual was repeated to allow all to dash out again for the night. If you were a military observer, you went back by jeep each evening to Seoul; a shell could always get you on the roads. If you were Press, you drove back to the cold, cramped railway-carriages parked outside Seoul, your home for the duration. About thirty war-correspondents travelled back and forth daily with the officials at the truce-tables. Even those nerve-testing hours were a respite from the war.

The truce plain, when I first saw it from the front seat of an army jeep, which had bumped its way up from Seoul, looked indescribably lovely as we huddled by the side of the road, awaiting the signal for firing to stop so we could drive on.

I thought of Braque then, and I still do. The colours of the terrain, the markings on it, the tents and equipment would have done justice to his palette. The land was mustard green and *puce*. The area was marked off with devastating casualness by four narrow strips of *cerise* plastic, laid on the earth and held down by stones. From each of their corners (to mark the area from air-attack) helium-filled barrage-balloons were anchored – waving joyously in the sky overhead. These were *silver*. At night, four searchlights threw beams into the sky to define their glitter.

The truce tents, looking like blobs on a Cubist's palette, were either *dark brown*, *white*, or *black* canvas. When *khaki* and *black* jeeps and *khaki* and *navy* planes composed themselves in tight little groups alongside them, each added superbly to the Cubist composition. The colouring certainly was pure Braque.

Panmunjon's truce area itself was thick with languages; being a linguist was a very special luxury. Apart from the delegates, the press corps was a large U.N. in itself: Americans, French, British and South Koreans mingling with Japanese. On the other side were the Communist contingent, including the dapper Australian I met, Wilfred Burchett, who was a freelance reporter out there. He was easily spotted by his Russian fur cap. Alan Winnington was there too; he also wrote for London's *Daily Worker*.

Fraternization between Press on both sides did take place – but only gingerly, being openly frowned on by the Communists. Winnington talked to everyone. His job seemed to include passing out the propaganda being handed out by Communists over the conference tables. Whenever this happened inside the tent, the Allied delegation tended to get up and leave. (When meetings ended normally, the Communist delegates just got up and walked out in a stiff procession – never relaxing their frozen expressions.)

While I was in Korea, the temperature was 20° below zero. Wind tore inside the weather-beaten tents (warmed with electricity furnished by Americans) where a team of five Allied faced a team of five Communists across a narrow table. Despite the formal, highly unfriendly manner of these meetings, the men knew that world peace was involved in their discussions. Six months after I left in January 1953, they succeeded.

The end came in July; temperatures by then were so hot and humid it must have been as uncomfortable as the cold. I tried to imagine the wild azaleas and convolvulus which would be in bloom after I left, covering mine-fields and death-traps.

I never think of Korea without recalling the story of Secretary of War Frank Pace's visit to the front lines there. He was inspecting evacuation procedures for the wounded (and they were remarkable). A mobile surgical unit reached men very promptly after injury; first-aid care was quickly given; helicopters then brought the wounded back to Seoul, where hospital attention was ready. Intensive-care cases were flown to Tokyo – some back to the U.S.A.

While talking to the wounded just brought back from the front lines, Secretary Pace bent over a badly wounded, dark-moustachioed soldier, who was lying on the ground utterly silent and calm. 'Don't worry. We'll soon get you to hospital in Tokyo,' he soothingly promised.

With a look of downright contempt, the man grabbed the curved surgical needle from the hands of a field-doctor working on him. Without a second's hesitation, he plunged the needle through his palm – in one side and out through the back of his hand!

'Me Turk. Me no hurt,' he growled back at the shattered Cabinet Minister.

Painting
Section

ALL of my adult life, collecting paintings has been a consuming passion. For the years of *Look* and *Flair*, 1946 to 1955, I edited the art pages of both magazines, and during that time a steady stream of work crowded my office excitingly. I used to appear more like a gallery executive than a magazine editor.

I began serious buying then, searching to discover and publish the unknown as well as the known. My homes are a treasure-chest of such memories and experiences. Every painting tells a tale of encounters with painters. They still go on.

I became a painter myself after moving to England. Before then, I had painted sporadically – usually to document a place whose sight I loved: a barn I was fond of, an antique shop (furniture ageing outside in the snow), a holiday home I once lived in – perched on a pier on Cape Cod. Photographs would have been simpler but would never have satisfied my unconscious craving to paint, which I stifled successfully during those years. When I began seriously in England, I threw the technique of documentation aside (and I describe the reason why on a later page).

Thus, it was quite natural for me to get to know many painters; some of them became close personal friends. I could go on forever recounting anecdotes connected with them, but I have disciplined myself to select a few. I chose Paul Dufau, Graham Sutherland, Georges Braque, Camille Bombois, Rufino Tamayo, Picasso, Enrico Donati and Salvador Dali; they offer no repetition.

One enchanting experience I like to recall involved Daniel, the five-year-old son of a painter whose work I once went to see. His father, Alan Wood, had invited me to speak one evening in 1970 to the students and the local Arts Society at Cardiff University, of which he was then head of the Art Department.

I brought many slides for my lecture; in addition I had about

69

thirty ektachromes of the latest ones I'd painted, to show Mr and Mrs Wood after lunching with them. Danny was the most fascinated as I described each colour film in turn—holding it to a light, giving its title and details. I always handed each one down to the serious, interested youngster.

I came to one—a very carefully painted lion's head floating in a bright, sunlit yellow background. 'That's a portrait of Tom,' I explained as I held it to the light (my husband being a Leo, my 'portrait' of him was a lion).

'Who is Tom?' Danny asked.

'He's my husband,' I explained.

The child was put to bed for a nap, but after an hour, I asked if I could say goodbye to him. He was brought down in pyjamas—wearing an anxious look.

'I've *thought* . . . and I've *thought* . . . and I've *thought*,' he announced in carefully chosen words as he looked straight at me, 'but I don't believe I have ever . . . *before* . . . met a lady married to a lion.'

I'm often asked why I am so interested in surrealists. Like the chicken and the egg, I'm not sure whether my interest came before I decided to write a book about Surrealism's most curious character, Salvador Dali, or after—as a result of the effort.[1] Whichever it is, I still collect surrealist tales. I brought one of them back from a remote corner of Brazil.

It concerns one of that country's greatest literary figures, Jana Guimares Rosa, who died two years ago (when his book *Stones* was still on the bestseller list in the United States). Rosa came from Minas Gerais, in the interior of Brazil. People there still think in mysterious ways and are often so sad they invent a world to replace their own. Rosa even invented words which, to the intellectuals (who understood them), were considered poems in themselves.

Four years before, he had been elected to the Academy of Letters in Rio. For two years, he refused to take his seat. When pressed for a reason, he confided that he knew he'd die if he did. Finally, in the third year, after much persuasion, he gave up the struggle and took a chance at immortality.

Four days after the ceremony he was dead.

Other art stories may be less surreal, but not less fascinating.

[1] *The Case of Salvador Dali* (Heinemann)

This is another of my favourites: I flew over from London to Paris to see an important exhibition of *Les Naïfs* in a converted ancient house, now a museum. I had come a long way and had no intention of settling for a brief glimpse. I spent hours wandering from room to room and floor to floor, seeing most paintings several times over. Rousseau, Bombois and all my other favourite *naïfs* were represented in an irresistible collection.

I was not the only one who seemed captivated by the exhibition. A very strange man, tiny enough to be Toulouse-Lautrec himself, was in the main room when I arrived, and I left him in the museum a few hours later. Wherever I went, I found him nose to painting. He carried a tiny notebook in the palm of his tiny hand and he filled the pages with minute sketches.

Bursting with curiosity, I determined to find out what was being transferred to those tiny squares of paper held so neatly in his child-sized palm. Details of which paintings, which buildings, which birds, which animals, which flowers?

He was totally oblivious of everyone; nor did it interest him that he was being observed. I had been shoulder-to-shoulder with him constantly, but he never looked up or tried to stare me away. He kept his mind on his notebook.

Finally, I edged near enough to look into the palm of his hand. There (at eye-level with the lower corner of most paintings) he was, laboriously and skilfully copying the *signatures*! The little man was, quite obviously, a priceless link in a vast 'forgery-factory'. He was the all-important signature-maker!

Experts boast they can detect a copy from the real thing by studying a painter's signature. You think it is easy enough to copy a Utrillo, Modigliani, Bombois? Not really—without a proper signature.

I Began to Paint

Most things I write are journalistic in nature; they *happened*. Only in painting did I begin to create a private, dream-like world of my own.

In 1969, I began to paint professionally. My style and technique were literally shoved into being by a young Italian painter, Dominico Gnoli, whom I had invited to a party in London, because I admired his work and wanted to meet him. He had an exhibition coming up, and I knew he needed to widen his audience. He had been introduced to me by Arthur Jeffress, in whose gallery I eventually had my own first exhibition.

The young Florentine, a member of the Gnoli family of poets, writers and painters (known to many as 'the Sitwells of Italy'), soon became a friend of my husband's and mine. Though Dominico died tragically in 1970, I will always be indebted to him for his strange, harsh treatment when I began to paint. It was a push in the right direction.

He was spending a weekend with us in Sussex and decided to paint. I asked if I might also paint with him. 'Yes, of course,' he replied, 'but only if you can meet my conditions!'

'And what are they?'

'*One*, that you sit opposite – so that you don't attempt to copy what I do; I hate that and it wouldn't benefit you in any way. And *two*, that you paint something original.'

I agreed – and simply began, using brushes and paint borrowed from him. I sat across the room, composing a still-life. He looked at it in contempt. 'No! You simply cannot paint those things,' he announced.

'But roses and shells are things I love,' I explained.

'Just the same, I can't allow you to paint something so banal!'

'Very well. If *you* know so much, what do you suggest?' I demanded, irritated.

'For heaven's sake, anyone who has had your background and created a magazine like *Flair* must have imagination—*and* memories. Use them both!' he snapped back. '*Create* something!'

I did. I painted a dream-like version of flowers in the sky.

From that moment on, I have tried to test my memory, to call on my own visual images, to uncover what is subconsciously memorized: the flowers, insects, landscapes, birds, butterflies, trees, leaves, all the animals—and the way they behave—all of which seem impressed on my mind. I never draw. I never compose. I never have a plan. I sit down, pick up my board or canvas and paints, and the memories that Dominico Gnoli insisted I command, *do* respond.

Never knowing in advance what I shall paint, I am always intrigued to see what results. It is exciting to think of a once plain white board or canvas transformed. Sinyavsky, according to Bernard Levin, said, ' "Paper exists to enable a man to forget himself and its whiteness." '[1] 'Say "art" instead of paper,' continued Mr Levin, 'and Mr Sinyavsky's is a considerable achievement, for man has been trying to define art ever since he invented it.' Every painting, good or bad, was once just a blank surface. To me, sitting in a theatre watching a good play, the wonder is that it too was once only a blank sheet of paper.

I now paint three full days every week. A stream of consciousness seems to direct what I'm doing and conversation with guests neither interrupts nor disturbs my work. I am thoroughly disciplined, never altering this three-day schedule. Through the summer holidays, I paint all the time.

Like the primitives (although I don't paint as they do) I am completely self-taught. Like them, I paint things remembered, but unlike theirs, my paintings are never anecdotal.

I started by principally painting flowers in unusual settings. The first painting, for which Dominico Gnoli was responsible, was a clump of earth floating in the sky, from which brilliant cyclamen grew. Tiny rootlets hung from the soil against the pink sky.

[1] *The Times*, November 20th, 1973.

After that start, I've never been able to paint flowers conventionally; instead, a vivid red carnation may be plunged into a dark green tree like a boutonnière, or a rose is so tall it becomes a tree; flowers fly through space with butterflies, insects, bees and birds clustering around.

Next, I began to paint the jungle cats, probably inspired by the sinuous Abyssinian cat my husband gave me in 1957, before I even began to paint. In the short period he lived with us in London, the handsome animal used our home like a jungle, prowling stealthily around the furniture, leaping on armoires like trees, hiding inside wastepaper-baskets, watching me from the corner of my desk. I mentally photographed his every movement before we reluctantly gave him away to live as a country squire with a family in Hampshire. Everything he did had been imprinted on my mind's eye — how he sat, how he walked and how he *eyed me*.

Soon beasts and flowers grew together in my paintings; my favourite is a lion almost hidden by his own giant bouquet. Another shows a family of tigers under a tree, a bouquet under the paws of the mother. In still another, two tigers have a serene rendezvous in a beached rowing-boat by the side of a satin-smooth African lake. There is a painting called *Weekend House-Party*, in which three tigers sun themselves on the rocks outside a Brittany cottage. Also another of two polar bears standing on ice floes, carrying poppies. In another, a Noah's Ark flying through the air, all the animals perched on a huge log; a garden grows out of a chimney, with a tiger hidden under an oversized leaf.

It is possible I may have unwittingly absorbed something of Dali's meticulous *style* (though never his subject-matter) in my own painting, which I began a few years after writing a book about him. Nine of my paintings were exhibited in the XVI Biennale in São Paulo with the SURREALIST group, hanging alongside such masters as Klee, Chagall, Labisse, Tanguy, Miró, Chirico, Delvaux, Neatta, Magritte, Ernst, Picasso, Picabia — even Francis Bacon! One critic called my work 'the innocent among the wicked'.

Since the Dominico Gnoli episode in Sussex in 1959, I have had twenty-two one-man shows, five of them in important museums in the U.S.A. and Brazil. Twenty-eight paintings, done during a ten-year period, were the subject of a parable written by Robert Vavra, with an introduction by Yehudi Menuhin – a book called *Tiger Flower*, which still sells steadily five and a half years after publication.

Its successor, *Lion and Blue*, also Robert Vavra's invention, with an introduction by the Prince of the Netherlands, is written around thirty-odd lion paintings.[1] I was delighted to be asked to contribute a painting to be part of a beautiful book written by Beverly Nichols, *The Art of Flower Arrangements*. It is one among eighty colour plates, each discussed by him.

For me, painting fulfils a lifetime's dream. As a busy American career woman, I was foolish enough, in the past, to think I could never find the time to paint. Today, I use time as my weapon.

Perhaps I paint the way I do, without concern for school or style, because of my own personal attitude towards collecting other people's work. When I came to live abroad, I made two decisions – which meant collecting in a new way: never to buy any painting merely for its 'name' or 'label', and never to hang a painting unless I knew or got to know the painter personally.

Apart from some fourth- and fifth-century Persian and Indian art, every painting we own has its own anecdote. Some of my most fascinating friendships have resulted from getting to know the artists. Much of my travel time is spent with them – often searching for unknown talent, to help a painter, to make a friend. This, to me, is very pleasant modern patronage.

No one wants to go back to the time of the Medicis (unless for the unmatched treasures produced in that golden age) but I do believe strongly in personal patronage. In the Middle Ages, it meant life, recognition and guarantee of work to artists. I don't want to labour the point, but I do wonder why personal backing for painters has gone out of style.

Oddly, Big Business has emerged as today's new patron, liberal-minded enough to collect the unknown as well as the 'big labels'

[1] Collins, 1974. *Tiger Flower* was published in 1969.

to hang in offices and boardrooms. Banque Lambert in Brussels comes to mind, an enormous and beautiful modern office built by Baron Lambert—it will be Belgium's museum of tomorrow. Everywhere in the U.S.A. 'Big Business' collects. Fortunately for the progress of art and for the enjoyment of the public (whether in museums or in corridors of business offices), these purchases are tax-deductible there.

Money considerations are reason enough to buy lesser-known painters: many who have done so have been superbly rewarded. One of the most famous collections 'bought for a penny and sold for a pound' was that of Captain Edward Molyneux. He asked and got a million dollars from the National Gallery in Washington for the collection he had picked up for a song many decades before. Before he died, he started a new collection, and I was delighted to see, in an interview in the *New York Times*, that he had singled out my work.

I have a special love of modern *naïf* paintings. To me, they are an organic part of painting's history. An anthropologist of the year 2075 will have to think twice before ignoring their anthropological aspect. Such artists are taking up their brushes all over the world, quite unaware of each other's existence, yet all producing innocent and anecdotal documents of our time.

To major collectors, I ask: are the modern *naïfs* not waiting in the ante-room, waiting to be discovered?

Georges Braque: the secret 'vice' in his life

I adored my visits to the great French painter, Georges Braque. He was a tall, erect, dignified man with deep-blue eyes, his head topped by a shock of cropped white hair — one of the most beautiful of men. I met him in 1950; eventually, after a few years, I was able to break through his wall of shyness and we became very friendly before he died in 1963.

I used to visit him with Simonne Gauthier. She managed *Look*'s Paris office and was much loved by all French painters. We called on Braque together; indeed this became a routine on my Paris visits. As a rule, we went to his Paris house, going straight up to the top floor to meet him in his studio and to examine his latest work. Sometimes we drove north out of Paris to Varengeville, near Dieppe, where the Braques had a lovely, beautifully situated old farm, surrounded by fields, near enough to hear and almost see the Channel. These were sybaritic pilgrimages, and how we savoured them!

If we went in winter, we generally ended up inside Braque's huge fireplace, sitting near the glowing logs having a farm tea — I've never had better. Hovering somewhere near by, there was always the maid, Marietta — whose mother was housekeeper. Between them, the two had tended the old master for many decades.

Wherever we were, we always talked painters and paintings. We would go on to discuss his latest canvases (several of which were going at one time). I also commissioned work from him: the paintings and bas-relief I now own are the treasured results.

One afternoon, sitting on our small stone seats inside the farm's fireplace, I could tell there was something on Braque's mind. He

77

had fallen into silence, concentrating on the long, straight twig he held over the gently burning logs, a slab of bread impaled on it. He was toasting it for me before it would be smothered in butter from the local dairy and home-made jam.

Suddenly Braque looked up and asked impulsively, 'Would you like to know my secret vice?'

Coming from that serious face, it was a shock. My mouth slightly open, I managed to mutter, '*Your* secret vice? Do you really want me to know it?' Though longing to hear what he had in mind, a warning had quickly been radioed to mine: don't let him tell you something he may regret later. His friendship is more valuable.

Fortunately, Braque didn't wish to be put off. One could see the idea growing in his mind, as with eyes literally twinkling he said, 'Come with me — *Suivez-moi*!'

In single file, Simonne and I followed in his slow firm footsteps: we took a path outside the side door to the back of the house, over the yard and down a small hill — where a large barn suddenly loomed up. We were soon before the huge doors, obviously closed against something mysterious inside.

'Do you really want to see the great vice of my life?' he asked, now grinning.

'I'm not at all sure, are *you*?' I asked him, with terrible visions suddenly flashing into my mind — all, I admit, of a highly unpleasant nature. (Could he be harbouring an idiot-child — like those of legend, hidden in so many Welsh cupboards, the offspring of incest? No. That was ridiculous. He'd never expose it. Some horrible animal — *snakes*, maybe? That would be unbearable. Someone in chains? A 'painting-factory'? A second studio? What was his secret.)

I didn't have time to think further; the doors were flung open. There before us was a gleaming, beautifully kept racing car!

'Fast cars are my only vice. At night, I sometimes take this one out and drive like a maniac along the hard sand on the beach outside Dieppe! I feel young and dangerous — and it makes me happy.'

All his life, Braque had had this one impatient passion. He indulged in his first fast car as soon as money allowed — but he never drove publicly nor allowed that car to be part of his image. It was never described, never displayed, never discussed – except in personal photographs.

Maid Marietta has kept a record of Braque's life with his friends, a photographic diary of remarkable completeness. Since she was thirteen years old (when Braque placed an inexpensive camera impulsively in her hands and said 'Go ahead and snap!') she *had* snapped – with his consent and collaboration – all the family's friends and all their social occasions. A vast collection of famous faces has been accumulated; all the men and women who made up the art movements since the Impressionists were replaced by Cubists (such as himself and Picasso) are there. The collection remains a potential photographic history of the great names in art. I was meant to edit the book.

Braque painted the cover of the book; it was to be called *Braque and His Friends.* The framed painting hangs near my bed and I still hope to produce the book if difficulties which have arisen since his death can be overcome.

Graham Sutherland: we discuss his 'lost' portrait of Sir Winston Churchill

Late in 1970 I wrote to Graham Sutherland in the South of France to ask if he would tell me (for this book) whatever happened to the missing Churchill portrait he once painted. The portrait was being worked on when I visited Chartwell with Bernard Baruch and all of us talked about it at length, and enthusiastically.

The portrait, commissioned by a joint Parliamentary Committee (Chairman, Sir Charles Doughty), has since disappeared, lost somewhere in limbo after apparently having been seen only by the family and a few associates very briefly at the presentation. No one has ever explained its whereabouts. Graham Sutherland has been silent.

Would he talk to me about the experience? To my delight, the elegant Mr Sutherland gallantly appeared at my door in London a week or two later, ready to discuss the touchy subject. Because of his facts, I put our conversation on tape – so that he could 'vet' it before publication.

Of course, the greatest risk was actually in this suggestion itself. I simply cannot use a tape-recorder. If there is a way for me to ruin anything technical, I do; on both previous occasions when I'd tried to use it in an interview, the elusive little machine wasn't really working. I had to end up trusting my memory – with not even a note for guidance.

Fortunately I hired a reliable tape-recorder and better luck accompanied Mr Sutherland's remarks: some circumstances and the disappearance of the portrait, as far as the distinguished painter recalls it, were recorded. Needless to say, I was touched by Graham Sutherland's confidence, and delighted to have had this evidence of it.

His visit helped dispel the rumour that 'Churchill used to doctor up the portrait every night'—which proved to be a canard. Graham Sutherland never left the actual portrait behind: it was painted at his house in Kent from studies. He does not normally let a sitter see the final portrait before it is finished, or the studies. He took the studies home with him every evening.

It was also fascinating to know how Churchill wanted his portrait painted. He said to Mr Sutherland at the outset, 'Are you going to paint me as a bulldog or a cherub?' 'This depends on what you show me!' replied the painter.

Churchill insisted on sitting on a dais to be painted—something no one else had ever asked the painter before. 'I saw a great deal under the chin and under the nose!' Sutherland admitted before he went on tape. We continued as follows:

GS. We have been talking about the family.

FC. And about the difficulty of sitters who 'prepare' their faces for action.

GS. And about Mary Soames and Soames.

FC. Mary Soames and Soames—were they very helpful and co-operative?

GS. Yes. The eventual difficulty may have come from Lady Churchill.

FC. Is it known that she put her foot through a Sickert?

GS. That's what he told me.

FC. He said so himself, yes? Was this to intimidate you; that you'd better make it right, or else she'd do the same?

GS. I don't think so. We were talking about the number of portraits he had had done of himself.

FC. How many had there been?

GS. Oh, lots. 'I couldn't count them,' he said. I said, 'Well which did you like best?' He said, 'Well, I rather liked the Sickert that was done of me.' And I said, 'Well, you worked very well with Sickert.' And in fact he did, perhaps better under Sickert than under anyone. As far as art is concerned he was very impressionable. If some quite bad painter said he should work in a certain way, in that way he worked. He was very malleable in that way; it was a strange sort of modesty—even to the extent, towards the end, of taking advice to work from photographs projected on to the canvas.

FC. Chameleon-like? ...

GS. No, not just changeable, but from ignorance and modesty.

FC. He didn't feel superior?

GS. He'd take advice from any painter who happened to be there. But not in anything else but painting. There was no question of that. And he said as to the Sickert portrait, 'Well, Clemmie didn't like it all ... she put her foot through it.'

FC. What I am really interested in (now that you've been able to disprove the crazy notion I had that he did 'doctor up' his own painting—and how sad I am to lose that anecdote) is, how ever did the story get around?

GS. I don't know. It is conceivable that I *had* accidentally left something there during my daily visits to Chartwell, but I know I was very careful to take things away every day. Careful because, as I told you, he'd asked me to show him every day's work and I was determined not to. He said, early on in the sittings when I had explained that I showed neither the day-to-day studies nor the final work until finished, 'Come on, be a sport, after all I am a fellow painter.' It puts me off terribly for people to see my intermediate stages—even how my thoughts are developing (which are always tentative at that stage ... that's the whole point of making studies). So I had to compromise. I would show him something innocuous every day. I tried to make a substitution by putting the real study I was doing underneath it. I succeeded in doing this most of the time.

FC. You seem to have got away with it?

GS. All but once ... I made, one day, a drawing, and he looked at it and said, 'Oh, oh this is marvellous. Why, this is going to be the *finest* portrait I have ever had made.' The next day he happened to see the real one—which I was working on. 'Oh no, oh no, no, this won't do. I haven't got a neck like this. You must take a quarter of an inch—nay,

half an inch — off my neck-line. I want to be painted like a
nobleman.'

FC. This is so revealing. I consider this to be a kind of mental
touching-up of a portrait. In effect, he *did* touch up your
work, by making an attempt to direct it.

GS. Of course.

FC. This, in fact, was what he was attempting to do, even if he
never got his brush to the canvas.

GS. I think he might have liked to touch *anything* up, because
being another painter it would be almost irresistible not
to feel that he could do it better himself.

FC. Now tell me about the man that you met during those ten
sittings of an hour each: did close scrutiny reveal a man
you liked better or less after that?

GS. Better.

FC. Better?

GS. He was always considerate, always kind, always amusing and
co-operative. When he wasn't co-operative, he didn't
know he wasn't being co-operative. I think this is fair to
say.

FC. And he actually *meant* to be?

GS. He meant to be co-operative, and in fact often was. We talked
about everything, not only painting, but politics and so on.
I think we got on well. He likes to paint out of doors with
people, you know. He would say, 'Oh I do wish that you'd
come out with me and we could do the same subject.' But
it didn't turn out like that with me, owing to the circumstances surrounding his dislike of the final painting.

FC. How could he be against it? Did he actually watch it con-
tinually — despite it not being your practice to allow it to
be seen?

GS. He was only against the portrait when he first saw it. But I
think he was suspicious of what it might become …

FC. Did he actually press his way to see it at a stage when you
would normally not allow it to be seen?

GS. No, he didn't even do that. By the time he saw it, the actual
portrait was finished.

FC. And then what?

GS. I have explained that the actual portrait was not ever at Chartwell. It was done at my house in Kent. He *said* that he was not shown the portrait before the presentation. I can only say that it was delivered to Downing Street twelve days before the presentation.

FC. Is that fact known?

GS. Whether it's known or not I don't know; he did write to me after the trouble to say it was not so much that he didn't like the portrait, but that I didn't show it to him before the presentation. This to me, to this very day, is the great mystery because, in fact, it was delivered by my own carrier, as I said, to Downing Street, between ten and twelve days before the presentation.

FC. Well, the mystery remains; *what happened to it?* (a) did he really see it and wish to claim he didn't, or (b) do you think it was deliberately kept from him?

GS. It might have been kept from him. I just don't know.

FC. What happened at the presentation?

GS. What happened before the presentation might interest you — on the day that Lady Churchill came down to my house to see it (Randolph had previously seen it) Willie Maugham was also a guest, and Willie was very kind and helpful. He said 'Graham, it would be very embarrassing for you to see it in front of Lady Churchill. I will go up with her to your studio and if she likes it I will whistle down for you. If she doesn't like it you'll hear no whistle.' And so Willie whistled down, and I came up and she was in tears, saying 'I can't thank you enough,' and 'it's absolutely marvellous,' etc. etc., and I was pleased, naturally. And when we came downstairs, she said, 'Now if Winston wants to know what it's like, have you got a photograph?' I said, 'Yes I have — but I would personally advise you not to show him a photograph because the portrait will be delivered in the next three days; my carrier will be coming; and there is no reason why he shouldn't see the actual thing rather than a photograph.' However, she decided against that. She wanted the photograph. So I gave her the photograph.

FC. In black and white or in colour?

GS. In black and white, which is never accurate (and it wasn't a very good photograph anyway). At nine o'clock that evening a big black car drove up to the house. A large, very important looking letter was handed in by the chauffeur. It was a letter from Churchill which said 'Dear Mr Sutherland ... ' (I'm paraphrasing slightly now.) 'While I would always be happy to have my features delineated by you, I do not think that what you have done is a fit subject for a presentation portrait. The ceremony, however, can go on because my friends in Parliament have all signed a very beautiful presentation book. Yours sincerely, Winston Churchill.'

FC. Good God, how awful! Would you object to my quoting the letter exactly?

GS. I may not be able to put my hands on it.

FC. But was this the accurate essence of it?

GS. It is a paraphrase. You probably should see the actual letter; you would find it almost identical. If I could find it I would let you see it. There's no reason at all why you shouldn't, and I would like to be dead accurate. A copy may have been kept. This was a handwritten letter.

FC. I hope you still have it. It's a letter you should have kept.

GS. Well, I'm sure I've put it away. I keep my things sometimes *too* carefully, and then I can't find them, but this was the gist of the letter ...

FC. How hurtful to you ...

GS. Oh no! But I immediately got on to the Chairman of the Committee (the portrait hadn't then been presented to Sir Winston) and I told him what had happened. He said, 'Oh, this is very serious. I must go straight away down to Chartwell.' He telephoned me at about quarter to eleven that evening and he said, 'Sutherland, forget entirely about that letter. Everything's all right.' I said, 'What have you done? This is marvellous,' and he said, 'Well, I don't know, I'm not a lawyer for nothing.'
So the ceremony did go on. After, we went to a party in the evening at Downing Street and Churchill was very

nice. He said, 'Well, Sutherland, we may not agree about matters of art, but we shall remain friends.' That was that.

FC. Was the presentation of the portrait made at the ceremony?

GS. Yes, it had already been made in the morning. Willie Maugham was extraordinarily understanding and was shocked about what he thought was bad treatment. He said, 'You know they are really awful ... this is too much ... they behaved very badly to you ... you mustn't mind,' and so on. I didn't mind, oddly enough.

I said, 'Well, what about Lady Churchill crying with pleasure in my house?' He replied, 'Well, now she says she was crying from disappointment!'

FC. How extraordinary ...

GS. It is not without amusement, I suppose!

FC. I think it's a fascinating story about how a great man behaves when personal vanity is concerned – or how a situation can be created around a great man.

GS. You must never think he really behaved badly to me, but the situation was funny. I didn't take real exception – even to the letter. Randolph, I think, was silly and more than silly. He made matters worse when I met him on Onassis's yacht; he said, 'Oh, I'm rather sorry to meet you because I feel the family have treated you so badly ... '

'Not at all,' I replied. 'Why? Everyone has a perfect right to dislike a thing if they want to.' It's written into my contract always.

He repeated, 'Oh, well, I think – we think – we behaved badly. But *why* don't you write to my father and say how sorry you are that you didn't please him?'

FC. What an idea!

GS. So I thought. But, still, I had nothing to lose in doing so, and it might have pleased – so I thought – an old rather bemused man.

I did write to the old boy: I said, 'I'm sorry I wasn't able to please you, but if I had the portrait to paint over again I wouldn't do differently. None the less, I'm sorry that you were not pleased by it. I would have liked you to be pleased.'

A letter came back saying, 'It was not because I didn't like the portrait but because you didn't show it to me before the presentation.' That was the last straw. I thought then, well, one can't go on forever arguing with a mind already made up.

FC. It seems an act of petulance – because you *had* sent it to him.

GS. Can you imagine my not showing it to him before a presentation? It would be the very last thing I would do. But then, I was dealing with such a mercurial character, a little suspicious, as I am myself.

On the whole, I got on with him well. I liked his company. I sometimes lunched alone with him. Quite alone.

FC. The studies which Beaverbrook bought from you for the Churchill section of his museum, were they, in principle, more or less the same?

GS. Oh no, they were enormously varied – some in Garter robes, because he wanted at first to be painted thus; then he changed his mind. He thought he'd rather be painted as a parliamentarian. And then I had made one of him smoking a cigar; another one, in duplicate, of him reading a letter. I suppose there must be, including drawings, about eighty items altogether in the museum.

FC. How incredible – eighty sketches in connection with one portrait!

GS. Not far short – not all done at Chartwell, and sometimes from memory when I got home.

FC. Are they now mainly in Canada?

GS. They're all in Canada in the Lord Beaverbrook Museum. Max Beaverbrook sent an envoy down to search my studio to see that I had sold him the whole lot.

FC. A very crafty man!

GS. A little naughty perhaps – even crafty, but I was fond of him. And a bargain was a bargain; I had agreed to sell him everything.

FC. And so the scraps of paper were all picked up?

GS. Yes, except for one or two that the envoy didn't find.

FC. That pleases me for one reason: if the painting has been destroyed and gone permanently, perhaps there's a sketch somewhere which is similar to it?

GS. There is one study — it is more close to your word sketch, more, perhaps, a compositional 'layout'.

FC. And where do *you* think the portrait has gone?

GS. As to the whereabouts of the portrait, I think that the Committee has been very weak with Lady Churchill. After all, they had the right ... he was to be the owner during his lifetime only.

FC. Should not Parliament have been able to say where *is* it — to inquire after its conservation?

GS. They say they will not do anything until Lady Churchill is dead; but, that's all very well. Foreign countries want to borrow it. It was specially asked for by the Germans for my Retrospective Exhibition last year. And I wrote to Mary Soames to ask if she could do anything. She said, 'Well, I'll ask my mother, but I can tell you straight away that I know she will never yield.' So that was that. But it was a nice letter, not unpleasant at all. She has much of the old man's occasional sweetness. Part of his greatness was that he was often very funny. Do you remember about the special food for the goldfish? You know all about that? Bought at Fortnums!

FC. Yes. He told Mr Baruch and me about it, once.

GS. About the Communists?

FC. No.

GS. Well, you know, he would take a great big handful out of the tin and fling it into the pond, but the throw wasn't big enough for the ones at the back to get it. So I mentioned that this seemed a little unfair. 'Oh well, you know, that's life,' he replied, 'I mean to say, the Communists expect everyone to have everything equal. But life is not like that. The ones at the back don't necessarily get a share!'

Camille Bombois:
a great painter 'repays a debt' to me

The late Camille Bombois was a *naïf* painter who may one day be considered another Rousseau. He was born in poverty and died in similar circumstances, though quite needlessly. As with Georges Braque, Simonne Gauthier and I used to call on him regularly.

The elderly man and his wife lived in a poor quarter of Paris, in a tiny, sparsely furnished and very ugly little house. Bitterness prevented Bombois from enjoying greater comfort and recognition before he died; he often went so far as to refuse to give his work to dealers (whom he thoroughly distrusted). His suspicions almost isolated him. He preferred not to sell at all rather than be, as he thought, 'exploited' by the entrepreneurs. But in a locked closet in the house were many of the finest fruits of his labour – a treasure-trove which, if sold, would not only have provided wider acclaim, but many luxuries denied to the lonely pair.

He had endured a lifetime of hardship which began with the years he served as a labourer in a circus (the background to his early paintings of clowns), so he clung tenaciously to most of his canvases as an insurance for his old age.

Hard as his grip was on these paintings, his wife's was firmer, quite understandably. Her husband was very old; he had suffered several near-fatal illnesses. If death came, his widow would feel safer with a long, narrow, crowded cupboard. Here, indeed, was plentiful insurance. Actually, she died in 1964, before Bombois, of heart failure, leaving him lonelier and more bitter. He had lost most of his sight through carbon monoxide poisoning from his boiler.

Each time Simonne and I came to see the old man and his wife (about twice a year), we always brought along *pâté de foie gras* or some other delicacy. It would invariably be rushed out of sight to some secret hiding-place to be relished after we'd gone. We'd sit in a fairly empty parlour, discussing his work and his bitterness towards dealers, which I tried to placate in his own interest. Slowly, over the years, a feeling of trust developed.

I, at least, was able to buy some of his paintings at the current market price. Among these paintings are several I commissioned, including one of lions: there are also three which I actually roughly sketched out for him to interpret in his own style. I particularly love one which is a stiff parade of earthenware flowerpots, each planted with a different stiff solitary bloom (my ten favourite flowers).

One spring day, Simonne and I arrived to find the man close to tears, obviously frightened into a state of near-hysteria. What had happened? we anxiously inquired. Apparently the French income-tax authorities had just discovered his existence. What could he do? He'd end up in jail, he moaned, wringing his hands. His white-faced wife was even more certain of it.

As this was in the early 'fifties, before French income-taxes were taken too seriously, we finally persuaded them that the tradition for French painters to ignore taxes was an accepted fact. That he wouldn't end up in jail. That no other painter had. And that I would arrange for *Look*'s French attorney to look after M. Bombois.

This was done. The case was resolved as all other income-tax matters concerning French painters seemed to be, at least in those days. I never asked what had been done: I was told by the *Maître* to 'forget it' and I did.

About five months later, I was back in Paris and went out to see the old couple. This time we were greeted by warm faces wreathed in smiles. A round table was quickly drawn into the centre of the terrible little parlour which smelt of ersatz linoleum. Upright chairs were drawn to the table for four to sit around. This was something new; obviously a conference was in mind.

After a few moments both M. and Mme Bombois got to the point: How could they possibly thank me for what I'd done? For months, the painter explained, they both worried and fretted about 'how to repay the generous American lady who saved me from jail'. No matter how I insisted he would never have been imprisoned, the fact wouldn't register. They had come to a decision. I simply had to be repaid.

Oh Lord! They're going to offer me a painting, I quickly thought ... I couldn't possibly accept it ... I mustn't accept it ... They had the whole thing out of proportion ... I must discipline myself not to take anything – not to let them over-estimate what needed to be done.

'Madame Cowles, we have thought it over, my wife and I, and we have at last found the solution,' Bombois firmly announced.

'Please! There is no need for one,' I insisted.

'We've made up our minds. You know that painting you have always wanted – the one which I've always refused to sell to you?'

'Yes, of course,' I admitted.

'Well, to thank you, we have finally decided that you can *buy* it. The price is high because we don't really want to sell it!'

When I could regain my composure, which took a little doing, I finally extended my hand to thank them both warmly. In their way, they had made a great gesture. In fact, they had done me the greatest possible favour, for the painting was certainly one of Bombois's and his wife's favourites as well as mine.[1]

Bombois didn't live to realize what a 'gift' he'd really made. About fifteen years later, in the winter of 1970, an American dealer offered me a great many times what I had paid for it.

---

[1] A Bombois, it seems, was also a favourite of Sir Winston Churchill's. Eve Arnold photographed Lady Spencer-Churchill in January 1973, seated under the perfect painting, a bulldog. It had been presented to him by Camille Bombois in the most desperate days of the Second World War.

Rufino Tamayo: the making of a portrait

One portrait of me is by Rufino Tamayo, one of Mexico's greatest living painters. It brings to mind an anecdote, and is a symbol of the friendship between the Tamayos and myself.

Tamayo has painted very few portraits, but of the few he has done, none could have been painted under more amusing circumstances. It was Tamayo's suggestion in the late 'forties that he should paint me. He and his wife telephoned my secretary for an appointment in my office. Very strange, I thought; they come regularly to my home, why the office? But the appointment was made; they insisted on making an 'official' call. They wanted a conference.

'We would like to make you a gift of a portrait of yourself,' Tamayo announced (the 'we' making it clear that the idea was his wife's as well as his).

'But that is too generous of you – and very exciting!' I exclaimed.

Silence. Both were unwilling to proceed with their next point, so I urged them on.

'How do we begin? And when?' I pursued.

Tamayo's wife spoke up: 'The point is, we don't know how large you'd like the painting to be!'

Putting the burden on me to choose the size of a gift was terribly embarrassing. Pressed for an answer, I decided to brave it out.

'Oh, about this size,' I replied hesitantly (very loosely indicating a square shape with my hands, about two feet by two feet).

No joy resulted from that, to judge from both Tamayo faces. With a certain nervousness, they asked me several times if I was sure that size would be all right. They then thanked me and left promptly, after arranging for the first sitting at eight o'clock the next morning. It had been an odd encounter.

I was living in a seven-storey New York town house, the top two floors of which were a studio-room used for entertaining – large enough for a projection-room and for dancing. It could be reached by taking a lift; thus it was possible to arrive unnoticed on the top floor, taking the lift on the ground and proceeding unnoticed through the house. This was essential; one condition was that 'not a soul is to know about or see the portrait until it is finished'.

The next morning I found both Tamayos upstairs at the appointed hour. They came without paints, brushes or canvas. 'We're only here' (the twin-act still in use in conversation) 'to discuss what you'll be wearing. How do you want to look (clothes make all the difference)? May we look through your wardrobe?'

'Of course, come down and we'll go through it together,' I agreed.

The next hour was taken up with the anxious details of dress. Finally, a plum-coloured, Dior chiffon evening-gown was chosen. They then agreed to start the next morning.

Again, I noticed a certain oddness in their behaviour; they were alarmingly reserved and this was not at all the vivacious Olga I knew, nor the Rufino of the dry wit. I couldn't understand.

The sitting began (I was already dressed in their chosen clothes) but the atmosphere was still so noticeably cool, I had to do something about it: 'For heaven's sake, something's wrong with both of you! What *is* it?' I demanded.

After making a few ineffectual denials, Olga finally broke down and blurted out, 'It's obvious you aren't really interested or excited in having this portrait. If you were, you wouldn't ask Rufino to do such a small one. You really gave it away when you asked for a two-foot-by-two-foot canvas!'

I nearly choked with laughter until I realized that to the Tamayos it wasn't funny. 'Can't you understand that it is impossible for anyone to ask for a huge portrait when it is offered as a gift?' I demanded.

'Is that all? Would you really like it bigger?' they both replied.

The penny dropped; they finally knew and believed my reasons and they were soon wreathed in smiles. After a round of hugs and

93

kisses we were again friends. 'Tomorrow morning we'll return with the right size,' Olga promised.

Before leaving, I got a lecture from the painter himself: 'When I paint you, you'll be the real *you*. First of all, I'll bring you out from behind your dark glasses (there won't be any in my portrait). Everyone will be conscious of the beautiful eyes you hide.

'And there won't be any of that "famous lady" bit; I'll paint you as you are, the tiny, feminine person we know and love.'

I was far from annoyed by the outburst: though I've worn dark glasses ever since first ordered to do so by my doctor in 1940, I said I would be pleased to be painted without them. Size? Until I came to live in England my waist was nineteen inches, my top weight seven stone, so it was pleasant to have Tamayo paint me as a feminine creature and not as some sort of Junoesque symbol of success.

They arrived the next morning with a huge, heavy object; it was the full-sized wooden door on which I was to be painted. The result is unique for any portrait, and particularly for one by Tamayo. Known for his brooding dark canvases, he painted this one entirely in sepia and black on white (the white-painted background rubbed into the door so painstakingly the wood grain shows through). Tiny? Definitely not: I look at least six feet tall and long-waisted (which I wish I was but am not). But I am serene, my hands relaxed in my lap. The eyes? It is quite impossible to say they aren't the most important feature: they're painted as if carved in marble, without *pupils*. I am completely recognizable, though staring eyelessly at viewers. As a portrait it is remarkable and mysterious; as a painting it is one of Tamayo's most original.

Many years later, Rufino Tamayo had a chance to paint something else in Sussex when he and Olga came for a weekend. It was haymaking season and there was much activity on the land.

'Everybody works here,' my husband chided the male guests.

'But I can only paint,' Tamayo replied.

So my husband gave him a pot of paint and a two-inch brush, pointing to our garden gate. It was painted in no time at all by Tamayo and it will be many, many years before anyone has the temerity to do it over and paint out the great man's work.

Pablo Picasso: is he a giver?

Apart from what must be the qualified statements (or should one say complaints) of the women in Picasso's life, he has shown much generosity in giving paintings away. There is one (apocryphal?) tale of the huge 'eye' painting sent by him as payment to a Paris doctor – who is supposed to have taken a piece of flint from Jacqueline's eye while on holiday in the South of France. The doctor's wife got terribly sick of the 'ugly eye painting' but finally gave in to its presence by deciding how lucky she was not to be married to a gynaecologist!

Picasso always responded to his great friend Roland Penrose when he asked for an original drawing for a raffle to benefit London's Institute of Contemporary Arts. For this, I am particularly grateful, as I once won one.

In 1970, Picasso gave what may well be the greatest art gift in history when he ceded legal claim to the massive collection of Picasso paintings hanging in the Barcelona Museum.

A few years ago, in London, a small but charming gift of another sort surfaced. A mural he had drawn in an undoubtedly exuberant mood on a friend's wall came to light when the building was demolished. Picasso had been in London and gone to a party given by Professor John Bernal, a physicist and crystallographer of international reputation, who then lived above his laboratories at London University. Perhaps the creation of the mural followed an overdose of liquid refreshment, but regardless, he did paint it. The mural was salvaged by construction workers in the late 'sixties. It was cut out, intact, and presented to an obviously perfect permanent home, the I.C.A.

But, back in 1951, Picasso made one of the most extraordinary gifts of his life to two relatively unknown young people, an act of staggering but eccentric generosity. In an outburst of unbounded good will, he turned their tiny two-room flat in Vallauris into a Picasso Museum. The modest, somewhat dreary house to which the flat belongs must be a most valuable property in southern France.

Jean Ramie, stepson of Mme Suzanne Ramie (who owns the ceramic atelier which produces Picasso's plates and ceramic pieces), married one of his fellow artisans in the atelier. He and his bride, Hugette, chose a simple, cold-water flat over a vegetable shop in the town as their home.

A wedding gift for them? In a playful mood, Picasso went to the still bare flat, armed with brushes, buckets and paints. With a sweeping bravado and great good humour, he transformed every wall. Large Picasso paintings, complete with make-believe frames and hanging wires, were painted on all the walls. On some areas he introduced such *trompe-l'œil* objects as ivy hanging over the fireplace, ceramic 'Picasso plates' over the cupboard and – hanging in the right places on the wall – even make-believe tiles to cover bad cement patches.

In the young couple's little sitting-room, he topped his output by painting an eleven-foot mural, an unusual one for Picasso. It is allegorical and romantic, depicting the bride herself as a medieval lady, waving from her castle balcony to Jean, her new husband, a knight in armour arriving on horseback.

It is said that the whole vast museum of Picasso paintings in those rooms took less than an hour for the great man to paint. Anyone who has seen the film of Picasso making an almost instantaneous painting knows that such a feat is possible for him.

As a final impulsive gesture before he left, Picasso gave the newly-weds one of his most exquisite *découpage*-paintings, *La Dame aux Poissons*. The real painting was hung up alongside those painted directly on to the walls.

Enrico Donati: a painter joins a union

Enrico Donati, the closest friend I have, is a painter living in New York. He started in Paris as a surrealist, creating an important place in the movement for himself. He left Surrealism behind to paint dimensionally in marble dust, eventually becoming one of the most respected and successful artists in the New York School, his work now hanging in important collections everywhere. A few years ago, he added sculpture to his activities, producing shining molten pieces like abstract stones and ancient primitive objects. I've collected his works through every change in style and they always evoke compliments.

Any similarity with any other artist must end with the above description. Enrico Donati neither lives nor works like any other artist. He paints and sculpts in his vast studio overlooking New York's Central Park from one to seven o'clock daily (unless, on rare occasions, he lunches elsewhere). From early (sometimes very early) morning until noon, he is Chairman of three companies (one of them the important, elegant perfume house, House of Houbigant). His family, in Milan, have great wealth — but he has little interest in it: he too is a self-made millionaire, many times over. He is, in fact, a most remarkable person.

His first wife and I became instant friends in 1959 — and they and his present wife and I have become like sisters and brother. Nothing is too much for him to do for me or I for him (a statement put to the test with warming proof many times through the years). In the late 'forties, I had the chance of helping him over an artistic hurdle, when he was being frustrated by the Union of Paperhangers and Scenic Artists in New York. The Marquis de Cuevas, then the grand patron of ballet, was to present the Ballet

Internationale in New York with sets designed by Salvador Dali, Marcel Vertes, Du Bois, Boris Aronson and Enrico Donati (whom the Marquis chose after seeing and buying two of his paintings).

Donati's assignment was to do the décor for Ravel's *Bolero*, choreographed by Mme Nijinska. To his dismay, he discovered that no artist could work in the theatre without first being a member of the union. He was frantic; the deadline was close.

He came to me, desperate over the problem. Being in publishing was a great door-opener. Within a week I succeeded in getting him the information he needed to study in order to pass their exams – and, more importantly, I succeeded in persuading the union board to nominate an extra-curricular examining board just for the purpose of passing him into the union (at a time of year they never convened).

Their fee for the privilege of taking the examination was $500. Membership in the union, provided Donati passed the exam, was another $500. I wonder what it is today?

The union headquarters was well over to the West Side, on New York's colourful Forty-Second Street. Neither Donati nor I can remember precisely if it was over a butcher shop or a fish market, but it was one or the other and we did go together, he did pass the exam and he did design the sets and costumes for *Bolero* – a very happy man. It was an amusing experience to listen to his replies to the odd questions asked.

This may be the only thing in this book which is written in envy. I long to design for the ballet myself ...

Paul Dufau: the shy farmer

Late in 1963, I sat down to a meal among farmers in the great hall of a converted mill in south-west France, a guest in the house of a friend who had deserted Paris for a forgotten little valley, Agen. All around us inside the house was a collection of paintings and *objets d'art*. Outside were the smallholdings of the district, the producers of the cattle, preserved fruit and stuffed plums for which Agen (population 35,000) is famous.

Next to me at the table, the hostess had put Paul Dufau, a local farmer. After hours of discussion about his farm and his beloved prize-winning sheep, Dufau rose to go. Putting his gnarled, workman's hand in mine, he added with shyness as he turned away, 'I also paint.'

The next morning, I drove early to his farm to see his work. If I'd expected (and who wouldn't, of a French farmer of sixty-seven) the innocent, anecdotal painting of an ageing, lonely man yearning to put memories on paper, I was wrong. Here was a sophisticated painter of stature, who painted as if in the same studio (at least a part of the same milieu) as a Mirò or a Debuffet or even a Klee. Braque was his idol, whose influence was obvious.

Many of the works I found piled in deep heaps on a barn floor were years and years old, many were dusty and worn. A remarkable sophistication existed in all.

Paul Dufau's painting on an easel in the neighbour's house was the first genuine recognition he'd ever had. He had never *sold* a painting until I arrived and I chose many. Some he simply declined to sign ... 'they aren't worthy'. He tried to refuse payment. 'They're not good enough,' he insisted.

The money I put in his hand, after a *great* deal of persuasion, 'will go towards farm improvements,' he mumbled tearfully, as I drove away.

Paul Dufau's face, even in repose, was masked to hide tragedy: he was the farmer who insisted, for some reason, on painting. For what good reason no one knew. A little-understood man, pitching physical energy and the need to eat and survive against a restless, imaginative inner impulse to create. The quarrel between the two described his long and frustrated life.

'The world is either Jeanne d'Arc or Christ or Napoleon and we poor mortals are put down on earth between them,' he explained to me sadly.

He was born in Agen in 1897, a son of an itinerant sabot-maker. As a youngster he was apprenticed to his Aunt and Uncle Dufau, to work on the same farm which he ultimately inherited. As a boy, he was paid a pittance. The book of accounts, kept by his aunt in the punctilious calligraphy of the turn of the century, shows (among columns of out-going expenses) Dufau's wages: ten francs a month. The money, incidentally, had to be used for buying his shoes from his own father.

He used to lie on a cot in a stable (which is now his atelier) and stare through the window at a huge oak tree outside. A strange bond grew between the tree and the child and he used to conduct an endless dialogue with 'my only real companion'.

Nothing on the 200-year-old farm was more primitive than that stable-bedroom. There, under an oil lamp, he began to draw when he was ten, and he has painted in that room almost every night of his life since then.

Whatever stature Dufau had in his local world came from rearing sheep, a 200-year-old breed of crossed English and French stock, some of France's finest animals. More than a hundred prizes were tacked on to Dufau's farm walls, adding a vivid pattern to a drab world.

In 1963, after a lifetime of struggling, Dufau and his wife Renée and his thirty-eight-year-old son Michel could barely make a living. Wife Renée did the planting and digging of potatoes, and grew the corn to feed the sheep and hens which gave them the meat and the eggs and the occasional chicken in the pot. After I had arranged his first exhibition, in London (a sell-out) at

Grosvenor Gallery, the house (certainly one of the crudest in France when Dufau inherited it) at last got an occasional bulb on the end of an electrical cord and the comfort of a water tap inside the kitchen sink. Ten years later, there was a tractor, and even a small car. Also a refrigerator and, of course, the ubiquitous television set on top of it. After dinner, when farmer Dufau went to his studio, Renée and Michel settled down to its entertainment.

When I first saw this ninety-acre farm, nothing was commonplace — not even the animal population. A miniature comic zoo of fifteen cats ('beware, they are *très sauvage*!'), many dogs and geese and a bird-world of a hundred chickens and one glorious cockerel (tame enough to allow only Dufau to stroke him), two goats (Blanchette, and a shaggy white one, Fantasy, who looked more like a llama). There were, of course, about a hundred valuable breeding-ewes and eighty tiny lambs.

The hundred hens had been taught by Dufau to roost in the limbs of the wonderful old oak tree outside the farmhouse's front door. They say chickens are stupid, yet this flock had learned, with Dufau's patient training, to climb what looks like a heap of rubbish at the foot of the tree to go up to bed — a broken portion of a spiral staircase which Dufau found in a junk yard is the starting point. At night, the chickens slowly marched up, one at a time, settling first in lower branches and gradually getting to the top. The darkening sky shadowed them into dreamlike silhouettes against the night.

There is little that is extraordinary about the nearly eighty-year-old Dufau's face; what magic does exist in his own secret world is hidden. His looks mirror his life as a sheep-breeder, not as a painter. For years, he went into the fields in the French labourer's rugged brown corduroys, big boots, and heavy jacket, shepherding his flock until daylight disappeared. Inside his pockets were the pencils and crayons and the tiny two-inch notebooks that fit inside the palm of his hand. The faces, the attitudes, the anatomy of the sheep and their lambs (or the ducks and geese which follow them) were always recorded, to be translated later — in wax and oil and sand — into semi-abstract paintings.

Paul Dufau has had to be his own judge, the hardest thing for any painter. He has never had an audience, or a critic — except, in her own way, his wife. 'Though she didn't like everything, she didn't insist – she never expected me to dance for my soup!' 'You don't have to please,' she would say to him.

I asked Dufau (in 1963) who his favourite painters were. 'Courbet, first, for the sensuality of his brush, then Picasso, for his verve, his acrobatics and facility and for his sense of humour – Braque for his philosophy. He is the most spiritual,' he responded, without hesitation.

Dufau knew without doubt whose work he worshipped, and he went on trying to find out how to express himself. He took difficulties for granted. 'It is necessary for an artist to find things difficult. Surface techniques are more and more mysterious. I go on experimenting.' (Not long before he died, Braque used almost the identical words in a conversation with me.)

In the evenings the silent shepherd retired alone to his atelier; he might have gone there to think something out or to examine the tiny sketches made that day in his notebook. Or to enlarge on an idea painted in miniature, or to try out some technique that fitted the paucity of his equipment – or, finally, even to make a painting. When he did, the wild pace of a traveller before a storm would be comparable in speed.

Little was conventional in the barn studio except for the poverty itself. Dufau lived and worked in a world of permanent make-do. The cheap mounting-board used by photographers was his normal canvas, although, occasionally for his large, half-sculptured texture-paintings he exchanged this cardboard for inexpensive plaster-board. *Not once had he been able to afford canvas.*

The stable looked more like a printing press than a studio; in fact the two most photogenic pieces of furniture in it were huge old-fashioned hand-presses on which Dufau turned out an occasional commercial assignment for a restaurant, or for the illustrated menu, or lithographed Christmas cards he sold in Agen. The studio was always knee-deep in paint-litter and in paintings – years and years of unseen, undiscussed and unsold work gathering dust.

Though he lived in the centre of pristine beauty, he never painted the landscapes around him. The river valley is fertile and cultivated; the slopes of the low hills are covered with orchards.

Even vineyards (in Marmande and Nerac, where brandy is produced) are there to paint. But his mind was set only on the
problem of transforming form into matter, and matter into form.
How can it be done, he kept asking. 'Since I work so alone, there
is no response. I continue in ignorance.'

Just before the Second World War began he inherited the farm
from his uncle. A decrepit house and land were left to him, but
without money—which had all been spent in a burst of travel
before the relatives died. Though it had been a Dufau farm for
more than a century, it was in a terrible state. Paul and Renée and
their son moved into an unheated, unlit, waterless home—
'surrounded by rats, rats and more rats!' The farm now belongs to
his bachelor son, who is still doing the hard manual labour.

As soon as war was declared, a period of great danger began for
the family. The Dufau farm became a hide-out for the hunted.
Agen produced stocky, hardy, fiercely independent and self-
reliant people. Not only the Dufaus, but many other families kept
the German Occupation busy. The area was a staunch pocket of
resistance during the war; the fiercest S.S. troopers had to be
deployed there to deal with the peasants and the Maquis.

Dozens of Jews lived all through the period with the Catholic
Dufau family. With each warning, the refugees fled to the coal-
forests nearby, to return when the S.S. went away after their daily
search for stragglers.

Mme Dufau still remembers vividly her concern that the
Germans should not find things left behind in the house each time
hidden refugees dashed to the forests. Quickly she'd unpack their
bundles and mix the miserable contents with her own meagre
things, to 'lose' them.

Though desperately poor, there were always twelve or more for
the Dufaus to feed at table. 'The Maquis not only expected to find
a *potage* on the stove whenever they slipped in, but took away
apples and potatoes for a rendezvous with others in hiding.
Giving food away was not a suggestion but a mandate; it was
requisitioned not only by their own side but by the Vichy government—who helped themselves to a percentage of all animals for
the national supply.'

So generous were the Dufaus to the Jews, they were once

warned by one of them not to take so many in. 'You'll expose the farm as a hiding-place and then where will we go?' he pleaded.

Some very well-known Parisian intellectuals must remember to this day that the Dufau family saved them. After the war, one man offered to help launch Dufau in Paris as a painter – but, sensing an attempted pay-off for an act done without premeditation, Dufau refused the only thing he ever really wanted in his life. 'I don't want to be known out of gratitude,' he explained, in declining.

Anyone (including critics) who has seen his work on my walls has singled them out. All admit that Paul Dufau's work commands the respect and attention for which he had waited all his life.

'Do not stop loving my work,' he pleaded with me as we said goodbye after my first visit. I never have. I often go back.

Salvador Dali: a respectable art hoax

Here is a capsule close-up of a strange man, beginning with a little-known tale of an official art hoax, done by Salvador Dali as an important commission. It isn't often that a great collector gives the stamp of approval to a copy of a great painting, nor that he has the wit and panache to do so openly. But everything happens to Salvador Dali, including the experience of creating an official hoax.

One of the most fascinating stories about Dali concerns his copy of a painting by Vermeer, the great Dutch painter. He did it for 'the Grand Seigneur' of medieval art in the U.S.A., the late American banker, Robert Lehman, who discussed the episode with me just after the painting was finished.

Dali's temperature always rises at the mention of Vermeer and has done so since he was a boy. His feverish idolatry for his chosen god took an unexpected turn when Robert Lehman (whose world-famous Renaissance collection was recently willed to New York City's Metropolitan Museum of Art) commissioned him to 'Make me a Vermeer!'[1]

Mr Lehman originally got to know Dali in 1934 when the surrealist arrived in the U.S.A. A mutual friend introduced them, knowing both had a passion for realism and for the paintings of the Middle Ages. Dali was overwhelmed by the Lehman

---

[1] The Lehman collection was worth over fifty million dollars many years ago, and probably has at least doubled in value by now. It was gathered by the Lehman family on a scale so grand it may never again be repeated. Tapestries, jewellery, furniture, bronzes, enamels and boxes were collected as well as great masterpieces in painting. When an exhibition of 293 pieces out of more than the 1,000 he owned went to *L'Orangerie* Museum in Paris in the mid-'fifties, an editorial in *Carrefour* pointed out that it 'represented a taste so severe' they hoped it 'would inspire the French Museums'.

collection. 'But your collection's incomplete, monsieur. You haven't got a Vermeer!'

'You are right. One has never been put on the market,' Mr Lehman admitted. 'I have searched the world for a Vermeer. I know that one is badly needed to round out my collection.'

Suddenly, he had an impulse. 'Why don't *you* make a copy of a Vermeer for me, Mr Dali?'

The painter was overcome, too vain not to be flattered. 'It is impossible, monsieur. Impossible! Even I could not do it!'

The suggestion lay fallow for a very long time. The men met frequently in the following twenty years but it wasn't until the mid-'fifties that Lehman repeated his offer. This time Dali took the bait, with a surprising admission.

'I'm just working on Vermeer's *Lace-Maker* now — one of the most beautiful paintings ever created!'[1]

'I'll buy it if I can see it first,' Lehman said.

'Of course I will show it to you,' exclaimed Dali. 'I will do it at once! But only on one condition: you must pay me as much for this copy as for a Dali original. Ten thousand dollars.[2] I will make you a perfect copy ... '

Dali was, in fact, actually working in the Louvre on the copy, faithfully, painstakingly (no doubt, with banker Lehman's earlier suggestion in mind). But he didn't sit down to paint without doing the usual Daliesque things. When I asked the painter to describe those efforts, he listed them this way:

'First analyse Vermeer colours ...

'Then ask Louvre for analysis of pigments ...

'After, order some canvas to be woven ... just like Vermeer's.'

Before starting on the canvas, Dali also claims he asked the Louvre what ten books Vermeer loved best (and then to have read them!), to have absorbed everything he could about the Jesuit ritualism of Vermeer's period, to have read every reference book which Vermeer had presumably consulted about perspec-

---

[1] A. Reynolds Morse (who has established a vast Salvador Dali museum in Cleveland, Ohio) told me he has discussed Van Meergeven, the famous Dutch impostor who copied Vermeer, with Dali. Dali claimed that he recognized them as fakes from the start and was able to say 'I told you so' to Morse later.

[2] The price, in Dali's market today, was low. Dali would certainly ask $50,000 now.

tive. Finally, he examined, with microscopical care, how Vermeer applied his paint.

He tried to discover exactly what size brushes (down to the number of hairs in each) Vermeer must have used in order to paint with his exact precision. He even tried to determine why Vermeer frequently put maps into his paintings. He read the geography of Vermeer's time. Probably no other person or painter knows more about the man.

When Dali finally conceded that his own painting was a flawless copy of Vermeer's masterpiece, he submitted the work with his usual devastating bravado to Mr Lehman, who promptly bought it. The banker later described the copy to me as 'glorious'. 'Everyone', he pointed out, 'agrees it is a remarkable example of Dali's craft, a perfect Vermeer!'

Mr Lehman asked Dali why the canvas was so coarse. This baffled Dali, since he had ordered one to be made to the Louvre's detailed specification of Vermeer's original. Ted Rousseau, of the Metropolitan Museum of Art, pointed out that the original Vermeer canvas at the Louvre had been lined and had shrunk flat, and that time had done much to it in the centuries since it was painted.

Dali's reaction was to order that his canvas be relined, pressed, and flattened out as well until it was conceded by *everyone* that it was a magnificent copy. The 'masterpiece' had been done without hoaxing a single person at any stage of the game. It is signed, quite simply: 'Vermeer by Dali'.

The England
I Know

ALTHOUGH I moved to England in 1955, I'd been coming to England regularly while still living in the U.S.A. (both as journalist and, eventually, on frequent errands for President Eisenhower). But my real personal attachment began in 1953, when I attended the Coronation of Queen Elizabeth II. Good fortune followed in its wake. Twenty years after the event, I feel it important to recount – if only to a new generation who may never see its like again.

I am now fortunate to have a city life in London in the pre-Adam mansion called Albany, built in 1770 by Lord Melbourne for his bride, and a weekend country life spent amid the gentle, rolling, green hills of Sussex in a Tudor farmhouse. One is elegant, the other cosy, each a superb contrast.

The life I now lead is so different from the frenetic and somewhat exaggerated one of the United States, where my world was in and around journalism. Yet here – building a new life in a new land with a new husband – I found an even greater creative existence.

England, in terms of personality, is unique, eccentric and practically unpredictable. But the atmosphere is amicable. London is a crossroads; friends from everywhere arrive to enliven the core of my local social life in many non-overlapping circles. 'Foreigners' (in art, the theatre and politics) are the icing on the cake, if one is entertaining. An element of surprise can always be provided.

England is a country where history is part of everyone's life. Hogarth's characters still walk about on the streets. Some of the world's greatest paintings are in small museums north and west of London. Parliament and the House of Lords is always crowded by Members. The eternal Tower of Babel in Hyde Park sustains free speech. The sudden unexpected meeting with the gold Royal Coach and Horse Guards trooping off from stables to the palace is

England's best tourist attraction — and the sight of the Queen tops it all . . .

Here, old clothes are actually popular — and new junk is a girl's best friend. Wealth is immaterial (though helpful). Rolls-Royces are generally driven by pop singers and ambassadors from the world's smallest countries (some of the nicest people having absolutely no money at all). Small-town life exists in the tiny villages of the huge city. A garden can be dug right in the heart of London; no one needs to exile himself to suburbia to grow the tuberose-begonias and honeysuckle he covets . . .

My Appointment as Ambassador to the Coronation of Queen Elizabeth II

When it was announced that I had been chosen to attend the Coronation officially as Ambassador representing my country, the repercussions were not exactly earth-shaking but a certain rumble was plainly heard. Apart from the honour and excitement of the experience, jealousy and enmity (even one case of downright paranoia) had to be met. The announcement certainly separated friends from enemies.

One woman's attitude can never be questioned: Clare Booth Luce's — whose idea it was that I should go. 'A remarkable young woman is going to be made Queen. This is an assignment made to order for a woman — and you, Fleur, are that woman,' she said quite firmly when the news of the Coronation was first known.

A whisper in the President's ear was all that was needed and that assignment to England, for which I am eternally grateful, was the first of many to come from the White House.

The reaction to my appointment as Ambassador ranged from the glee of a few genuinely happy friends to a comic pretence at being pleased from others, and an ugly vendetta from one woman — all of it most revealing. Some of it was soul-destroying (for at least fleeting moments). But, whatever else happened on the human side, the event brought the warm and valued friendship of a great man into my life, George Catlett Marshall, who also went to the Coronation — as President Eisenhower's personal representative.

In the course of doing our rounds in England together, General Marshall and I had hours and hours of companionship, and while making conversation on all fronts to strangers (attempted in every conceivable language), we managed to get to know a great deal about one another.

Among the most disappointed by the appointment was the late Elizabeth Arden, the dyed-in-the-wool Republican cosmetic queen, who lavishly entertained candidates and gave generously to campaign coffers. When my name was bruited, quite furious, she made it abundantly clear that this was impossible: *she* deserved and *she* expected to be named instead. It was a very long time before she talked to me again after she realized she wasn't going to get the appointment.

One very distant 'relative' became so enraged over the news (it was diagnosed as jealousy by many who knew us both) that she drew on the nearest acid pen she could command, Drew Pearson's. The two invoked a happily futile attack on me through his poison-pen column in newspapers. But despite any efforts to the contrary, my appointment was absolutely final by the time it was made public. Not even Drew Pearson could prevent my departure to England.

I was utterly conquered by what I saw and did. Nothing interfered with my ultimate pleasure there. The experience was unforgettable.

On my return to the United States, John Foster Dulles wrote:

I should like to express my appreciation for your services as the President's representative to the Coronation of Queen Elizabeth II. The dignity and understanding with which you fulfilled your mission contributed greatly to the maintenance of those close and friendly relations between the United States, the United Kingdom and the Commonwealth of Nations which are of such vital importance at this time. I hope that for your part you found the experience rewarding.

It was nice to be a stitch on a piece of historic embroidery. My account follows.

For the Coronation, and for the seventh time in English history, *God Save The Queen* came back into the language and habits of a large block of the world's population. After fifty-one years, the English world was getting a Queen again. Her awesome but tiny predecessor, Queen Victoria, had played her role with such greatness men would never again question female ascension.

I *saw* a beautifully embroidered pageant. For once, and for good, bloodless history. Ancient ritual, reaffirming its place in a modern world; gilt and plumage instead of aluminium and helmets. Length and ceremony instead of brevity and dispatch, happiness instead of despair.

Rain did pour down on millions standing on wet streets; cold winds chilled bones, blew hair, went through heavily wetted clothes (June was like November) but never were the English enveloped in so large a smile.

Art Buchwald called it 'England's wettest hour'. The phrase was a moving bouquet; a historic event has been more lavishly described before, but not more pointedly.

It's almost impossible to frame the Coronation in the context of the world today, yet it did dominate the minds of most of Europe at that time. I can only recount the highlights of the experience (it would take a book to tell them all) and ask you to see in them a small reference to the world twenty years ago!

General Marshall, ex-Secretary of Defence and ex-Secretary of State, was head of our American delegation, which also included the Governor of California, Earl Warren (later Chief Justice of the United States), and General Omar Bradley, representing the armed services.

Cheers rang out whenever General Marshall was spotted by the crowd; court circles also held him in awesome regard. That venerable 'Mr England' himself, Winston Churchill, made a splendid chip in the flawless Coronation ceremony when he spied Marshall in the Abbey, sitting in what was without question the finest place in the church. Churchill, almost lost inside an enveloping huge cloak of the robe of Knight of the Garter, suddenly recognized his old friend. Stepping out of line, he simply clasped the General's hand affectionately. Bent over, Churchill looked like a royal red cabbage. Of all the dignitaries he was the most extraordinary sight as he marched in the slow, difficult rhythm of the processional down the blue carpet of the Abbey. Spotting Marshall, he behaved as he always did; he ignored rule and circumstance. It was an amazingly impulsive gesture, which few knew happened.

General Bradley, in his quiet way, modestly accepted smiling faces that surely tied him to memories of Normandy. Governor

Warren brought a family who radiated apple-pie Americanism. None of the Warren family had ever been abroad before and their excitement and pleasure was infectious.

As one of the very few official lady delegates, I was treated most kindly by the English. The Queen was especially pleasant; once when I talked with her about her visit to the United States, she admitted, with genuine nostalgia, 'I'd like to have seen more of your American Alps, your American desert, your "big river", your great farmlands, your Pacific.'

Though I was absolutely astonished by her beauty and dignity in the Abbey, her poise and pretty English looks were a delight to see in an informal close-up at Buckingham Palace later.

About six other delegations were being presented when ours was there; I watched carefully as she moved slowly across the room. Nearest the door was the Greek delegation, including the coiffed nun who was her husband's own mother. Next was that *bon vivant*, Prince Bernhard, head of Holland's delegation; then the French delegation: General Juin of Morocco and M. Henri Schuman, France's Foreign Minister, heard from her how much *she* enjoyed the courtesies of their president when she visited France.

Listening to her superb French, I couldn't help thinking of her predecessor, Elizabeth I, who was the most learned of English queens. The formidable monarch spoke Latin, French and Italian fluently, Greek modestly. Her Latin was so good that when a bishop thought he was insulting the royal dignity secretly by giving his sermon in Latin, he was promptly arrested as he descended from the pulpit. The new Elizabeth, dressed in simple yellow cotton, reminded me that the first Queen Elizabeth, so passionate about clothes, left a thousand ball-dresses at her death.

All of us were greeted with equal poise and interest, superb briefing having accomplished its mission. When the Queen reached us, General Marshall made a little speech at the request of the English Speaking Union, to announce that they had raised $300,000 as a memorial to her late father in the form of scholarships in Marshall's name. Her eyes lit up.

When I was presented, she smiled and asked, 'Are you having a good time?' 'Yes, you have given us a wonderful experience and very special memories,' I replied. 'But, of course, all America has a wonderful memory of you from your recent visit to the United States.'

Of all memories of the event the picture which lingers most is of the crowds asleep on the kerb-stones (some for as long as forty-eight hours to stake out their space on the Coronation route). Three faces still stand out: the American man from Connecticut, who pitched a canvas shelter on the Mall for himself and crouched and shivered inside it for two days, as excited and intrigued as the British. Fortitude and curiosity knew no nationality.

The second was a *very* old lady, who parked her little stool on the pavement in Park Lane facing Hyde Park twenty-four hours before the great morning. I stole a moment to talk to her. 'This will be my fourth Coronation, and the most important one of all,' she told me. I found it very hard, very hard indeed, to slip inside my linen sheets and fluffy eiderdown on the cold, rainy night before the event, when I knew she was sitting out there in the cold and damp.

Just outside the Abbey, there was a last memorable face of the tiny little boy perched on his father's shoulder, one arm around his father's neck, the other one holding on for dear life to his father's nose. Children were everywhere (schools were given a place of honour on the route), but this little boy and his patient father stand out. They were still there, in the same place, and in the same position, many hours later when we returned from the 'Queen's Luncheon'.

The Queen, though hostess, was absent, riding in the State Coach through the crowds, to be seen with her new crown. After the ceremony her guests dined in Westminster Hall. The dark stone walls were hung with huge pink and orange garlands. I never got over the beauty of that combination: pink and orange is an unremarkable twosome today but Constance Spry seemed to have invented it then, working through the night on flowers which had been flown in from Africa.

The most colourful sight of all, to me, were the Zulus, Arabs, Indians, Chinese, Nepalese, Germans, tribesmen, Russians and coroneted English nobility—mixed like tossed confetti, side by side, in a never-to-be-repeated tableau. Wrapped turbans, tropical plumage and emerald beacons punctuated a sea of conventional diamond tiaras and veils. The view along the aisles in the Abbey was staggering.

Every colour of skin was arrayed on the canvas. Imperturbable foreigners blended with royals, broad smiles with grim-set jaws. Participants of bitter feuds and members of happy political entanglements sat side by side, most of their differences at least temporarily resolved by the biggest show on earth.

England somehow managed to break psychological if not political barriers with the event. I watched disparate elements of their colonies as they arrived at function after function – before and then after the Coronation. On arrival, they stood aloof, like stalks in the crowd, never mingling, seldom speaking. I saw the gradual melting until, before leaving, one could detect an unspoken smiling desire to claim ownership of the Queen. As we know, all political frictions weren't automatically erased, but they were certainly softened.

Public ardour wasn't just crowd-hysteria. The excitement remained after the gold coach had passed. Ten days later, I sat in the House of Commons and heard a Member of Parliament demand that decorations remain up for all of England to see for many weeks more. All this was quite understandable. The Monarchy, to an overwhelming number of the English people who were alive in June 1953, was a natural form of human society – perhaps not a necessary one, but absolutely natural.

The Queen was their connection with history (hers is one of the oldest offices in the world after the Papacy) and she was also the symbol of the future (which, that year, she certainly took for granted would be ruled by her own descendants). The little princess had become head of every branch of the nation's life, the Supreme Commander of the Armed Forces, the last recall in justice, the 'fountain' of honour, the patron and 'visitor' of ancient universities and royal academies and societies. She became, in fact, the head of society in all its aspects. Though she had no power herself, she was there to see that the actual possessors of it were kept in their places.

Trooping the Colour took place nine days after the Coronation yet all the main streets of London (some of them miles away from the scene of the event) were clogged and jammed with traffic and by crowds. Many people had come the night before to get kerb places on which to stand – only a few of them would ever see any part of the ceremony.

I watched from Anthony Eden's big room where I was over-looking the show from the back of the Foreign Office. Yet thousands who stood all over London to cheer the changing of the command could only tell it was happening by the sound they heard of guns. They merely wanted to be in the crowd, to watch the official cars go by. They didn't *need* to see. Incredible? That was England in 1953.

Enough time has elapsed to write of a few undisclosed incidents: how, through strong encouragement from George Marshall, I got to know the Queen of Greece. And Mrs Marshall's 'Wrong-Way Corrigan' drive, in reverse, on the Coronation route itself, while the ceremony in the Abbey was in full swing.

Mrs George Marshall's drive (in reverse) during the Coronation is a very long story. I should begin first by describing the marching orders given us every morning by our Gentlemen-in-Attendance, General Sir Leslie Hollis, Commander of the Royal Marines, and his assistant, Denis Greenhill[1] of the Foreign Office.

Each morning, quite often it seemed like dawn, our exhausted group was given an enormous chart, twice as wide as it was deep, which would have done justice to an army landing.

Worked out in minute detail were the strategic points of each day's events: exactly what time we were obliged to leave the hotel (and never a moment later), when to eat (and where), when to go to or leave a party, when expected at the next port of call, when and if a change of clothes was required (and if so, *exactly* what to wear – down to jewellery), who, if any, of the family which might have come to London was invited to a given event (or whether the wives or children were meant to sight-see or visit and how much time *they* had).

The logistics involved in 'fitting' our Coronation car into the Coronation procession are worth describing. Because of General

---

[1] He recently resigned the post of Permanent Under-Secretary of State for Foreign and Commonwealth Affairs, and is now Lord Greenhill of Harrow, G.C.M.G., O.B.E.

Marshall's age and position, it was arranged that he and I should be in the car next to the last in the procession of foreign representatives. This would mean a slightly longer night's rest as well as the shortest possible wait in the Abbey.

The first arrivals (the staff officers) had to be in the Abbey at six in the morning, it was therefore a great luxury to be near the end of the line. (The only ones to follow after our car were maharajahs, sultans, Commonwealth prime ministers, princes and princesses of royal blood – and the Royal Family itself.)

All had been rehearsed down to split seconds. We knew what time we were to be awakened, when breakfast would be at the door, when lifts were set aside – even the order in which we got into our motor car (not to lose a moment in unnecessary politesse).

We left at the exact moment. The speed of the drive was fixed so that we arrived at the second when, without interruption to the moving Coronation procession, our car would simply turn and glide from our street into the empty space being maintained for our car in the parade itself.

But it was long before this that Mrs Marshall's day began and during which the amazing, unknown 'Wrong-Way Corrigan' episode took place. Mrs Marshall and the General's affable A.D.C., Colonel George, were given seats in a stand just outside Lancaster House, on the route. In a gesture to Mrs Marshall, General Sir Leslie Hollis gallantly offered to sit with her, sending Denis Greenhill to the Abbey in his stead. Apart from anything else, General Hollis feared that Mrs Marshall's bad back could act up after sitting and standing too long.

At 8.00 a.m., these two were already in their places on the stand, having been taken there in taxis. The day was wet and cold. At 10.00 a.m., Mrs Marshall was already feeling uncomfortable. Would she like to go inside Lancaster House and rest? No. She was determined to see the Queen go by. Finally, at 10.45 they were able to move inside for a short rest.

When asked what she'd like to do then, Mrs Marshall looked General Hollis straight in the face and said, 'General, I would like to go *home.*'

Home meant her hotel at the opposite end of the Coronation route (which, quite naturally, was entirely shut to traffic). All guests were, in fact, in an area sealed-off from the rest of London by nine-foot high barricades.

General Hollis realized he must get her there. The Lord Chamberlain's officials were in Lancaster House; that helped. With a great deal of difficulty, a taxi was actually produced, but it was left to Hollis to find a way for Mrs Marshall, Colonel George and himself to get down the Coronation route in reverse direction!

The first obstacle was the enormous Royal Engineers' Band waiting at the bottom of St James's Street. Hollis had the fun of asking the commanding officer to move his band, to let them through.

The route stretching before them was totally empty, a huge traffic lane packed on all sides but deserted down the middle. Suddenly the crowds saw a tall black taxi scuttling down the Mall —a car going at the fastest possible clip in the opposite direction (that is, *between* hurdles. They still had three bands and two lots of troops to manoeuvre out of the way). Finally, 'Wrong-Way Taxi' reached its hotel.

Hollis told me later that day, almost in tears, that he had missed the entire Coronation of his Queen. Years after, in his autobiography, the late General was less anguished by the memory but he did admit in it, without qualification, that it was 'almost with relief that the Coronation assignment came to an end on Derby Day, June 6th'.

Whenever I am asked how I came to be so close to the Greek Royal Family, I thank George Catlett Marshall.

One day, he took a long, hand-written letter from his pocket and showed it to me. 'This is from a remarkable woman I want you to know,' he stated, and he saw to it that I did. It was a political document written to him in great confidence by Queen Frederika of Greece. That letter led to my friendship with this extraordinary family, which I value highly.

During those days together I had ample opportunity to talk to him, to get his views on all subjects of the day, of his life in general. Joe McCarthy, whose record in wounding Marshall needs no reminder, was then at the peak of his trouble-making career, a source of such embarrassment and disgrace to all our group that it cannot be exaggerated.

Life in Albany: where I live

A very old gentleman, William Stone, was once described as 'an impregnable stronghold of old London'. He lived just below us in the notable private building in London, the historic monument called Albany, which has also been my home since I came to England. The mansion, tucked beyond the noisy Piccadilly traffic, is still controlled by a 150-year-old trusteeship; it is charmingly riddled with ancient rules and regulations which have set it apart from all other London dwelling-places (perhaps from anywhere else in the world), making it a unique and desirable place to live. It had been erected in 1776 as a town house for Lord Melbourne.

Albany is as much a landmark as the Circus close by; a peaceful paradise on the edge of surging Piccadilly – a serene, idyllic oasis where romantic past and influential present are guarded by the National Trust for the future. Some say it is one of the world's wonders – a residence with its own laws, its own standards of living, its own wonderful traditions, its own great ghosts of former residents of the past.

It was temporarily presided over by Mr Stone when he was appointed Chairman of the Trustees in 1895 who, in the course of his lifetime, slowly acquired almost half of the vast estate. When he died (aged over a hundred) he left thirty sets of chambers (mainly in the Rope Walk, which leads from the main mansion to Vigo Street) to his university – making Peterhouse College, Cambridge, a most unusual landlord.

The old man was quite a curiosity. Even when he was alive, tales were rampant about his miserliness and his eccentricities (he left a large collection of Georgian jewellery, including a tiara which was reputed to have been worn by him occasionally). There was also his incredible vitality: although he padded off to sit in the flagstone garden below my drawing-rooms daily (to be read to by a nurse in a voice of necessity so loud I was often an unwilling audience), the most incredible sight was his daily departure for Regents Park. He'd shuffle off at a slow steady pace for a walk of *miles*. He did this until about a year before he reached his centenary.

With this event, a celebration was in order. Reaching the century mark in England tends to develop into a tribal ritual, and celebrating Mr Stone's achievement was no exception. All the tenants of his vast residence (most of them living in the Rope Walk area behind the mansion in which he and I and a few others lived) and all others, in fact, who knew the old man, realized their obligation. On January 14th, 1957, a vast birthday party took place.

Committees had to be formed: one was for the libations and cake decorations ('Many Happy Returns' was voted down as unsuitable); another committee was named to work on the greetings (a birthday telegram from the Queen had to be arranged, the custom when any of her subjects reach that great age); another committee worked on choices for speeches (*who* would be selected from an awesome list of Oxford dons, publishers, and intellectuals among his own Albany tenants?). Another dealt with the invitations (not too many could be asked, in consideration for his age). The orchestra of the Welsh Guards was engaged to play outside in the garden, so that sounds of music should drift in through the windows. Their repertory of songs was a fascinating revelation of Mr Stone's personal taste in music, which included Mozart's *Eine Kleine Nacht Musik*, and Ketelby's *In a Monastery Garden*.

His health was, quite naturally, a primary concern. Could the frail old boy really survive the excitement? Decisions were taken with tender felicity: just so much but not too much could be risked to tax his uncertain energy.

The party was held in what were then the chambers of his tenant, Mrs Frederick Roe (whose doorway was opposite Mr Stone's), who had a sufficiently large drawing-room. Mrs Roe, an old friend of mine, decided that (though I was not one of his tenants, and did not strictly fall into a category for the normal invitation) I simply must be on hand. A vote was taken before an invitation was issued to me.

Not being a 'normal' guest, I made myself as invisible as possible on arrival. The party started at five o'clock and lasted until seven to enable important gentlemen from the city and government to participate.

The old man was led in gently and placed at a carefully selected post in a high-backed armchair set in the big bay window. There, in the afternoon light, Mr Stone would be in full view. He had a way of instantly rising to his feet as soon as he was set into the chair (someone had to be placed alongside to push him gently back each time he rose). The bobbing up and down would have been hilarious had it not caused such concern. Whatever else one was thinking, everyone prayed that he would last out the afternoon.

Speeches were made, short and slightly pompous. The guest of honour seemed far away, not even listening. Where *was* he? I kept asking myself. The Queen's telegram was read, followed by a short burst of applause, then other messages followed; still his mind was not with it. The cake was brought ceremoniously. The decoration on it, after much discussion, read 'Happy Birthday'. A toast was drunk to his 'continued good health' and the guests lined up to shake his hand and say a word or two before they departed.

For most it had become an Albany reunion—a chance to chatter and ask many questions of one another in a community of intriguing dwellers who put privacy so high on their list of amenities.

I tended to cling to corners, watching discreetly. It was a happening so singularly English I couldn't get over it. I had only arrived from America about a year before and felt very much an observer. But my own turn in the queue finally arrived. I was the last; everyone else had left, the room was emptied except for the overwhelming presence of the tired old man, the hostess and fluttering committee members. All seemed dazed with delight that the strain had not proved fatal.

Finally, I stood before him, observing the morning suit which hung on bony shoulders, the long chicken-neck with obtrusive Adam's apple, the wandering, watery eyes. I tried to be brief.

'Mr Stone, you don't know me; I'm *not* your tenant, I'm an American living in a set of chambers I own above you, but I've been allowed to come to your party. I just want to add my best wishes for the day,' I explained.

'*You're an American?*' he croaked out. As he did so, he bolted up again from his high chair, took my hand in his and headed like a slow turtle for the other side of the room. The destination was soon obvious: it was the long, soft sofa he had obviously eyed all afternoon so longingly.

He never looked elsewhere. He never said another word to me or anyone. As he slowly reeled round and drifted down into the sofa's soft pillows, he took me down with him. I dropped, without a murmur, on the floor below him, his hand still gripping mine.

He finally let my hand go, pushed his Adam's apple back in place, arranged his stiff, butterfly collar and cravat and then boldly attacked, looking me straight in the eye:

'Do *you* remember Beauregard?' he asked in deadly seriousness.

'No,' I whispered back (more in shock than in doubt).

'Well, your people were very unkind to Beauregard after the Civil War,' he reprimanded me firmly.

'I'm so very sorry,' I demurred.

'Do you know what General Grant said to Beauregard after the war was over?' he pushed on.

'No, I never really heard,' I whispered, hoping to show some regret.

'Grant said, "Beauregard, you go back to your farm." The nonsense of it! Beauregard had no farm!'

'What happened then?' I whispered.

'He joined the mercenaries and fought on the British side in the Sudan. *I'll* never forget Beauregard!'

That point settled, I looked for an exit. But he was not ready for departure. Settling back quite happily, he then searchingly inquired:

'Were *you* on the Pony Express?'

'Good Lord, no! It was slightly before my ... '

Before I could point out the matter of age, he interrupted: 'Of course you weren't! I know exactly who *was* on that first journey.

You do realize that a very great friend of mine invented the combustion engine?'

'Quite frankly, I didn't know that,' I feebly admitted.

'Yes, and I can tell you who was in every seat on the first trip. Let me see; it was Johnson on the right window seat, and on the left ... '

'Please, you must be very tired,' I murmured, as I jumped to my feet, longing only for the door. I felt as if I was on Mars ...

I kissed the hostess warmly and fled to the comparatively modern confines of my own eighteenth-century walls above.

Actually, in these hallowed Albany chambers, the rules in very fine print hover charmingly over life there. No music — no sounds at all — after eleven o'clock. No children. No dogs. No cats. An Edwardian atmosphere is maintained with astonishing success (and most of us who live there are grateful for the restrictions).

Something happened many years ago to typify the attitude: it was midnight. A poker-faced porter unlocked the heavy door to let a tiny woman through. There was Judy Garland, who had come for a midnight snack, looking tired and unglamorous in rumpled trousers, with rumpled hair, with a rumpled manner — but with an unexpected difference — she was actually unusually gay. This was a pleasant moment sliced into her usually neurotic life. Once let inside (after proving she was really expected) Judy started skipping through the hall, singing. *Singing!* That's against all the rules *any* time of the day — but at *midnight!*

'I'm sorry, Miss, you simply cannot skip through these halls and certainly you cannot sing here,' the porter announced. She stopped dead in her tracks, burst into gales of laughter, and said: 'You must be kidding! I'm Judy Garland! Anywhere else, I'd be getting $20,000 for doing just this!'

'There, there now, Miss,' he said, patting her gently on the back. '*Not here.*'

Sussex: living in the country

I made a pact with my husband just after we were married: we wanted a weekend house but we would never buy one we needed to discuss.

When we saw ours from the top of its Sussex hill, we both mentally bought it on sight. It was a beautiful April day in 1956; we'd left the main road a little more than thirty miles from London and wandered two miles down a private road, along the high-hedged lanes so peculiarly English.

The house suddenly came into view inside its own soft valley, hidden from the world by its extensive grounds (the house in the dead centre). A very old house, it had been a mere débutante when the Spanish Armada sailed in to attack England – neither cottage nor castle but something very manageable in between.

After taking in the pinkness of old tiles on the house itself, we turned and saw the larger 'black', weathered wooden tithe barn smothered by rhododendrons – and clematis over the old tile roof. Centuries ago, the local church stored its 10 per cent of the estate's crop inside. Three years ago (fifteen years after we bought it) we restored the weakened and damaged barn. When we first saw it, the doors were open and we walked straight through it to see the two wings of the barn beyond, closed in on the fourth side by a blazing copper beech hedge. In the court inside this square we now have a swimming pool. And we've completely restored the rest, saving it from falling down.

Centuries ago, whoever planned the garden had help from a fast stream running through the land; it helped the terraced rock garden which dropped down to the dammed-up lake, and shaped it like a small amphitheatre. Peter Brook saw it and said he'd like to produce *A Midsummer Night's Dream* there. The actors would have had at their backs the wooded copse of the far side. Many times we've seen Margot Fonteyn leaping from stone to stone in something akin to a private ballet.

My husband has since made three more lakes in the valley, flooding them (with immense scientific care) to produce three more areas of water, each cascading over a waterfall to a lower body of water. Each will eventually have its own garden to give homes to wild birds. Harold Macmillan reminded him recently that he was merely continuing the tradition of the Georgian gentlemen who would always re-level and re-landscape their land to add a lake.

Under the sunlit trees near the smallest one, daffodils, kingcups, bluebells, fritillaria and azaleas abound. I constantly add tulips and all bulbs to the meadow gardens near the others. I've also planted seeds of all the disappearing wild flowers. Now water gardens are being designed around the other three lakes, to reflect the colour.

Elsewhere, I have lived up to English tradition by planting masses of roses: a hundred and forty-six 'Elizabeth of Glamis' line the walk to our door and remind us of the Queen Mother. Recently I've added my own proud collection of fifty 'Fleur Cowles' rose-bushes, created by Gregory's in my name. A cream rose blushed with pink—and fragrant—looking as if Fantin-Latour designed it.

Our front door is shadowed by a yew tree the same age as the house, planted in 1572 to provide the bows which were the weapons of the yeomen of England. Inside are the wooden beams which served first at sea. Fine wood was precious so our house was built from the discarded ribs of old ships—so tough and so calcified one can't drive a nail into them today. My husband (whose business is 'timber') loves each and every one.

The obligation to any *monument historique* is to preserve it. This we have done but we have brought lavish internationalism into its interior décor, using furniture and objects collected on travels over the years. We find it all beautiful and peaceful.

Why do I love the English countryside so much? The reasons are countless — but I'd like to name two:

The weather: Though often really grim, it can also be a painless paradise — particularly when sunsets bring smoke and grime and sun together in the burning haze immortalized by Turner, or where white cumulus clouds boil in a sky of baby colours (rarely dramatic, always soft and *blue*-blue). Long, sad sunsets are noted down by farmers more reverently than radio's meteorological reports.

The counties: Where else, in such a tightly crowded area, is such infinite variety? In a space smaller than many states in America, one can find different architecture, different landscapes and wildly differing natural characteristics. For instance: the savage beauty of Cornwall (Cape Cod in the U.S.A. is a pale copy) where stone houses sit precariously near the sea on one of the world's stormiest coasts. Then there is the lush, manicured green of Sussex, where an Elizabethan world still exists in tiny towns. Walls are an amber glow in the Cotswolds, where ancient French stone houses perch alongside the high green hay. In Kent the marshes and lowlands are filled with lazy cattle and sheep by the sea.

The stuff of poets ...

An Evening in 1948
on the House of Commons Terrace

During 1948, when the cold war with Russia began seriously to hot up, I was in London on a fact-finding trip.

On June 24th the Russians had stopped all rail and road traffic from the West to Berlin. Power stations in the Soviet sector stopped the electric current. Seven days later (after a meeting of all four military governors, who failed to come to an agreement), a complete blockade followed.

Brinkmanship, Dulles's word which later became so commonplace, described a very tense month of Russian provocation, which ended in an incredible airlift mounted by the United States and Western Allies in response to the virtual siege of Berlin.

Whenever I flew to Europe that year, I started my journey with a vague apprehension; would we be lucky to get through? Both the East and the West seemed close to accidental destruction.

On one such journey, whilst in London on a particularly tense day, I was invited by the late Sir Alan P. Herbert ('A.P.', author, playwright and one of the most original Members of Parliament) to dine. We went to the House of Commons. 'You'll be nearer to decisions and nearer to news,' he explained.

The night was grey in the misty way Turner knew so well and made so famous. After an early meal, A.P. unexpectedly sat me down at a table on the great stone terrace outside, which goes along the river side of the turreted House of Commons. 'I'll go upstairs and send people down to you one at a time. They'll all enjoy meeting a lady editor. Just sit there. Before the night is over, you'll see a great many men whom you've never known before, men on all sides of the war issue,' he announced as he bounded off.

He left me alone. I found myself in a setting most unreal. It was so familiar yet almost unbelievable. I'd seen it so often in paintings: the river, the bridges, the haze, the late sun burning through. But an overwhelming tension added a dimension never put there by paint and brush. It was lonely. It was somewhat eerie, even frightening. Would the first bomb fall as I sat there? Would the Third World War be declared? Most agonizing, would this beautiful great building, which had been bombed but survived the Blitz, actually fall now?

A.P. had sat me down directly opposite the private door which opened on the narrow, upright stairs leading to Members' Chambers above. Although I never knew who A.P. would send down (each man merely introduced himself), I always knew a lot about them by the time they arrived. I could tell them by their gait.

I first saw their shoes, then their trousers, then, finally, the whole man emerged from the stairwell. The slow and careful step would be someone older and more profound (more worried perhaps?). The fast step (sometimes a trot) turned out to be someone gay and undaunted, less experienced (perhaps even elated by the drama of coming events).

I talked for nearly two hours with Members from both sides of Parliament, every moment of it completely fascinating. Each man had a highly personal answer to questions about Russia's intentions, about the bravery (or, to one, the ridiculous rashness) of the colossal American airlift,[1] about the readiness of America to face Russia (and Britain's willingness to unite with her) in outright war (nuclear?) against an enemy so recently on the allied side. Most were deeply concerned, certain of war.

Some men stayed four or five minutes, some fifteen. A.P.'s ingenuity, persuasiveness, even playfulness, must have been at its peak, to judge by his choices. I was exhilarated and, I might add, overwhelmingly grateful and flattered by the originality of the idea.

Soon darkness began to appear. In the last days of July, daylight went slowly. I knew in the twilight that someone terribly

[1] The airlift began in July 1948. By mid-February, in 1949, the Allied airlift had brought the millionth ton into Berlin and evacuated over forty thousand children. On May 12th, all restrictions imposed by both sides on road, rail and river traffic in and out of Berlin were finally rescinded—and the 'war' changed climate once again.

preoccupied had started down the stairs. Every step was slow and deliberate, even hesitant.

'You didn't really want to come,' I said to a handsome, silver-templed, deeply ponderous man, 'this is obvious.'

'You are right, I did not – but A.P. insisted,' was all he said, as he sat in heavy silence, looking up the river.

I didn't disturb him. We sat there like detached strangers for at least five long minutes, when he suddenly turned to me:

'This is a grave evening. I'm terribly worried. Do *you* like Shakespeare?'

'Of course, of course!' I responded, ignoring the oddity of the question. Somehow, I knew how much that would please him.

For the next half-hour, looking straight ahead at the river (and without interruption), he recited Shakespeare. I remember most of all the excerpts from *Romeo and Juliet* and *Hamlet*.

He got up without another comment. 'Goodnight, Miss Cowles – and *thank* you,' he said as he turned slowly to walk back up the stairs.

That poetic gentleman was the Rt Hon. William Shepherd Morrison, P.C., M.C., K.C., LL.D., Conservative Member for Gloucestershire since 1929 and a former Minister who became Speaker of the House of Commons in 1951. In 1960, after eight years there, he became Governor-General of Australia. He died in 1961.

Shakespeare's works were such a part of his being, he was always known as 'Shakes' Morrison to his friends, A.P. explained a few minutes later when he rejoined me. I was still in a pleasant state of bewilderment.

Important Gentlemen

I HAVE met countless important men and have often mused what made them so. Even the most noted can be hard to analyse; they often surprise us, acting just like other ordinary mortals.

I'll never forget the frosty Foreign Minister of Great Britain whom I invited to dinner in New York. He had just flown in to attend a U.N. session and was obviously tired by the journey. A very changed man left after coffee; clasping my hand unexpectedly in his, he bade me farewell at the door, thanking me so effusively and so irrationally I simply couldn't resist asking him, what on earth for?

'Why? Because you gave me Garbo! I shall never forget you for that!' he exclaimed, in a state of complete euphoria.

I had seated him between her and me at table, evidently the greatest possible thrill. He never seemed a formidable man after that.

Other big men come down from pedestals in different ways; Winston Churchill, for instance. I knew one of his remarkable wartime secretaries well, but she would never confirm (or even discuss) the common gossip that he dictated from his bath.

Importance can be shown in many ways. I can think of two examples. One, a friend from Portugal, Dr Antonio Judice Bustorff-Silva, was once officially invited to France to visit President de Gaulle after the end of the Second World War. The tall French leader and the Hogarthian banker and industrialist walked round the gardens of Versailles together (one of the rare times when another man's height almost equalled the General's).

Dr Bustorff was being thanked officially by de Gaulle on behalf of the French Government for looking after the Portuguese property (and possessions of the Government and other French nationalists) during the war. He never took a penny for doing it.

'What can the French do for you in return? You may choose anything you like. You name it; France will gladly give it to you!' de Gaulle pointed out.

Dr Bustorff stopped short, quite unprepared; they were standing alongside a lovely lily-pond, filled with glistening fish. He looked slowly around him.

'I'd like those two Chinese carp to be sent to me in Portugal,' he announced with a grin – to de Gaulle's shocked surprise.

The two fish were his price, nothing more. A dignified reaction to the idea of accepting any repayment, by one of the most generous men I know. The same carp, larger and fatter, swim in the similarly beautiful lily-pond of Dr Bustorff's *finca* outside Lisbon. For me, this story makes Dr Bustorff a very important gentleman.

The other man is Lord Chief Justice of England, Lord Widgery. He had come to the bench via the army, a rare road to travel to the top. The elegant jurist revealed his character in an intriguing way when my husband and I were his guests at the annual induction of new barristers in Westminster Abbey. Every judge in the land was on hand – from Justices of the Peace to High Court judges. Each man (and each of the few women) wore the robe of office his station allowed; from wigs over black cottons to wigs over black silk with purple and scarlet ribbons – the sight cannot be matched elsewhere.

Before going inside for the ritualistic ceremony we stood with Lady Widgery, watching the judges file in. When the Lord Chief Justice arrived, resplendent in wig and lavish robe, he greeted us.

'I've just had an awesome thought,' my husband announced. 'Not a court is sitting in England today. No justice of any kind is being meted out!'

'And no injustice either!' was Widgery's prompt response.

One can hardly hope to find a better clue to the state of British justice – or to a man's greatness.

Stories about a few other gentlemen I have known take longer to tell; their length doesn't necessarily make them more significant. They follow.

Gamal Abdel Nasser: the man I knew

In the early 'fifties, I tried once, crazily, to persuade Gamal Abdel Nasser to consider meeting Prime Minister Ben Gurion of Israel on a neutral ship in neutral waters to discuss their problems. I tried, another time (and nearly succeeded), to persuade him to lend the Tutankhamun treasures to the National Gallery in Washington (although I hadn't consulted anyone beforehand). This might have been one politically acceptable way to get him to Washington – where he could begin to be involved with the West. There were other attempts. I argued for hours to persuade him not to go to the Bandoeng Conference: it would be his first trip outside Egypt; it would inevitably tie him to the East at a time when the West still hoped (although they did little to ensure it) to keep Egypt in its camp. I *did* get to know the man (and his family).

Once, in jest, I replied to his question about when I was next coming to Egypt, that I'd do so whenever he promised to see me *on time* – 'when you can take the time to show me some of your projects!' The next time I went there, the invitation came through official channels, and he made good his promise.

On one visit, I was Nasser's guest at the feast of Ramadhan, the traditional dinner given to celebrate the end of the yearly religious period of fasting. Since early in Egypt's history the armed forces have given a banquet for their monarch on this evening; for the first time in history, a commoner and not a king was their chief. As far as I know, I am the first woman to have been invited. I found myself the one female face in a full-page photograph of thousands of officers published in the Cairo newspapers the next day; many frowned on the female intrusion. In fact, when I'd accepted Nasser's invitation, I'd had no idea where I would be dining.

After five visits to Cairo, I decided not to go back to Egypt. The men around Nasser were irritated and there were immense obstacles to overcome before they would ever agree to any plan I offered their leader.

First of all, I was the wrong sex to be in the limelight in an Arab country. Secondly, I was American, and that became more and more of a handicap (the States were already looked on with suspicion when I first went there in the early 'fifties). Lastly, when it became known that I had Nasser's attention and had gone frequently to his home, I began to feel hot breath on the nape of my neck. I never went back after the spring of 1955, by which time U.S.A.–Egypt relations had really deteriorated.

My first introduction to Gamal Abdel Nasser was in 1952, when I made a trip to Cairo as a travelling editor; United States Ambassador Henry Byroade arranged it. I got on well with the powerfully-built man (confirmed when a half-hour appointment became a two-and-a-half-hour visit). After that experience I went back with specific objectives, usually at President Eisenhower's bidding.

I only once came close (very close) to achieving any objective. I met disappointment in all, despite Nasser's friendly behaviour. There was hardly anything I could say which would offend him, although the same sort of discussion with a Head of State might normally have made an ambassador on post *persona non grata*.

Whenever I went to Cairo, I stayed with Ambassador and Mrs Byroade. Every time an appointment was requested for me to see Nasser, a message would come down through official channels – naming the hour though never the place – and then the cloak-and-dagger trip to meet him would begin.

These rendezvous had their element of suspense until one got used to the conditions. I always began the journey (alone) in the ambassador's black limousine. At a certain point, usually at a large, crowded two-storey café, I would leave the big black American Embassy Cadillac to have a drink with Dr Mohammed

Hatem (I believe he is now adviser to President Sadat). Ultimately (and only after the Embassy limousine moved safely away) a small, decrepit car would draw up to take us to the heavy, high doors of the fortified army post in which President Nasser lived until he died in 1970. It was only a mile from the centre of Cairo, but it seemed very far away indeed. The unfamiliarity of the route gave one the feeling of added distance.

The first time these gates opened, I had little idea what to expect. Like everyone else, I had heard that Nasser and his wife and a fairly large brood of children lived in absolute simplicity. This was no exaggeration: the house was small and mediocre, the rooms were the size of large boxes, the furniture sparse. In the parlour reserved for special callers, the ubiquitous brightly-coloured, brocade-upholstered suite (brilliantly gilded pieces of furniture of the type so favoured by Egyptians) was the sole decoration. There was, in fact, something touching, if not ridiculous, in a Head of State jamming a very large family into such small quarters.

At one time, the Nassers and their three sons and two daughters and I spent hours being photographed together — very active little boys and girls flitting around like mosquitoes. The child who caught my fancy was then his father's pet, a wild-eyed, frisky boy of six or seven whom Nasser had nicknamed Jimmy Cagney! The timid Mrs Nasser was only persuaded to have a real conversation with me after several visits.

What about Nasser's personal characteristics? *The charm?* It abounded. *His handsomeness?* By Western standards, his nose was huge — but one flash of a smile and the nose disappeared. His eyes were his best feature but unlike his nose they could not be caricatured. *Dependability?* I tried not to challenge it. Perhaps he was intrigued by my straight talk. Were our political conversations, in fact, his first with *any* lady? Was I not, in any case, the first Western lady he'd ever come to know? *Educated?* More than most Egyptians (though obviously less than his successor, President Sadat). He was a voracious reader, his mail including a subscription to that favourite of America's political intellectuals, the *Foreign Affairs* magazine. He spoke English.

He paid me the compliment of total concentration, doubling

over in his chair as we talked, looking intently at me. From time to time that broad grin would punctuate the conversation and when it did, I knew I was losing the game. His goodwill wasn't my objective. Nudging him into action was harder.

If he was terribly anxious to reply, he'd grab my wrist – to make sure of my attention. He may have had dozens of people waiting (as he made me do when I first called on him in his office in Cairo) but he gave no sign of impatience; I never got the impression I was being hustled on my way.

In 1972, many years later, when the Tutankhamun treasures came to Paris and then to the British Museum, I was irritated by the irony, remembering how hard I had tried to get them out of Egypt in 1953. At that time, Nasser flatly said No to my suggestion that they be lent to Washington's National Gallery. 'The Egyptian people would lynch a leader who would send away their natural heritage,' he announced.

If they'd been lent to Washington, Nasser could have made the acceptable 'cultural' journey – without an official White House invitation – and political discussions at White House level might have changed Middle East policy. Perhaps averted two wars. Hate was not so hot then; negotiation might have had a chance.

Nasser was then probably the world's youngest Head of State; he was thirty-five when I met him after he had deposed General Naguib. A year before, as a lieutenant, he had master-minded the army *coup* that led to Farouk's abdication.

The *coup* which overthrew Farouk was accomplished without bloodshed. Nasser admitted to me the Revolutionary Command Corps only meant it as a *feint* to test Farouk's strength. But Farouk left the country instantly, and abdicated. The monarchy was abolished and a republic proclaimed. Farouk's five-million-dollar annual income, his four palaces, his two yachts, his fleet of planes, his carloads of erotica, his palaces – one with rooms full of gifts for amours – were all inherited by the state.

The Revolutionary Command Corps which had devised the revolt was composed of twelve men, led by Abdel Nasser; all of them were young, most of them majors. Another four hundred young men were in the group called the Officers' Committee and together they became Egypt's ruling class.

They were all too young and too low in rank to choose a leader from their own group when Farouk fled. The regiment's own general seemed the logical person to meet the requirements of the unexpected victory. General Naguib was over fifty, looked like a good, solid father-figure, was kind, unassuming and un-ambitious. And he readily accepted the revolutionary group's invitation to become President of the newly-formed republic.

Nasser went to great lengths to explain to me why he took the Presidency from Naguib himself so soon afterwards. The move was not at all unexpected; Mike Cowles and I had been in Cairo just after the *coup* and were visiting the British Ambassador, Sir Ralph Stevenson. 'Keep your eye on the brilliant young man behind the President. *He's giving the instructions. His name is Nasser,*' Ambassador Stevenson pointed out. I recalled this conversation every time I saw Nasser.

Naguib, Nasser told me, was 'too simple-minded; he soon fell in love with the public's attention. It went to his head, and when he began to negotiate secretly with our natural enemies, the extreme right-wingers, that was the end. Those crafty old men had never done anything for Egypt but "milk it" — yet Naguib was completely taken in, and soon could have become *their* man. So for Egypt's good, we placed him under house arrest.'[1]

Nasser replaced Naguib a few months after he had been con-sidered too young to do so. Nasser was only two years older than the roly-poly Farouk he replaced, looking for all the world like an inconspicuous young man leading a handful of young zealots in uniform. He soon became the most powerful personality in the modern Arab world, using the dictator-principle to try to carry out reforms (a controlled press and an army behind him).

Even disaster and defeat by the Israelis didn't harm his total appeal to the masses, for whom he had become a god-like figure (one might call it success by default). Even in the caves and mud-houses of Muscat and in the desert of the Hadhramaut in Arabia, I saw Nasser's photograph hung inside those rough walls, a passport of brotherhood between Arabs.

In attempting to change their world, the Nasser government became the oppressor itself; innocents were jailed and a new

[1] Where he may still be, more than twenty years later.

feudalism was installed in the name of freedom by the king-makers (and their new 'king').

At that time, Nasser seemed a man spurred towards revolt, as so many dictators before him, by his own childhood poverty. He had enormous intellectual capacity, seemingly incapable of personal corruption. He constantly referred to his mother when talking to me; 'She often went hungry to send me forward.' His own book describes this devotion to her.

Nasser became a revolutionary in that best of all revolutionary breeding grounds, the student riots, when he was seventeen. He wanted to become a lawyer and to use the knowledge for political reforms but he changed his mind at twenty, when he was commissioned in the army to fight for the first time against the Israelis in 1938.

A possible turning point may have been in 1942, when the British sent their tanks against Farouk's palace, with good cause. Though Nasser loathed the king, nationalism reared its head: Farouk was the monarch and Nasser was riled by this affront to Egypt's dignity. Exactly ten years later, he thought differently, dethroning the profligate king, using tanks to do so.

Nasser died a little more than five years after the Rabelaisian Farouk had a heart attack (and a sordid end) in a Roman restaurant. In that very same week he had been re-elected President of Egypt by 99.999 per cent of all votes cast. A very different Nasser had gone to his people in this election. He had become tired, cynical, pressurized and also ill, allowing no other candidate to appear on the ballots or in the headlines of his controlled press.

What had happened? He must have been terribly unhappy (if he still had the capacity to look back): his country was an example of the mismanaged state, his army had been shown up by the Israelis and his national economy was in tatters.

He had nudged his country slightly forward before he died – but not very far – and seen the situation with Israel brought to boiling point, leading to another war.

Bernard M. Baruch: a girl's best friend

I was fortunate enough to know Bernard M. Baruch well and to benefit from that friendship in ways that can never be fully expressed. I was described as one of his 'children' in the biography of his life, written by Pulitzer Prize winner Margaret L. Coit.[1] If I had been his child, he couldn't have cared more for my happiness and well-being.[2]

He was so many men and performed on so many levels, anyone who had his confidence and friendship was enriched by both, and I was one of the few women who were close to the elder statesman. Apart from his spectacular secretary and two remarkable nurses, the list was small but diverse. Clare Booth Luce was not only his most glamorous favourite, but he was genuinely in love with her.

Luce and Baruch met in 1923, at the Democratic National Convention in Chicago;[3] she was then the beautiful, blonde lady editor of *Vanity Fair* and she was slowly taking Baruch's dictation, typing with two fingers. Her beauty and mind fascinated him for the rest of his life.

Another female, Hedda Hopper, whose shrill reportage on Hollywood gave it occasional jitters, was also a great favourite of Baruch's; he was amused by her vivid character, her very special language, her crazy hats and her extreme right-wing politics (which must have been shattering even to a 'conservative' Democrat). She was a friend of mine as well and even I thought she was at least 180° to the right of the most reactionary politician.

[1] *Mr Baruch: the Man, the Myth, the Eighty Years*, Houghton Mifflin, 1957.

[2] Mr Baruch did, in fact, have three children of his own, Belle, Renee and Bernard M. Baruch jr.

[3] It was her first political convention but within a few years she was a speaker at another — a Republican, not Democratic.

To say Mr Baruch's taste in friends was catholic was an under-statement – judging by his male as well as female friends. The men weren't all 'kings' or 'king-makers'. One of the most colourful (and, to many, the most inexplicable) was Billy Rose – Broadway impresario, entertainer and big-timer, who boasted he was always welcome in Baruch's house and life.

Billy Rose also came under Baruch's surveillance via the type-writer, as an ordinary stenographer working at the War Industries Board. He began by bringing the austere Mr Baruch his 'afternoon chocolate-sodas' and ended up sipping gin and tonic in Baruch's palatial homes. Much of Billy Rose's great fortune was made on the stock market and although Baruch permanently denied being the brains behind it, no one ever really believed he didn't master-mind the operation.

Robert Ruark, famous both as a syndicated columnist, and author of bestseller books, was another whom Baruch loved. The feeling was reciprocated. Both men used to shoot together and talk politics, Baruch enjoying Ruark's colourful language and mind.

Miss Coit's 800-page book is an authorized description of Mr Baruch's first eighty years (he lived to be ninety-five), but on a few personal memories my own potted version is short and sweet.

First, the man's wealth: he made it on the stock market when in his early twenties. Once made, he gave up Wall Street for public service. Though a capitalist (who gave the Russian Marxists a real case of intellectual jimjams), his rich friends thought he 'deserted his club' by demanding higher taxes for national welfare and crusading against profiteers. He gave his own money freely.

As a counsel: he was even consulted by the Soviet Union. He was official adviser to six presidents (and relentless advice was given to many who he felt needed it even when not asked for). He influenced governments in Europe as well as his own – and it would be hard to make an official count of Cabinet members, high-ranking military gentlemen, diplomats, local politicians and congressmen who came to him for help – which was given either in his office, from his elegant flat – or sitting on his famous Central Park bench in New York City (hence his most familiar American nickname 'Mr Park Bench').

Although he consistently refused a post in government (knowing that it usually 'kissed off' a man's potential influence), he wrote countless official reports and headed many missions, including the United States mission on Atomic Energy in the U.N., in which he gave a historically tough battle to the Soviets. His Baruch Plan for control of atomic weapons remained American policy for years.

He purposely stayed away from politics 'as such', mainly because he wanted to be of service, regardless of the party in power. But he did take on some big jobs: he chaired the War Industries Board in the First World War, controlling the entire industrial establishment of the United States; he had an important voice at the Treaty of Versailles; he was close to Woodrow Wilson in all economics, labour and agricultural conferences and wrote a post-war plan for Roosevelt for use at the end of the Second World War.

To most humble Americans, 'Mr Park Bench' Statesman was the thin, tall, grey-haired figure who sat on a bench in Central Park outside his New York apartment, acting as trouble-shooter when things went wrong. Few Americans didn't know that for at least half a century he was an influential force in their lives whether or not he represented their own particular hopes and views. Many didn't like his straight talk, often in the vernacular. 'Bunk' was his best known one-word comment whenever he disapproved.

Mr Baruch and I met in 1946 and I often used to wish it had been sooner. I had gone for the weekend in Port Washington, to stay with friends in a little gatekeeper's cottage on a large estate belonging to mutual friends. On Sunday, Alicia and Harry Guggenheim asked us to lunch in the main house. The great man was there, already seventy-six years old.

In the nine fateful years before I moved to England, he took much time out to be my friend. Advice poured forth and with one exception – his contention that I should go in for politics – I took it.

Very soon after our meeting he told me he had looked me over and decided I was 'a damn clever girl'. He offered to help me get into political life properly. Since the idea of elected political office has always been anathema to me I said, '*No thanks.*'

'Well, you're in the right business anyway. You can at least keep an eye on politics, so make the most of that,' he ordered. Needless to say, being in the publishing world interested me more: 'getting to know' wasn't difficult. And a lot of 'getting to weigh it' was funnelled into my mind by the old man himself.

Whatever he knew he'd pass on. Advice just seemed to fall from him, and not always in an obvious manner. He had a way of sharing information: he never gave me the impression that he either knew it all or was supposed to be the only one to know it.

There was one habit he got into which I'll never be able to appraise sufficiently – although I do know that few other things sharpened my mind and increased my knowledge so immeasurably. He used to telephone me early in the morning, just a few minutes after he knew I'd reached my office. Being deaf, he used to shout (which in itself would make me sit up mentally). His questions were always penetrating.

'Fleur,' he'd bark. 'What do *you* think the g–d–Russians are up to today?'[1] Or he'd shout, 'What the hell is the stock market up to today?' 'Did you hear the President had removed controls yesterday – what the hell for?' 'Who *is* ready to take on unilateral action against Red China?' ... 'What's your view on old-age pensions?' ... 'What's today's news from Cairo?' ... 'Who the hell really thinks Tom Dewey is going to win the election?'[2] and 'We may not know the score from Korea' (the morning that gunfire first sounded there) 'but just the same, you'd better start thinking about it.' ... 'You know Harold T——; what do you think of the Kefauver inquiry?' And so on and on. I never knew what he'd ask.

Can one possibly estimate the value of such a tribute? I'm sure it was a calculated game of teaching. The result of this constant questioning was to 'scare' me into knowledge: I never dared give a knowingly stupid answer. I never dared pass over a pertinent piece of news (who knew – perhaps it would be just what he'd

[1] Shortly after Hiroshima, when he was made the American representative on the United Nations' Atomic Energy Commission, the Russians obviously inherited the majority of his curses.

[2] Baruch was the one prophet who always knew Truman would be elected. Although Baruch and Truman's friendship had cooled almost to the point of an open break, Baruch was probably the only man in America who knew (and bet money on it) that Truman would beat Thomas E. Dewey in the Presidential campaign in 1948. He sent me a handwritten note many months before for the record. Truman's own party treated him with contempt.

be asking about the next moment!). I never knew where that volatile mind would perch or what question I'd be expected to answer.

The exquisite side of the agony was the occasional pleasure of hearing him answer his own question. And then he'd hang up. The call was always brief and to the point. I learned to be precise.

Because I loved my old friend and never wanted to let him down, I soon discovered how often sheer intuition (or some other inexplicable magic) came to my rescue. I found myself saying things I didn't even know I knew. The important thing was to be intelligent enough that he'd keep on calling, and keep up the routine. In the end, he had taught my mind to grab facts quickly and to analyse them fast. No other method could conceivably do more to train a mind on current events.

When I came abroad to live, I lost that ritual; I missed those 'frightening' telephone calls. I could only talk to him when our paths crossed in the U.S.A. or Europe and there was never time enough to make up for the months lost in between. Conversation, face-to-face, was always leisurely. On the telephone it had a machine-gun rapidity. No one could ever take his place playing that little game. Fortunately for me, we played it for a long time.

He took a great interest in my career, and though he read and discussed what I was doing as an editor and was especially proud of the magazine *Flair*, he never let up on his desire to see me as a full-time diplomat. Whenever I did something for President Eisenhower, he was pleased.

Once when he was at Little Hobcaw, his shooting-lodge in South Carolina (which he gave as a gift to his nurse, Miss Navarro), he wrote to say he was feeling sorry for himself as he had flu. He ended the handwritten letter with: 'You lay low and keep quiet and your number will come up. Best to you. You rate O.K. in my book and my book is a good book.'

At another time, he was angry at what he termed a lost opportunity. I had been asked to testify on a Saturday before the Senate Foreign Affairs Committee about the state of our Information Programme around the globe. The trip to Washington interfered with a weekend on which I had promised to take Mike Cowles's three children to Bermuda, so Senator Hickenlooper, head of the committee, reluctantly agreed to accept a written statement for the record, rather than demand my appearance. I sent a copy of the report down to Mr Baruch, telling him *why* I wrote it instead of reporting in person. He was furious.

'Dear Fleur,' he wrote back instantly. 'I could spank you for not appearing before the Foreign Affairs Committee. This was a tip-top statement. You would have established yourself as an authority and opened a post like Sweden or Switzerland for yourself. Bang! Bang! Bang! Three spanks!'

When I discussed the possible embarrassment of a post to a woman's husband, a conversation I once had with the President, Baruch thought hard about it. Finally, he decided: 'You're right. A girl's got to be somewhere in back of a man — not the other way around.'

My friends used to ask me if I knew how Mr Baruch kept from growing old. It was no secret. He took immense care. He did his daily dozen. He always had a dedicated and attractive nurse, first Blanche Van Ess, then Elizabeth Navarro, both of whom cosseted him but treated him firmly. Neither of them allowed much nonsense when it came to his health. 'I might have talked back to Presidents but never to Van Ess or Navarro,' he once admitted to me, proud of their care.

It was no secret, either, that Mr Baruch was a patient of Dr Niehans, to whom, at his death, he left me a handwritten letter as a strange legacy. The letter asked the Swiss doctor to look after me personally. I was not to be 'passed on to any assistants', and he ended by pointing out it was a favour he had only asked for *me*.

Dr Niehans had long intrigued (and frightened) me. Many of my own friends, male and female, mainly actresses and of varying ages, have been to him and sworn by his youth-fixing process. Two very famous old men, Pope Pius XII and Doctor Conrad Adenauer, were helped to longevity by Dr Niehans. Willie Maugham as well, and (by common gossip) the Duke of Windsor.

I never presented the letter to Dr Niehans (and the doctor has since died), although Mr Baruch admonished me to 'go quickly. Niehans prefers them young so he can keep them that way —

instead of waiting for all us old ones,' he kept reminding me.

Although few doctors I know have been against his method (injection of embryonic tissue from just-born lambs) not one has been willing to guarantee me against *future* harm – hence the letter still gathers dust on my desk.

All through those years, I went to Mr Baruch regularly for advice – and especially when I was personally troubled. He knew all the family secrets; he was full of wisdom when I needed to be put on the track again. Every time I got his suggestions, he'd thank me for asking for them. He gave his advice with such firmness it was more like a command, straightforward and efficient – but he was always a little surprised to find it carried out.

I brought Tom Montague Meyer to him just before we were married. I didn't need his blessings but I knew how much it would mean to me to get them. I was so terribly happy to see how quickly they were impressed by each other. We left for Europe with Baruch's warm friendship given instantly. Apart from a personal liking, Mr Baruch was fascinated by my husband's knowledge of China (gained from his own business experience and interests in the Orient). Until the old man's death, both men always 'talked China'.

Mr Baruch used to use me in different ways; he often 'talked out' an article or a speech to me. I tried to be a good listener. The ritual was unchanging. I would arrive at his beckoning, for tea, for lunch, for dinner. When he had something on his mind, it came out after food was over and he had deposited himself in his special chair in the main drawing-room and I had pulled up a small upright chair to sit, knee to knee, to 'hear him think', as he used to put it. Because he was deaf but hated to have his hearing-aid turned up high, one had to sit as close as possible.

The atmosphere was conducive to lucid conversation. The apartment was intensely civilized in style (and in management, thanks to the skill of Nurse Elizabeth Navarro). A Chandor portrait of Churchill, commissioned by Baruch, dominated one drawing-room; it also dominated my favourite photograph of Mr Baruch and me – his arm around me (with Churchill peering down at us, glowering). Churchill's painting of a landscape hung in the drawing-room, one of the few paintings he ever gave away.

Everywhere, one was surrounded by beautiful English furniture in a formal but personal atmosphere, 'busy' with relics and mementoes, expensive but never showy.

I can't begin to count the hours I spent there. Once or twice, he even called *me* for help. One year, just a few days before Christmas (and fortunately, while I was in our New York town house), he woke me up by telephoning me late at night. He was alone; Miss Navarro was out. He didn't feel well. Would I come right over?

I rushed out of bed, pulled a fur coat over my pyjamas and hurried out of the door. We lived at 47 East Sixty-Ninth St; he was at 4 East Sixty-Sixth St — just three-and-a-half short blocks away. I was there in a few moments and the butler ushered me to his bedroom.

I was stunned by his appearance. He lay quiet and unmoving on the bed — all of him (and he was so tall) stretched out on the long bed. He didn't even open his eyes. He was so white and still I thought for one terrible moment he was dead.

He knew I was there. His arm finally stretched out and his hand found mine. He started to talk and continued for hours. I couldn't even concentrate because part of me was listening, part of me watching his physical condition. I despair over the lost phrases.

He talked of Hoover and why he liked him — what he thought Hoover had done right (and how much was hidden behind the cloud of criticism of the man). He talked of Truman and his eventual dislike of the President (sadly nurtured no doubt by Truman's gradual rejection of Baruch's advice and service). He spoke of Eisenhower: 'Never forget it, Fleur. Behind Ike's grin is a man of iron.' He spoke of Woodrow Wilson, the one man who he felt survived the test of years (and survived the public's praise as well as its abuse as far as Baruch was concerned). He thought President Wilson had a radar-piercing mind, that he was one of the few men who could look into the future (a *not* commonly held view of Wilson).

I left Baruch when he seemed on the verge of sleep; I slipped away with a heavy heart as I had a feeling he was dying. But he lived twelve more happy and active years, dying in 1965 at the ripe old age of ninety-five, five years older than his great friend Churchill, who died the same year.

Winston Churchill:
this is the story that wasn't

This is the story of the 'story that wasn't'. One week, early in 1970, I gave a lunch to two famous widows: Lady Spencer-Churchill and Janet Murrow, whose husband, Ed Murrow, was one of the greatest radio and TV reporters of all time. At luncheon an old story came to light again.

Like all really old great ladies, Lady Churchill's mind loves to wander in the past, with the incredible clarity that can come with age. Anecdotes were her favourite topic and so we all did a lot of reminiscing. She greatly enjoyed one which involved her late husband, Winston Churchill.

For the many years I enjoyed the friendship of Bernard M. Baruch, I constantly heard about 'My best friend, Mr Churchill'. Although Mr Baruch was a few years older than him – and died just before him – he always felt himself the younger; each touchingly tending to act like a nanny towards the other. When Churchill came to the United States, Mr Baruch's New York apartment was often his home. On those occasions, I always had the good fortune to see him.

On Churchill's last visit to America he came to make a speech at Massachusetts Institute of Technology, an event arranged by Mr Baruch. Churchill arrived in New York one week before. His schedule was packed solidly from that moment onwards.

On the Tuesday, I was bidden to come and have tea with him and Mr Baruch. The circumstances that led to this invitation were somewhat harrowing, beginning with Mr Baruch's telephone call to me the week before Mr Churchill's arrival. He was in an obvious state of flap.

'You *know* the man,' he barked at me (being deaf, this was routine), 'so you'll have to stay away and let me get people in who have a right to meet him, too.'

I was stunned. I'd never even raised the question of a visit (although I secretly counted on the pleasure of it) but it was obvious that my aged friend was already getting into a state over the complicated programme.

'Don't worry, dear,' I placated Mr Baruch, 'get me off your mind. I realize perfectly what problems face you. Forget me. I understand.'

I felt like Pagliacci but I had the good grace to act properly. Four times, each day that followed, Mr Baruch telephoned to warn me he simply could not fit me in. Each time, I tried to soothe his anxiety. Finally, in a fit of irritation, I sharply reminded him that he really did not need to keep calling me, that his implied concern was enormously kind – but to *forget* me – that I would understand.

After the first call, I never really expected to see Mr Churchill, so the daily telephone calls were flattering, to say the least. Even touching. I realized that Mr Baruch was obviously always trying to fit me in – and only called me up when his own conscience pricked too sharply.

On the Tuesday, there was, once again, the familiar barking voice of Mr Baruch on the telephone. 'What are you doing at tea-time?' he suddenly demanded.

'Nothing!' I replied. 'I'll be there!'

At five o'clock, I made my way through the barrage of policemen, Secret Service gentlemen and other guards and found myself in the familiar long hall of Mr Baruch's elegant apartment. Though early, he was already dressed in white tie and tails for the stag dinner to be given three hours later in Mr Churchill's honour. He was pacing the floor, back and forth, non-stop. He was deadly pale. I knew something was wrong.

'What's happened?' I demanded. 'You look ill. Is *Churchill* ill?'

'No, he's fine – but I'm not. Here it is – Tuesday. He hasn't even put pen to paper to write the speech he has to deliver on Friday in Boston. It's all my fault for arranging this trip. Now it will be a failure,' he snapped back at me.

'Please, please, let us sit down and discuss it,' I begged him. 'You mustn't worry about *this* man's capacity to write a speech. If he isn't worried, why should you be?' 'Making a speech', I reminded Baruch, 'is something we know your guest tosses off rather easily—and always brilliantly. Will you please stop worrying?'

That Churchill 'came through' in those two days is now a matter of history, but poor Mr Baruch wasn't able to relax about it. I finally got him into his favourite chair in the drawing-room and sat down, facing him, urging him to rest.

I sat with my back to the door, huddled close to the deaf man, almost knee to knee. Suddenly, I saw his face turn green. I felt a presence alongside me. I looked down. There, beside me, were a pair of pink, waxy, bare feet. Above them was the great man, dressed only in a towel. There was no greeting—just a grunt as Churchill started to stomp around the room, constantly muttering his irritation about the awful nuisance of having to write a speech. 'I'd rather play gin-rummy,' he complained at one time. One hand held the towel in place, the other held on to the ubiquitous cigar. After a slow, prowling circumnavigation of all the furniture, Churchill finally left the room, waving his first greeting (and a farewell to me by name) from the door as he trotted out. Mr Baruch was ready to collapse.

The anguished Mr Baruch exacted a solemn promise that this tale was NEVER to be repeated to *anyone*. Reluctantly, I gave it. What a delectable anecdote to have to keep bottled up, I thought.

But I was released from the necessity sooner than I expected. Not many months later, I was visiting Mr Baruch in Paris. We were having tea in his rooms at the Ritz when Randolph Churchill popped in.

'What a hilarious meeting you had in New York with my undressed father!' he announced to me.

Mr Baruch turned pale.

'How do you know about it?' I demanded hastily. 'And let's establish it here and now that you never heard the story from me!'

'Oh, no!' he admitted, 'I have my own sources—and what's more I just published the delightful morsel in my own column!'

Mr Baruch was nearly ill—but, at least, he knew I had not

broken my promise. What is more, although I could never get a copy of Randolph's column (and even doubt if it was ever written) it freed me. I have often described the incident to my friends, usually acting it out.

Not very long after that, in 1949, when Mr Baruch was visiting his friend Winston Churchill at Chartwell, Mike Cowles and I were in London and received an invitation to join him there. At luncheon I found myself seated on Churchill's right at the dining-table, and tried to make conversation, never easy to do because he hated 'small talk' at meals — and in this case it was no exception. I decided to 'jump in' and discuss the last New York visit when all other chatter failed to excite the man.

'You *do* know, Mr Churchill, that *I* never told Randolph the story about the time I last saw you in New York?'

'*What* story?' he demanded.

'Oh, you know — that time you arrived in Mr Baruch's drawing-room wearing only a towel!' I went on, meaning to explain in more detail ...

I was interrupted by a red-faced and very angry man. 'That's a lie!' he announced. 'That *never* happened!' he thundered, as he returned in silence to his roast beef and brandy.

The atmosphere didn't remain cool for more than a few minutes. Soon after lunch was over we had the pleasure of a personally conducted tour of the beautiful grounds and house. (I'll *never* forget seeing the bust of Napoleon on Churchill's desk.) We had a view of the studio where he painted. The greatest joy of all was in seeing Churchill's affectionate attention to Baruch, expressed in extraordinary ways. For some reason, ordained by Mr Churchill but never explained, whenever we walked about it was always in single file: Churchill (bent and slow-moving) led the way, behind him came Baruch, tall, erect and slightly unsteady (he'd have hated anyone thinking so). At the end, we followed, one behind the other. Until there was something special to be pointed out, each contented himself with a steady close-up of the back of the person before him, walking Indian fashion. Whenever anything occurred to Churchill, he'd come to a full stop, slowly turn himself around to face Baruch, and then make an announcement for all of us to hear: 'This is the wall I built myself, brick by brick'

... 'Here are my goldfish, I know them all by name – come and see them answer to each one' ... 'This is my favourite view' ... 'Here's where I like to sit and make decisions' ... and in his basement studio, 'Here's where I paint.'

Often a 'dear' slipped out as he pointed to something in particular: 'Bernie dear, give me your hand. Watch out, dear – there's a drop in the lawn there' ... 'This is a very high step, dear – don't fall!' Never have I seen such unabashed sweetness, man to man.

The visit to his basement studio was memorable, for two reasons: one, that it was glorious to have had the chance to see his work and where he did it; the other, for the privilege of seeing the 'twin-picture' method he was using to produce the painting which sat unfinished on his easel. There was no attempt at secrecy; he was painting and we were welcome to see *how*.

Side by side (and facing us at the door) stood two equal-sized easels, parallel to each other. On one was his half-finished canvas, paints and brushes piled close at hand. To the left of this was the companion-easel, on which he had perched a black and white photographic blow-up of the landscape he was painting – the exact size of his canvas.[1]

---

[1] Though the photo-realist painters of today also use photographs to help them paint things as they are (using the camera to choose the way they crop their paintings, often putting several slides together to make one whole), they might not agree with Churchill's easel. These artists are attempting something very different – documentation in paint of the life-style of today's middle classes. Churchill would have loathed their subject matter: car carburettors, credit-card signs, motor-bikes, old boots, boxes, used car junk piles, car showrooms, pimply faces ...

Oswaldo Aranha: the 'Churchill' of Brazil

The word Aranha, in Portuguese, means spider. Anyone bearing it as a name embroiders a tiny one on his shirts, uses the insect as his coat of arms (and jewellery), and has every reason to be proud. For in Brazil, Aranha means Oswaldo Aranha, or, to be more precise, their national hero. I met this forthright, hazel-eyed man in 1949, and that fortuitous event permanently opened Brazil's doors for me as well as bringing a great friend into my life.

Like another different but fascinating man, Assis de Chateaubriand, Aranha helped 'boot' the sleeping, backward giant into the late twentieth century. Chateaubriand was a modern Robin Hood, who 'robbed' the rich for noble causes in Brazil. Aranha was a great statesman. Aranha, the elegant internationalist, scholar, parliamentarian and diplomat (who began life as a gaucho), was one of the first great men to see Brazil in relation to the rest of the world. He was, in fact, South America's first real internationalist.

He can best be described, in simplistic terms, as the Churchill of Brazil. His likeness to the great Englishman is intriguing; they share many qualities – particularly *courage* and *oratory*. Both reached their highest point of international prestige during the Second World War, both drove their countries against the Axis. Both were men of culture who thrived in the heat of the political arena, doing extravagantly well in it. Both were fearless. Both loved their countries with something amounting to an overbearing passion. Both were physically impressive, Aranha in dignified film-idol terms. Unlike most national heroes, they were idolized in their own lifetime (I have seldom been on the streets of Rio with Aranha without people trying to touch his sleeves and grab his hand).

Oswaldo Aranha: the 'Churchill' of Brazil

Though he himself was a Catholic, every Zionist is indebted to Aranha; it was while he was President of the U.N. General Assembly (and with his help) that Israel became a state. During the Second World War, he rebuffed every Nazi in Brazil (and there were countless in the government of which he was then Foreign Minister) by turning his country against the Axis. It was a perilous moment and most undeniably shortened the war.

The young Oswaldo Aranha in 1930 was the civilian leader of a revolution to unseat the country's leader, having personally chosen a military man, Joes Monteiro, to lead the troops in the national movement. But it was Aranha alone, who, with a mere handful of men in a brave and swift action, started it all by assaulting and taking over the headquarters of the Federal Army in Porto Alegre. Success in hand, the revolutionaries moved north towards Rio. There, joined by the garrison of Rio, on October 30th, 1930, they deposed Washington Luiz as head of the government – bloodlessly.

Monteiro, the strong, stubborn leader who so resisted change, was gone, replaced by the tiny friend of Aranha, Getulio Vargas, formerly a State Governor, who then conducted a benevolent dictatorship of his own until ultimately elected Brazil's President. It had been Aranha's second revolution, and he had completely engineered it.

Oswaldo Aranha was more than a diplomat and conspirator; he was a man of action, whose exploits as a gaucho and a revolutionary led to two bullets in his body, a legful of machine-gun fire and part of one heel shot away. Charm and *élan*, however, were never marred.

If instant friendship is possible, Dr Aranha and I had it. I was struck by his personality and patriotism; in me, he found a young journalist keenly interested in politics, *even Brazil's*. We talked non-stop. I soon knew more and cared more about Brazil, far more than most Americans.

It was a two-way street: I could and did interest important Americans in his country. Through him, I had a direct and friendly contact with President Getulio Vargas, which I was able to put to good use when on errands for President Eisenhower, conveying messages under exceedingly cordial circumstances. I was also helpful when the President's brother, Milton Eisenhower, headed a goodwill mission to Latin America, preceding him and his delegation to Rio.

President Vargas repaid my interest in Brazil by a delightful gesture, unquestionably instigated by Dr Aranha. I was made a Chevalier of the Order of the Cruzeiro dò Sul in the presence of the Eisenhower delegation.[1]

Oswaldo Aranha, it seems to me, was a born kingmaker, never seeking to be one himself. 'I like to influence events,' he used to say with a wry smile. He was right; he had an undisputed ability to do so, and we must be grateful that he could during the tricky war years when Vargas tried (despite a public which was passionately pro-Allied) to pretend a neutrality.

Although never 'top-dog', he was in seats of power for many years, serving as Minister of Justice, twice Minister of Finance, Foreign Minister, Ambassador to the United States, a delegate to the U.N., and elected President of the United Nations Assembly two times – the only man so honoured. In Washington, he had a very special connection with Roosevelt, who, like so many others, fell for his charm and erudition. To the American President, Aranha was a trusted, dear, personal friend.

There was one abortive, short-lived attempt by him to become President of Brazil, from which campaign he withdrew suddenly – but not without mentioning wistfully, 'I am tired of second place.' One can only wonder what he would have done as President to improve the depression-riddled, one-crop economy of Brazil which so frustrated him.

Despite the air, the style and the good looks of a socialite, he was nevertheless dedicated to the poor, to the troubled, to the unfairly-treated. His lovely home on the hills overlooking Rio never locked its doors. The front hall was always full of people (mostly strangers) seeking advice, in trouble. Politicians too, seeking his support, overflowed into the library, finding places to sit in the book-lined room. Legal troubles were sorted out, jobs found, homes saved and political strategies arranged.

[1] In May 1973, I had the great honour of being given the promotion to Commander of the same Order, the highest degree of the Grand Cross (given only, according to its by-laws, to Heads of State and Foreign Ministers) for my continued interest in Brazil and its affairs – this time, in the Brazilian Embassy in London, surrounded by European friends.

The dining-table was never considered set, (two or three or four extras could always be counted on to arrive unexpectedly) and food was always available. With impulsive generosity, he gave most of his wealth away; starting with hospitality, he was a permanent giver of gifts, ideas, money and books. My own library has been greatly enriched.

He didn't live to see the changes of which he dreamed or to measure the astonishing economic miracle of Brazil. Even so, during his lifetime, he never stopped trying to edge it on or to push his friendships in Brazil's interest. In those years, to forge a link with his country (or any other Latin American one for that matter) was fairly hopeless in the face of a disinterested world. Even Evita Perón's dramatic shenanigan couldn't really attract the interest of North Americans in the Argentine, as I found out after going there in 1949.

Some years after Aranha served in the U.N., Henry Luce flew with him into Rio. The editor of *Time–Life* Publications was overcome by the beauty of the harbour and city as they reached it – but even more by Aranha himself. He described him in his book, *The Ideas of Henry Luce*, as 'one of the greatest and most irresistible personalities I've ever encountered ... a sort of combination of Wendell Willkie and Franklin Roosevelt ... with the forthright, belligerent honesty of Willkie and the easy charm of Roosevelt, the inexhaustible animal energy of both plus a love of beauty and philosophy which neither of the Americans possess.'

Like Luce, who flew in to Rio on a special Brazilian plane from New York, I too met Aranha while on a flying junket in 1949. Unlike Luce, who never went back, I have returned regularly, and the new Brazil he predicted over years and years of conversation is materializing at last.

It's hard to improve on Mr Luce's appraisal of the man, but at the risk of gilding the lily, I'd like to quote another observer: 'He is a man with the eloquence of Aristide Briand, the romantic dash of d'Artagnan and the Pan-American idealism of the great Simon Bolivar.' Others called him 'audacious', others 'oratorical' (his style was considered hypnotic – even, by some, theatrical). But for all that, a man who could fight in the streets was no parlour-politician. And perhaps I can add to the legend by stressing his incredible capacity for friendship.

He was a symbol of the lean and tough, storied gaucho; one of seventeen children, he was born on February 15th, 1894, on a huge cattle ranch in the prosperous Rio Grande dò Sul. After a military education he went to Paris to the École des Hautes Études Sociales, coming back for a law degree in Rio University. There, as class orator, he first displayed his political skills. From 1923 onwards, fire and brimstone were turned on for a new career as a revolutionary. Even in the U.N. many years later, he put those talents to good use.

In Rio, I used to be irritated by my inability to understand his speeches in his native Portuguese — yet another person's lack of linguistic skill never cramped his style. His gift of speech was equally colourful in French, Spanish and English, so he would casually repeat the speech to me in impeccable English.

Here it is worth repeating a story: When Aranha first arrived in Washington he immediately sought a teacher. On learning that Ambassador Aranha was studying at three in the morning, this teacher asked, 'But you speak so well, why do you kill yourself?'

'Because I want to learn enough English to talk a lot and not say anything!' the diplomat cryptically replied, smiling broadly.

During the last war (Brazil was at that time a haven for agents and Nazi followers[1]), men inside and outside the government were mobilized in a tremendous effort to prevent Brazil from siding with the Allies. Aranha never doubted that the arrogant Axis would lose. He also knew that their victory would mean fascism in Brazil and he fought against them relentlessly. Inside the government he worked to prevent the formation of a young para-military organization of a fascist nature. He was the only one in the government not impressed by Axis gains in battle.

Vargas, in a speech on June 11th, 1940, proclaimed his own faith in the victory of 'the new order'. In his own Cabinet, many ministers wanted to break with England. Totalitarians of all shades rejoiced — and Radio Berlin sent warm praise of the South American Führer.

---

[1] There were also nests of agents who had to be hunted out in the Argentine and Chile in 1942, when Brazil took the side of the Allies.

The Italian Ambassador in Rio, Sr Ugo Sola, wrote to his own Foreign Minister (and the letter was reproduced in Brazil's Foreign Ministry's Year Book) to laud 'the inspired dictator'. 'I felt strengthened', he boasted, 'by the elevated words announced by President Vargas.'

Aranha threatened to resign publicly at the closing session of the Inter-American Conference of Foreign Ministers of the twenty-one American Republics in February 1942, which was held at the Tiradente Palace in Rio. Its purpose was deadly serious; could the United States delegation (forty-six men headed by Sumner Welles) hold the Atlantic from the Axis? (The Argentine and Chile, for example, were either neutralists or strongly pro-Axis.) Before the conference, Aranha was America's firmest ally; he even made a whirlwind journey to other Latin American countries to try to bring them into line before the meeting.

When it was obvious that things were going badly because of the Axis-friends in Brazil, Aranha struck.[1] He told Vargas he was resigning, that he preferred to follow the people – 'rather than the whispered influence of the Nazi gang that dominate you.' Intimidated by Aranha's threat to resign in such a public showplace as an international conference, Vargas gave in – a bare few hours before the conference closed. Brazil declared war on the Axis. It was history.

If Brazil had not come into the war on the side of the Allies, the consequences would have been grim; the Germans would have had bases in North Brazil from which to bomb the United States (and they planned to do so); U-boats would have had fuel and shelter in Brazilian waters – from which it was an easy dash to North Africa; those same valuable bases would in turn never have been available to the Allies.

---

[1] In *The Goebbels Diaries* (Hamish Hamilton), the former Nazi official confirms Aranha's role:

'The Foreign Office has given me a report about the situation in Brazil. A bitter fight is going on between President Vargas, who is pretty much on our side, and Aranha, the Foreign Minister, who has evidently been bought by Roosevelt and seems to be doing everything he can to provoke a conflict with the Reich and the Axis Powers.

'We have, alas, no facilities for reprisal. We have about six hundred Brazilians in our hands whereas in Brazil alone there are 150,000 Germans. The possibilities of economic retaliation are also extraordinarily limited, as we don't own one-tenth as much Brazilian capital as the Brazilians possess of ours. So we have to be fairly careful.'

Getting those bases was a significant factor in ending the war; without the co-operation of Brazil, the Allies wouldn't have organized the Victory Corridor or flown planes safely to North Africa to protect the landings in Africa, nor would they have secured the flow of supplies. Few people in the United States or Europe realize that *one* Brazilian changed the course of the war.

Not all was serious during Aranha's term as Foreign Minister, as countless anecdotes indicate. Two linger on for their wit and brevity and for the way in which they describe Aranha's character. Both involve messages to him from diplomats on post: one Consul-General cabled him: 'The Attaché of the Consulate, Sr Annibal Graca attacked me today, using ju-jitsu — a sport, by the way, which I ignore.'

Aranha's reply was in his usual style: 'Attaché Graca is immediately summoned to Rio to answer disciplinary charges and you are yourself transferred to Yokohama in order to learn the aforementioned sport.'

Another diplomat was in the habit of sending exceedingly long cables; the verbosity of one message particularly irritated Aranha, who cabled back: 'The substance of your message is contained in the first paragraph and you are being debited for the rest.'

Anyone with his talent for persuasion was born for diplomacy (which he once described as the art of letting the other fellow have your own way). His two daughters have provided a suitable family succession in the diplomatic world: one married one of the most able ambassadors ever sent to the Court of St James, Sergio Correa Costa (whose grandfather was Poet Laureate of Brazil); the other married Ambassador Antonio Correa do Lago, who represents Brazil now in Uruguay.

Through this friendship, I have been handed a Brazilian family, having been 'adopted' by the Aranhas. Today, I have a wonderful collection of sisters, brothers, nieces and nephews in my life, all irrevocable ties to Brazil.

Like them, I was bereaved by the death of Oswaldo Aranha in 1960. The rancher-statesman died of a heart attack, leaving many deeply grieved by the news. Few men ever left fewer enemies or were remembered for their urbanity, intelligence and diplomacy by more friends or more countries. He was buried with the full honours of a President of Brazil.

One thing he told me lives on vividly: 'When I dream, I am sure I shall live forever; when I'm trying to achieve that dream, I act as if I am going to die in a minute.'

Assis de Chateaubriand:
the eccentric modern Robin Hood

I have already described Aranha as the statesman, but 'Chateau', as his friends knew Assis de Chateaubriand, I can only regard with astonishment and affection as a lovable brigand, a modern Robin Hood. He, like Aranha, helped mould his country – in a very different fashion.

The easiest description of him is to liken him to William Randolph Hearst or Lord Beaverbrook or Lord Thomson – but none of these three power-houses in communication could hold a candle to him as an eccentric. In scale, his empire measured closest to Hearst's; when I met him in 1950 he already had over fifty newspapers, many magazines and many radio stations. To this empire he later added a television network – and then watched with consummate glee as internecine warfare sprang up between them all.

He lived like a sultan and certainly looked like one; he was short, squat, big-nosed, dark-skinned. Those black shining eyes below a mop of black hair must have been his great allure (for allure he had, to judge by the glamorous women in his life).

He travelled about the world as if he owned it (and he once had enough money to feel he did). Space didn't count. Neither did expense. He had a way of scooping up whole planeloads of people (providing he thought them attractive) and flying them off in his own huge plane to some distant post. It could be from Rio to Paris or New York or London (or vice-versa). Or, in a smaller plane, he might fly up to the Amazon if there was a foreigner to whom he could show his plantations. He came to London as Brazil's Ambassador in the early 'sixties and presided over the most bizarre of embassies, often providing the diplomatic set with a hair-raising example while making countless friends.

We had both been in London on one of his most colourful journeys, at the time of the Coronation of Queen Elizabeth II, when he represented Brazil, and I the U.S.A. I could write a comedy around the many hilarious attempts he made to persuade me to present (on his personal behalf) a necklace and ear-rings of diamonds and aquamarines which he had brought from Brazil to give the Queen as a gift. 'You're a lady. A lady should make my presentation,' he kept insisting. The first time he tried was at seven o'clock one morning during Coronation week (the only free moment in our crowded schedule of beautifully organized days), when he asked me to meet him in the hotel lobby and tried forcibly to put the box with the fabulous jewels in my hands. He was quite upset when I declined but eventually I got it across to my generous old friend that official guests to the Coronation were not expected to bring personal gifts (that they could not, in fact, be accepted).

Chateau eventually had the great pleasure (it took many years) of seeing his jewels on the Queen. After he became Ambassador he altered the status of the gift from a personal one to an official gift from Brazil and it was accepted.

He was certainly Brazil's most colourful export. The world knew him well. Though eventually completely paralysed and speechless from two massive strokes, after he left his ambassadorial post in England he continued to travel until he died. Moscow was probably his last long trip, to look at beef stock in Russia.

Physically, he was almost a cabbage, but his brain was ticking over like a machine-gun. After months in the Stoke Mandeville hospital for paraplegics in England, he regained the use of one finger on each hand. He arranged to have a typewriter hung from the ceiling on a shelf, then had his hands placed into stirrups which also hung from the ceiling – and slowly but persistently he pecked out a daily column for his papers. And read voraciously.

He managed to communicate with people in an incredible fashion and by superhuman effort – by moving the muscles of his stomach. His two nurses 'read' his words by putting their fingers on his torso. Unbelievable? No, I've been witness to it many times, including when he was last in London. At a Claridges Hotel suite, the bedroom wall opposite his bed was hung with photos of the bulls he was thinking of buying for his farm, 'to restock Brazil'. The last time I saw him was in his home in São Paulo. He invited me to be a director of his new museum but, sadly, died before he could implement my acceptance.

I had originally met him in Rio in 1949 while on an aeroplane junket with other Americans in publishing, who flew on Pan American Airways' first flight to South America. Each time I arrived in Rio after that (and I soon began to commute) there was always a roll of drums in Chateau's newspapers; printed bouquets were regularly tossed at me (and so were the real ones). Fortunately, I can't read Portuguese so I'll never know what embarrassing flattery had been printed, but I did make masses of friends overnight by the sheer weight of this newspaper coverage. This familiarity with my name (plus the introductions and sponsorship of Oswaldo Aranha) did me no harm whenever I went to Brazil – often on errands for President Eisenhower. I hardly dare think of how this could have irritated the ambassador on post.

I soon began to hear about Chateau's Robin Hood activities: with his vast communications system behind him, which he never hesitated to use openly as a weapon, he forced men of means in Brazil (whether nationals or foreigners) to pay for the things he decided were in his country's interest to own. Many of the first nursery schools were 'subsidized' by this kind of coercion. So was civil aviation, which he helped to introduce to Brazil. A 'gun in the temple' (merely the implied threat of exposure in his newspapers) brought Big Business to heel.

Since most companies had a skeleton tucked away in a cupboard (every skeleton somehow known about by Chateau), his system worked. It must have been foolproof as, to my knowledge, no one ever dared say no to the expenditure chosen for him to make by the publisher.

Brazil's great museum came into being that way, nourished by a great collection of masterpieces, from Goyas to Picassos. I was once a witness to Chateau's acquisition of one of its finest canvases – in his inimitable way. I had been invited by Chateau to lunch: he arrived nearly an hour late, nothing unusual. 'Never mind where we're going – it will be nice,' was all he would tell me, as he chattered non-stop (in terrible English) on a fairly long motor trip to a fashionable suburb of Rio.

I had good cause to question where we were going. Once before, after accepting a quite casual invitation, I ended up the only woman on the dais with the dignitaries at the celebration of a civic event. To my astonishment, and embarrassment, I discovered I was the topic of the speech he was making (completely out of context and obviously an intrusion on the purpose of the get-together).

To be certain that I understood what he was saying about me then ('why I was one of America's great ladies,' etc. etc.) he commanded the man at my right on the dais to stand up and translate into English as he went along. Who was that gentleman? He looked like Tyrone Power but he was merely the Governor of Rio Grande du Nord, Sylvio Pedroza. At the age of nineteen, Pedroza had originally achieved fame by becoming Mayor of Natal during the Second World War, when the port was used by the Allies as a jumping-off place for Africa.

He and I have remained friends since that day of Chateaubriand's speech, and I was particularly happy to see Brazil's new capital, Brasilia, through his eyes when it was opened. He had been appointed co-ordinator of the new city's construction by President Kubitschek.

The luncheon which Chateau took me to in the suburbs some years later was somewhat different and in many ways more dramatic than the public affair I've just described. Not only did he decline to say where we were going, he didn't tell the hostess I was coming, so general pandemonium met our very tardy arrival. The table had to be reset and seated. Only during the second course could I piece together that the host was the head of a foreign, highly profitable company, almost a Brazilian by adoption.

Quite unexpectedly, after dessert, Chateau was on his feet, eyes glinting. Without a lost word, he got right to his subject – a beautiful El Greco painting which he had recently discovered in Europe. 'This', he stated categorically, 'belongs in Brazil.' Out came the gun. I could see our host blanch. 'It is wonderful of you to buy this El Greco for the museum,' Chateau announced with a huge grin, raising his wine glass in a toast to his latest 'victim'. The El Greco soon hung in the museum.

His eccentricity stretched in many directions. It is a pity that his 'firefly scheme' was never realized; had it been completed, Rio would have had a perfect symbol of his imagination and daring. He had built a new office structure for his publications and for a year or more he worried about how to give it any special distinction in an already spectacular, neon-lit city. At last he had the idea and one day, when still Ambassador to Britain, he came to visit us on a weekend in Sussex to describe it.

The entire top floor would be a solarium, all glass, a greenhouse of immense size and scale. During the day it would be interestingly beautiful to look up and see. 'But, ah! at night – it would be lit by *millions* of fireflies!'

The unannounced guest he brought to Sussex with him on this visit was actually a botanist, an expert on fireflies – a man who knew their habits ... how long a firefly lives ... what makes it light up ... how often the rooftop population in the building would have to be replenished to keep it alight.

Light intensity and wavelengths were discussed at length over food. Exhaustive research had been done. The spectacle would speak for itself, wondrous stars in a penthouse firmament. 'It will be like heaven on a good night,' Chateau concluded.

Despite those fascinating discussions in Sussex, Chateau died before his plan could be realized. Had it been vetoed when the man was too feeble to insist it be done? I often wondered.

At the height of his vigour and power, Chateau used his network of papers in many ways to achieve many results. There is a fascinating story about how, very long ago, he did it to avenge a social snub from a friend in São Paulo, the wife of a Brazilian millionaire. The tale may be apocryphal but he told it to me himself, very often.

Dean Acheson, then U.S.A.'s Secretary of State, was on a state visit to Brazil. All stops were pulled out to make this stay a success. It was arranged for Mr Acheson to stay in the home of the American wife of a Brazilian millionaire in São Paulo, an obvious choice. The house had a ballroom, which provided ample space for a glamorous dinner-dance to be given in his honour.

Chateaubriand wasn't invited. The hostess probably decided that this was one occasion when he couldn't take his presence automatically for granted. She soon rued that decision.

Chateau telephoned her for an explanation and she quickly claimed immunity. 'The whole thing is being arranged by the *Itamaraty*,' (Foreign Office), she explained. 'It's out of my hands.' This was nonsense and the publisher knew it. He also knew a lot of friends who'd already been asked personally by her, and he reminded her of it. In a fit of temper, she blurted out that *she* (and not he) would decide whom she would entertain.

Chateau didn't go to the party but he made life more than difficult for the hosts and everyone who did — with an immediate and devastating revenge. Two days before the event, he placed an advertisement in all his newspapers, located in 'bull's-eye position' (top of right-hand column on page 3). To ensure its noisy visibility, the advertisement had a thick black border around it. It read something like this: 'LOST, TWO CATS'... the ad. then described the cats: One, a white Angora, the other Blue Persian. They could easily be identified by their collars. One collar, the ad. pointed out, was of square-cut emeralds, the other, of square-cut diamonds. The ad. was signed with the name and address of the hostess.

The result was havoc: during Dean Acheson's stay (and, most of all, on the night of the dance) the Communist Party had a crowd of banner-carrying, chanting members to protest angrily outside the gates. Marie Antoinette couldn't have been more reviled. There was no way to call them off. As soon as one group was dispersed by police, another filed in, dressed in rags. Robin Hood had turned mafioso.

Big
Little Women

CHOOSING important women isn't as easy as choosing gentlemen of distinction. Anyone reading the polls in the U.S.A. on the world's ten most popular women must ponder over the results with some amazement.

Have you ever asked women you know to name the ten women they think are the most important in the world (known everywhere — not just locally)?. Few I've asked to play this game have succeeded. There just aren't ten universally known women whom other women wish to name (although Golda Meir seems to make most lists. So does Lady Bird Johnson). I, too, have often found it hard to name the others, especially as the fortunes of women tend to be evanescent.

Here I've chosen a few whose lives and careers couldn't possibly be interchanged; the utmost in variety. All were little women who lived big lives (and not necessarily on any Top Ten list ...).

A certain tiny friend comes to mind in a flush of affection — the 4' 5" Anita Loos, author of *Gentlemen Prefer Blondes* and many other books. When I wanted to write my first book (about the Peróns) I had a terrifying hurdle to overcome: how does one write a book?

I was editing two magazines; much of my time was spent examining other people's manuscripts with a very critical eye. How could I possibly start, bearing in mind one's own vanity as a critic?

I asked Miss Loos to lunch one day, explaining that I had a secret to discuss. I was too shy to bring up the subject, so the meal was almost over and we had talked of everything else. Finally, Anita Loos burst out in good-natured impatience, 'About that secret ... stop putting it off!'

When I blurted out (in the greatest confidence) that I would like to write a book, she rolled around in laughter, 'And why not! Why the secret?'

'Because I don't really know *how*,' I admitted. 'How does one go about writing a book?'

'It's terribly simple,' she retorted. 'Just open up your pad, write your first sentence – and the book rushes right after you!'

A tiny woman, with a big idea that really worked: I got my first line down on a yellow foolscap pad and *Bloody Precedent*, my book on the Peróns and their Argentinian predecessors, quickly followed – thanks to that advice.

In musical circles, one very important lady is Gina Bachauer, the admirable *Grande Dame* who is literally consumed by music, one of the three or four women to have ever joined the ranks of the world's greatest pianists. Critics toss bouquets at her; few living musicians have been more thoroughly observed, judged and praised. 'Gina Bachauer is a phenomenon. If she didn't exist, she'd have to be created,' the *New York Times* music critic recently wrote of her.

She is more than a musical virtuoso; she's one's greatest friend, a mother-figure to many elderly relatives, patron to the young in her field – and, *par hasard*, one of the world's funniest comediennes (in fractured English).

An example comes to mind: we were in the superb, three-masted schooner belonging to a mutual Greek friend, John Carras, tossing in very rough Aegean waters (10,000 square feet of sail notwithstanding) during a *melteme*. Being a good sailor, I stayed on deck, but Gina Bachauer took to her cabin. After a few hours outside, enjoying the roughness, I went inside the saloon to sit out the long storm.

Suddenly, Mme Bachauer arrived, struggling against odds up the yacht stairs – dead-white, elegant and composed but dressed to the nines in city clothes (we were still in the middle of the sea). Selecting a firmly fixed armchair in the saloon, she sat in it – bolt upright, white knuckles on clenched fists, holding on for dear life. Nothing was said for a very long time. Finally, she broke the silence, ringing the bell for the steward. '*Please*,' she ordered the astonished man, 'order me please ah taxi.' I nearly fell out of my chair. The *melteme* seemed to disappear.

I've always been intrigued by another woman, Ayesha Jaipur – and by why the former member of the international jet-set who was born into and married hereditary power ever entered the turmoil of Indian politics. Few candidates had more political handicaps than the Raj Mata of Jaipur: first of all, her vulnerable internationalism, which to uneducated masses could be described as 'un-Indian'. She had even been brought up in the West, in itself a political drawback. She was very rich and very royal.

In fact, she won her seat in the Parliament by making flagrant use of all her handicaps, campaigning in silken saris and wearing extraordinary jewels without apology, turning her internationalism into an asset, promising to give the Indians what she had seen done for the poor by living elsewhere in the world.

Evita Perón: female rabble-rouser

To quote from my own introduction to the book I wrote about Evita and Juan Perón in 1950:[1]

> I vividly remember the attentive, hand-rubbing, handsome, masculine Juan Perón. But it is Evita who continues to haunt me ever since I met her and sat and walked and rode at her side and talked to her, though the time was short. I cannot obliterate the image of this woman-politico with too much power, too much rage, too many flunkies in high government places, too little opposition, too much greed, too much money; a woman too fabled, too capable, too sexless, too driven, too overbearing, too slick, too neurotic, too sly, too tense, too sneering, too diamond-bedecked, too revengeful, too hateful of North Americans, too ambitious – and far, far too underrated for far too long by our world ...

I will never forget standing alongside her near midnight one night in 1950, as she harangued a howling mob of the 'shirtless ones' she named *Descamisados*, in a meeting in a huge amphitheatre outside Buenos Aires. I was on a publishing junket to the Argentine and had somehow captured Evita's friendship, which she mistakenly thought was reciprocated.

Of course, like many women, I had been transfixed by her famed technique with crowds, the way she looked, the success which overcame a tawdry early life. But friendship was a ridiculous expectation. I later wrote a book to prove otherwise.

She thought that the Associate Editor of *Look* magazine was

[1] *Bloody Precedent* (Muller, 1952).

176

worth taking in. She liked my clothes. She admired my jewellery.[1]
She imagined I liked her although I never once gave the slightest
hint of it. She wanted to impress me and took me everywhere;
'Watch me in action and see how I do it,' she explained.

The particular midnight rally I'm thinking of – in the Royal
Opera House – was a nightmare. Waves of applause rose hysterically up to us on stage – conducted by her voice, which she
used as a baton. As a rabble-rouser, I count her second only to
Hitler. She started out in an innocent little-girl whisper, her voice
slowly rising to a shout, until she took full command with a
frightening blast.

Every speech began with a soft, self-effacing claim that she was
merely the voice of poor, overworked Perón, merely speaking
on his behalf to save his energy. 'He is God. He is our sun, our
water, our air, *our life*! We must pray for his safe-keeping.' Tears
poured down her cheeks under the full glare of arc lights. The
crowd reacted so violently, I felt frightened even for us! Would
they rush the stage, crushing everyone in their hysteria?

Slowly, she used her device ('saving' Perón, all the while
building her own image). The public never seemed to doubt her
motives in keeping him at his desk while she built a public
following for herself.

Her star-quality was so great she used luxury and glamour as a
virtue. Once when I was at her side, she pointed to her clothes and
her jewels (probably close to a million dollars on her fingers, neck
and wrists) and shouted out in a rage to the mob before her, '*Look
at me* – once I was as poor as all of you. I'll steal and take from the
rotten rich and one day I'll hand it all over – it will all be yours!'
Women in rags looked at her as if she were an angel, many
mentally counting their future loot in jewels and clothes.

Her main motivation was hatred and revenge. If she could make
a decision, large or small, to harm someone rich (and I saw her do
this with sweeping brutality at her 'People's Court') she made it
with relish.

It never occurred to Evita that close exposure to her would

[1] Once in the Pink Palace, when she and Perón and I were alone together, she asked to
examine a Fabergé brooch I was wearing. President Perón winked at me and said (in the
English she didn't speak), 'That's *one* jewel she'll never get,' and grinned from ear to ear.

lose rather than make a friend. She was terribly proud of her skill, her hypnotic power, the obsequious way even men in the Cabinet treated her, her bossiness of Perón himself, her immense collection of jewels, her lavish wardrobe (which she showed me with great pride) and lastly, the effectiveness of her war on *other* people's wealth.

Her Evita Perón Foundation, of which she was in sole control (and never gave an accounting), took in more than 100 million dollars each year, all of it passing through her sticky fingers. 'Keeping books on charity is capitalistic nonsense,' she replied in irritation to my question about how the money was recorded. 'I just use the money for the poor. I can't stop to count it.' I have dealt in detail with that astonishing remark in my book.

Bloody Precedent reveals the strange historical fact that an identical man-and-wife team, Manuel and Encarnación de Rosas, had ruled (or I should say terrorized) the Argentine long before the Peróns. The book is in two parts, starting with the story of the Rosas couple. Almost page for page (certainly detail for detail) can be interchanged in the Rosas and Perón stories. Everything the Peróns did had already been done by the Rosas pair *exactly one hundred years before*:

1. Manuel de Rosas was less tyrannical than his violent wife, so was Juan Perón. Both dictators left the cruel decisions to their wives, who made them with relish.

2. Encarnación de Rosas invented the term *Descamisados* (peasant followers); Evita claimed she did – and used the same term and the same group as the base of her political strength.

3. The de Rosas couple took over the press of their time, so did the Peróns.

4. Photographs of Encarnación and Manuel were obligatory everywhere; ditto the Peróns.

5. Encarnación died of cancer of the stomach. So did Evita.

6. Manuel de Rosas fled to England for his life after a counter-

revolution; Perón fled to Spain. A new chapter about Perón's dramatic return to the Argentine can now be written – to break the otherwise identical parallel of their lives.

Evita Perón came back into the news less than twenty years after her death – like an unspent explosive, erupting and bringing a new phenomenon into existence – a dead woman whose name and image could still tamper with history.

A cold breath blew in: even lifeless, Evita was a force. Lifeless, she still commanded a civilian army, still fomented a revolution, still remained an ally to a remarried husband with yet another ambitious wife standing in her old shoes. The new Mme Perón accepts the constant re-evocation of her predecessor's face, name, voice and record as a daily diet. If corpses could smile, Evita's would be smug.

In mid-1971, interest in Evita took precedence over the promise of the government's forward-looking legislative efforts; President Janusse's much-heralded Constitutional Democracy was of less popular interest than the subject of the whereabouts of Evita's bones. The Evita cult (some of it political, some of it religious, some of it even necrophilic) began to flourish, demanding as its slogan, the truth of what had happened to 'Saint' Evita's body.

Manifestations were curious. Not only was Evita news, dead, but also good for retail business. Dolls began to litter the news-stands, blonde-wigged creatures dressed exactly in Evita's style – down to the football-padded shoulders of her suits and platform-shoes which were her day-time uniform, as well as her heavily-beaded evening clothes plastered in costly jewellery.

Even her speeches, recorded years before on her personal order, were reissued after being brought up to date by Perónists. They seemed to bring back a nostalgic excitement and a quickening heartbeat to crowds who had either once loved that shrill female voice or had been told about it. The old, homespun attacks on aristocrats were popular again.

Unlike Hitler, Himmler and other deceased figures, no one doubted Evita's death. Many could remember the yellow-faced, terribly sick woman they had seen being propped up by two men in her last balcony appearances. They held her skeletonized body by each arm as in a weak voice she declined the office of Vice-President. Years later her husband's new wife accepted it instead.

Evita's illness was obvious; she was dying of cancer. She was dead very soon after, dying in 1952 when she was thirty-three.[1] The illness began when she was twenty-nine; in four years she had wasted away to less than six stone.

Before she died, she divided the Argentine with a sharp, cruel knife. The land she left behind had lost the great wealth she'd set out to destroy. In a few short years, she had shattered its assets as well as its reputation as an aristocratic colonial land.

She was born, probably illegitimately, in Los Toldos, a small, dusty, dreamy pampas town, 150 miles west of Buenos Aires. Her vulgarity was an asset; if she'd been less common, she'd have been less of a success because her beauty came of a flashy sexiness that made the public feel at home with her. Although the men who knew her in her prime said she was 'too tough' to appeal to them, the public found her excitingly beautiful. When I was there, Perón seemed to have cooled off as well, although it would have been political suicide to show it. When we were together, he used to kiss her each time on the forehead, a far from passionate welcome.

The secret embalming process which is said to have been made to keep her looking so beautiful took six months to complete, with a body no larger than a twelve-year-old's. It is back in the Argentine today, ready to be played as a trump card – the final role in the odyssey of Evita, long, long after her death.

[1] Another statistic: Juana Ibarguren de Duarta, mother of Evita, died on February 15th, 1971, of cancer, like her daughter. Evita was in her thirties; her mother lived to be seventy-seven.

Margaret Thompson Biddle:
Renaissance woman

Being an editor brought an unforgettable companion into my life, the late Margaret Thompson Biddle, who came to me for a job. This modern woman lived and spent her life like an ancient queen, an extravagant, splendid lady who had probably one of the world's greatest fortunes. Many English people knew her as the former wife of the United States diplomat who was Ambassador to the Occupied Countries in the United Kingdom during the last war, Anthony J. Drexel Biddle.

She spent her money impulsively on homes, paintings, *objets d'art*, clothes, gifts, travel, friends. Whoever made her clothes (and Balenciaga had the major share) must have considered her an important mainstay. Whatever she ordered was ordered in multiple quantities for each home, and she had many. Not only in many colours but with hats, bags and all the rest to match each outfit. If she liked a city, she made a home there, ending her life with a collection of mansions and leaving behind a priceless art collection and a massive array of jewels for her two heirs to sort out.[1]

She died in Paris, still quite a young woman, of mysterious causes. It was in the mid-twentieth century, but she had lived her life as a Renaissance figure. She was an impulsive patron of the arts, a rash collector, an international hostess, and even a king-maker of sorts (though no one could have looked less like one than this small, unsophisticated American). I can see her now: a tiny head, dead white complexion, pouting lips which enunciated every word with care, and two childlike hands always making a

[1] One of them, daughter Margaret, died of cancer at the age of forty-two, leaving her ex-crooner second husband Morton Downey and two children an estimated $150 million (after having divorced Prince Hohenlohe Ingelfingen).

point in mid-air. As for her jewels: 'She's covered in jewels,' her friends used to say, and not in derision. The sight of one small person, bejewelled and opulent, became a regular feature.

King-making took place in France, which became her adopted country. A woman pulling strings behind a man in high places is perhaps typical of France, but when the woman is an American, speaking bad French (with unfailing and beguiling lack of hesitance, with a Yonkers-New York accent), it is indeed a phenomenon. Political match-making was her favourite game.

Margaret Biddle came into my life in a most unconventional way, early in 1949, after asking her New York lawyer to invite me to lunch with her. We went to my regular table in the now demolished Ritz Hotel, discussing every item under the sun in a maddening refusal to get to the main subject of the luncheon.

'Why are we lunching?' I finally blurted out. 'It's delightful to meet you both, but what is the reason behind it?'

To my amazement, the frail little woman before me, who had actually managed to double an enormous inheritance, wanted to work for me on *Flair*. Her father, Colonel William Boyce Thompson, had left her the Newmont Mining Co., the gold mines which he founded.

'I've heard all about the new magazine which you're starting, and I want a job with you. Isn't there something I could do in Paris?' she pleaded, with the most appealing anxiety, pursing her lips in her childish way.

I gave her the title of Paris Editor of *Flair*, which thoroughly irritated all the professionals I hired to do the day-in, day-out work in Paris. It did make sense to use her connections as a constant private customer of the couture; they would be useful when *Flair* reported on the Paris collections. So were her other Paris contacts (her drawing-room was a magnet for the influential).

Although an amateur, she worked terribly hard, in fact, with often unwonted intensity. Politics, her real interest, were no part of *Flair* magazine. She set up a political research group of her own, which was so formidable that she was immediately hired by the Paris magazine *Réalités*, when *Flair* expired, and for them she wrote a monthly political column until her mysterious and untimely death. I felt I had done her a good turn in the end and we had become such good friends, although at times I was irritated by the suspicion that she owned the magazine. The same rumour followed when she went to work for *Réalités*.

In the beginning, to orientate her to the magazine field, I took her on my travels when I scoured Europe for talent and ideas for *FLAIR*. Although she brought along no retinue, potentate-instincts soon surfaced.

Certain habits were standard with her. She never ate what was served on a plane or train. She always bought extra seats around her to guarantee privacy (and to allow space for whatever she chose to carry). At least two extra seats were needed for her food, which was always taken aboard.

When transatlantic planes used to have a separate eight-passenger section blocked off in the front area for executives or family travels, she bought the whole section. The four seats on one side were for both of us 'to spread out in', she would explain – the other two seats were to hold the 'picnic' which always travelled with her – cold roast birds, pâtés, beautiful breads. There would also be the ubiquitous heavy gold box, an incredibly beautiful object which Tiffany had designed to order. The interior was compartmentalized to hold a complete service for tea or coffee, everything fitting in a neat, flawless square, a triumph of geometric design and solid gold. The only thing required of a plane or train's catering facilities was hot water, which would then be poured into her own gold pot. If alive now, Margaret Biddle would surely be flying about in her own huge jet, décor by Jensen of Paris.

Despite this lavish portrait, I keep a more affectionate and intriguing image of her in my mind's eye – one of her as she travelled with me on a fast-moving Italian train. I still see her, smiling and happy, climbing up into the narrow upper berth she preferred. She wore luxurious nightclothes but her head was a mass of rolled-up ringlets – made from torn strips of paper over which she used to roll up her hair. A less elegant or more beguiling figure simply didn't exist.

Though as rich and powerful as a rajah, inside the little room on a train she became just another American tourist, hair in curlers, climbing into bed. The expensive, romantic Continental train became a little country cottage. Probably in Yonkers.

Madame Chiang Kai-shek:
'the greatest man in Asia'...

I regret to say that Mme Chiang Kai-shek's name will always be coupled with the image of her pet boa constrictor, a terrible thought. I have good cause, after visiting her in Formosa during the Korean War. Mike Cowles and I were on our way back from Korea, dropped by a Navy plane in Formosa, from which one could island-hop (by thumbing a lift on other military equipment) as far as the Philippine Islands where it was easy to board a commercial aeroplane to the U.S.A.

Getting to Formosa enabled us to visit Mme Chiang Kai-shek, that oft-described 'dragon lady with a Wellesley College drawl', also to meet the Generalissimo (the 'Gimo') and other Chinese Nationalists who set up shop under Chiang's leadership after fleeing the mainland.

I was excited to think of seeing again the woman who had evoked so many labels – who'd been called variously: a lady of vast tact, a tragic figure, the most charming pleader, a straight-shooter, the greatest of divas, an exciting personality, a pleasant companion, one of the most explosive personalities of our time. Adjectives ranged from dynamic to touchingly feminine, from simple and genuine to sly, captivating, poised, assured, malicious, *masculine*.

By whatever description, Mme Chiang is now a grandmother, well over 75,[1] limping slightly from a leg injury in a car accident a few years ago. She seemed bitter when four of us arrived at her

[1] She was born Mayling Soong in 1899. Her husband was born in 1886, which makes Chiang Kai-Shek a very old man indeed. One wonders what kind of leader his Moscow-trained son and heir will make.

door in Taipei in the 'fifties, with a warm but somewhat embarrassed welcome. Given the option, I am certain Mme Chiang would have 'postponed' all visits, living as she was in much reduced style at that time.

The contrast was dramatic. This was the same woman whose extravagance even shook luxury-loving Americans, the same woman who brought her own, highly publicized, silk sheets to the White House while on a state visit during Franklin D. Roosevelt's tenure, ordinary sheets being unacceptable.

The American public had been regaled, down to the most minute detail, with the size of her retinue, the size of her wardrobe, the value and amount of her jewellery, her insistence on luxury. Though uncrowned, she acted like both queen and saviour of her people and was obviously richer than Croesus.

Looking back at the visit to her in Formosa, I realize how annoyed she must have been. There were four in our party including Jane and Justin Dart, whom we rejoined in Tokyo after returning from Korea during a round-the-world trip together. The change in status, the total absence of luxury, the mediocrity of her new surroundings, and the Formosan public's disinterest in her were open to our eyes. She must have choked in silent rage.

She was living in a nondescript suburban villa, too small for guests, furnished simply—not at all what one expected of the lavish lady. During the war, communications were almost nonexistent so long-range warning of our arrival could not be given. Mme Chiang's warm welcome must have required a lot of acting. The still beautiful woman insisted she was delighted to have us as guests.

She was obviously in a mood of tightrope tension and unleashed her fury at me one day over a cup of tea! Sharp as a polished steel sword, she hissed: 'You Americans are fools. You have the A-Bomb. Why don't you throw it on China?' I couldn't believe my ears.

She has been angry at the British also. In a speech in 1950, before she left the United States for Formosa, she had these harsh words to say about them: 'Britain has bartered the soul of a nation for a few pieces of silver. I say "For shame!" to Britain.'

Our party was sent elsewhere to stay: 'As you can see, there isn't enough room for you to stay here in town; I had planned to put you up in our summer residence on the mountainside, just up there overlooking Taipei,' she pointed out.

Their guest house had been inherited from the Japanese who built it during the occupation of Formosa in the Second World War. The vast house, in Japanese architectural style, climbed over and clung to the side of a cliff; it had been built as a holiday house on the hill, a 'reward' for surviving Kamikaze pilots.

The architecture, though beautiful, made life difficult for Western guests: it was built on many levels, hugging a mountainside. Steep steps were the only way to get about. I felt like a crab crawling up and down a precipice. The entrance was at the top of the house, high up the mountain, overlooking Taipei in the valley below. One climbed *down* to bedrooms, whose front façade was almost entirely 'concrete lace', open to the outside world. There were neither windows nor glass to protect us from the air and its flying population, and this fact plagued us for days to come.

We were sent from the town house in the Generalissimo's large black Cadillac to the mountainside, to permit us to browse around the home which was to be our dormitory every night in Formosa (days being spent in the city). Just as the car started out of the driveway, Mme Chiang beckoned the chauffeur back. I was next to the window on her side. The windows had been rolled up to keep distasteful fumes out (the air was filled with the smell of sulphur which came up through the soil). I rolled my window down.

'I just want to tell you not to worry about the rats, Fleur,' she announced. 'My housekeeper keeps a boa constrictor!'

Never have I spent four more agonizing nights. Although I never saw the snake, I could never see enough to be sure that it wasn't always there. Frequently, when I felt sure the boa was cosily coiled in the dark under my bed, it was too dark to find out, and putting on a light would have attracted other frightening objects if I had been brave enough to do so: *lights meant insects*. In those Formosa hills, insects were like flying birds, *enormous*. Not to mention the spiders.

The fog used to roll up the mountainside from the harbour in the late afternoons. We watched with fascination as it moved higher and higher that first day, eventually drifting into our rooms through the open-work walls. We slept on primitive beds which were thin slats on small platforms slightly raised from the floor (the right height, I realized, for a large snake to slither and coil beneath).

Neither the promised housekeeper nor the threatened serpent ever materialized, but I never ceased being tense. When I'd got down to the safety of the city, I could reason that neither of them probably existed. Down there, it was easier to assume the snake had been conjured up as a mischievous revenge by Mme Chiang, but all such comforting thoughts disappeared in the night.

Before we left Formosa, I concluded that horrid insects, flying or crawling, as well as the sanitation facilities, were so unspeakable that the snake was only one ingredient among many nightmares.

It was impossible for us to move away from the residence. It would have been not only difficult to arrange but highly insulting to the Generalissimo. We had become official guests and politeness required us to stay until the uncertain moment of departure from the island. That couldn't be done until an Army, Navy or Air-force plane, arriving with a full load, could fly out with sufficient space for four of us to scramble aboard, sitting anywhere. We eventually were picked up by the Navy and got to Manila on bucket seats, which then seemed the height of luxury.

I never think of that visit, and Mme Chiang, without recalling Fulton Oursler's comment about her: 'The greatest man in Asia is a woman!'

Marilyn Monroe: how she took London

This is not yet another autopsy of Marilyn Monroe. The story of her life and death is such public property it hardly needs retelling — especially after Norman Mailer. But I did know her and there are two particular occasions of her life (one spent in my home) which have not been described.

I shan't attempt to add a long analysis of her character, except to say briefly that though she may have been a drug of sex to many men, to me she was a consistently vulnerable victim of her own spate of narcissism and her own anguished insecurity, and even when at her flounciest and best, I thought she was close to disaster. She offered herself to life with a smile which hid many fears.

As an editor, I had examined hundreds of prints taken of her for publication, but I never saw her until she appeared, secretly and furtively, to hide out in my weekend home in Connecticut in the 'fifties.

She'd been brought there by one of America's most gifted photographers, Milton Greene, then on contract to *Look*. He had come a long way in her life since photographing her in Hollywood on an assignment for me; by the time he had brought her to Connecticut, he had become her partner and business manager in the newly formed Marilyn Monroe Productions.

Guided by him, she had the courage to walk out of her Hollywood studio contract — a phenomenal and widely-publicized sit-down strike in protest against bad films. All America was on the lookout for the sex symbol who suddenly disappeared. Every likely place was searched. Milton and Amy Greene had simply tucked her away in the unsuspected safety of their own country house, not far from mine.

188

She was 'lent' me for a short time.

Not an ounce of anatomy was in sight when she appeared, as bedraggled as a Charlie Chaplin bum, almost obscured by an oversize, baggy, man's pullover, wrinkled slacks and sneakers. The costume never altered, nor did her disposition. She was unreservedly merry, free, unconcerned, unobserved, perfectly relaxed.

We were not alone; the other house-guest was a lovely woman over ninety years old, pink-faced (with a halo of white hair), twinkly-eyed and utterly innocent of mind. The late Bertha Stafford Vester had come to America as my guest from Jerusalem, where she had lived and worked all her life, a life which had been devoted to Arab children, following in the footsteps of her missionary parents from Boston. The object of the journey had been a routine one for her—soliciting funds once again for her work in Jerusalem.

When Mrs Vester returned to Jerusalem after this visit to the U.S.A., she left dazed with delight. She'd gathered sums of money from supporters to help keep her children's hospital going, she had stayed in the same home with a famous, *real-life* movie-actress! And she'd actually met President Eisenhower.

I asked the President if I could bring the brave American lady to see him; when I took her by the arm into his White House office, she was shaking with excitement. She curtsied low to him ('he's my King,') and shook his hand, gloves still on.

'You should have taken one glove off,' I teased her later.

'Oh no, I kept that glove on for a purpose—I want to show my friends in Jerusalem the glove that shook the hand of the President of the United States!'

The three of us (and we were certainly an odd trio) spent our time in Connecticut in embarrassed mutual admiration. Marilyn was overcome by Mrs Vester, the first woman of her kind she'd ever met. Mrs Vester was overcome by Marilyn: 'How could a movie star really be so cuddly?' she'd ask me. Mrs Vester had my unabashed admiration; no one I've known has had her total indifference to age and her total lack of fear.

A few months before, after tea at home in Jerusalem, she and I had walked out of the front door through her garden, arm in arm. Gun-fire could be heard but snipers were hidden.

'Isn't this a dangerous place?' I asked rather tentatively. We were heading for the American Club across the way, which she kept open for visiting Americans.

'Oh, yes, it is!' she retorted with wide eyes, still smiling. 'My brother and I were walking on this same path a few weeks ago and he was killed by a bullet.' This sort of day-in day-out danger, while it never troubled her for a moment, made the rest of the Jerusalem visit somewhat less relaxing for me.

Meeting Marilyn Monroe was more frightening to Bertha Stafford Vester than shells or gun-fire, both of which she'd lived through without concern.[1] When I warned her that she'd find Marilyn Monroe in our house in Connecticut, she squealed with delight. 'But I would be such a bore to such a glamorous creature,' she worried.

Boredom never reared its head. Marilyn Monroe and the oldest American woman in an Arab country fell instantly in love. Photographs of them together show a light of joy in both faces. Once, after hearing, mainly from me, of Mrs Vester's courage and exploits, Marilyn took her hand in hers and made an impulsive vow to the lovely old lady: 'I must do good for the world in some way. I promise you I will never waste my life again!' After a few weeks back in Hollywood, that promise got brushed away by the trauma of life. I often wondered, especially in the grim, suicidal years that followed, how long Marilyn Monroe remembered Mrs Vester?

The next time I saw Marilyn was when she came to London and took it by storm. She arrived to play in a film, in a deal arranged for her by Milton Greene, co-starring with Laurence Olivier in *Sleeping Princess*. No public was ever readier for a real-life myth than the English when she appeared. The acting-merger of this unlikely twosome proved a field-day for the British press.

Since the visit to Connecticut, Marilyn (without damage to her press-coverage) had remarried, this time to her first intellectual,

[1] See her book *Our Jerusalem — An American Family In the Holy City*.

Arthur Miller, who was splendid copy in his own right. On the tarmac of London airport, where celebrities are a dime a dozen, nothing more extraordinary than the arrival of this twosome has since been seen.

Maintaining Marilyn's legendary tardiness, even the plane was an hour late. One hundred photographers, fifty reporters and two hundred curious people champed and complained behind a metal barricade which had to be erected. Ordinarily calm officials and airport police were ruffled for the first time.

The T.W.A. plane finally arrived. The crew got out. The passengers got out. The luggage was sent out. A sweater firm sent in a sweater over the arm of an airline hostess. A vast bouquet went inside. And minutes ticked away. At last, Marilyn came gyrating down the steps, looking radiantly happy. Applause, friendship, unbelievable attention, even affection, was there for her, and she knew it. Waiting in the airport lounge with ogle-eyed curiosity (none of it mean or vicious or even condescending) were three hundred others.

There had been one of the great publicity build-ups of the century; the result was a movie star whom everyone seemed to like in advance, though few knew why. One reporter wrote, 'Miss Monroe had burst through the grey clouds and gentle drizzle like a peroxide hydrogen bomb.' And for days to come all the head-lines belonged to her.

Deepest bow of all came from an unexpected quarter. The day after her arrival, 'Profile' in the *Observer* was devoted to Marilyn Monroe (an accolade normally reserved for serious notables). With more than usual space, it called her 'the brightest star of the decade ... ' in spite of the films she had made.

Front pages were tossed at her feet like so many roses. Hardened reporters at her giant press conference the next day still recall her performance. Dressed in character, tight black dress, with trans-parent nylon midriff, it is possible to say her appearance alone warranted all the ensuing newspaper coverage. But appearance alone didn't account for her peculiar magic with hundreds of experienced pressmen (who included, unexpectedly, many bosses who seldom otherwise left their desks).

There was her voice, *and what she said.*

I'd marvelled over Marilyn's voice for years, but it was amazing to see its effect on the press corps. They heard the small sound she made, a voice so full of honey, so whispery, so disarming and so vulnerable. They heard it in its full range – from sensual whisper to earnest small girl, pretty devastating from that Lorelei. And with her voice went a beguiling, wide-eyed honesty ('innocent paganism' one paper called it) which teamed up so unexpectedly with her undulating walk.

She knew she had the audience with her and the result was a spontaneous, infectious performance. She romped through it with cool delight. Friendliness brought out her own almost unconscious wit. Under that sexy dress, she revealed a warm and natural girl. The cold sweats, the psychosomatic ailments, the skin rashes, all the symptoms of the insecure Marilyn Monroe were gone. For a girl who had always been terrified by every encounter with the world, she conquered her concern with a lack of inhibition which was astounding.

Her press coverage was fascinating. The *Daily Mirror*, with the largest circulation of any newspaper anywhere, expressed its enthusiasm in a page-two editorial the next day. With a loud blast, they slapped *The Times* just for not even mentioning her, for overlooking that – 'The Wiggle had reached London, 35 inches given to "The Credit Squeezes" and not a flicker of an eyelash about Marilyn, the most creditable squeeze of the twentieth century. What hypocrisy! What stuffiness! What suppression of notable news!' the paper accused.

The funniest revue in London wrote Marilyn promptly into a skit. In *For Amusement Only* a Marilyn sang to an Olivier, 'Why do they call me the Seven Year Itch?' She answered the question herself in a husky Marilyn Monroe whisper, 'Because I always come up to scratch.'

Every move she made was headlined, occasionally crowding out such items as Suez and Stevenson and Soho gangsters. She liked to sleep in complete darkness – 'Marilyn likes to keep it dark in Surrey'. When in a public restaurant – between cooks – bold type announced it – 'Marilyn Eats Out', a front-page headline. It took eight policemen to control the crowds that formed on Regent Street when the word leaked she was inside the restaurant. When

Arthur Miller went back to the States for a few days with his children, full-page pictures and stories analysed (and photographed) every move, every kiss.

What she wore was also considered copy, whether or not good fashion. The most-photographed dress of the year was the astonishing one she wore for the 'Monroe Midriff Press Conference'. Even the Paris edition of the *Herald Tribune* described THE dress: 'Marilyn wore a black dress that fitted her as tightly as frost clings to a window pane. It was a see-through dress. You could see a strip of Miss Monroe's famous body, starting just above her hips to a position slightly south of her chest.'

Her transparent midriff was not only a star in her opening show but gave birth to a rash of copies. Home-dressmakers cut away waistlines to insert net.

One day, dressed in jeans with the same sort of bulky cover-up cardigan she wore unchanged for days in my home, with the same white tennis socks and shoes and no make-up, she went bicycling in Hyde Park. No one recognized her or Arthur Miller. The bodyguard on a bike behind them had no one to protect.

When she guilelessly murmured she'd like to do *The Brothers Karamazov*, she managed eventually to attract London's culture-circuit to her side. And critic Siriol Jones in the *Sunday Times* finally took notice of Marilyn in the most entertaining description of all:

> Mrs Arthur Miller, as the farthest eskimo now knows, is that blonde and gentle mocker of sex and all its works, Miss Marilyn Monroe, who speaks honey in a monstrous small voice. Blondes — even blondes who talk and read and attend Lee Strasberg's Actors' Studio, the All Souls of the New York theatre — are not popularly supposed to consort with intellectuals. In fact, since Solomon talked to a butterfly, Cleopatra studied campaigning in Caesar's winter quarters and Isadora Duncan made her generous offer to Bernard Shaw, intellectuals and belles-de-nuit have found each other mutually irresistible. Mrs Miller, who is sugar and spice and all things nice and has been called the most famous nude since Phryne, is perhaps neither wholly yesterday's Dumb

193

Dish nor today's Portrait-Of-A-Young-Girl-Reading-Spinoza, but just the personification of all women who have unfairly wanted to be loved for themselves alone and not their yellow hair ...

When asked whose music she liked best, Marilyn named 'Beethoven and Berlioz'. This did her no harm with the music-lovers. What actors would she like to work with? 'Brando and Burton,' (no harm with serious movie-goers). When she announced she'd rather play Lady Macbeth than any other role in the world, the idea was never seriously questioned. 'I hate to say this,' she told newsmen, 'because when I said I wanted to play Grushenka in Dostoevsky's *Brothers Karamazov* people laughed. But since you ask me what part I'd rather play, let me say it's Lady Macbeth.' She paused for breath. 'Please get me right. I don't mean I'd like to play her right now. But some time.'

I tried to analyse Marilyn's success in London. Few ever actually *saw* her, so the reputation as a social success (which she *did* achieve) was a gift. She made two furtive visits, with near riots, to the theatre. Once to see Vivien Leigh before she left the cast of Noel Coward's *South Sea Bubble* and another time to join the egg-heads with her cerebral husband at the Brecht theatre (when I felt very sorry for the actors. The very nearly topless evening-dress had everyone's mind and attention during the performance).

The one party she did attend after arriving was given for her by the Oliviers and Terence Rattigan, in Rattigan's Ascot home. One hundred guests were invited. Marilyn arrived dressed in the *Sleeping Princess* gown designed for her to wear in the film as the chorus girl who titillates a bored prince-regent (Olivier) in the Carpathian Embassy in Belgravia. She had to be poured into this Edwardian, ankle-length gown of white-beaded chiffon. Someone next to me described it as: 'as tight as the curves will allow — with seams reinforced.'

She stood at the top of the stairs leading to the dance floor, a symbol of curvaceous womanliness, in a dress that was loaded down with pearls and white-beaded fringe, with a skirt so narrow that every step had to be a geometric calculation. Her hair was piled up on top with a fake mass of curls. The sight was slightly unbelievable as she stepped slowly down the stairs, leaning heavily on the arm of Arthur Miller, blotted to his side. They couldn't have been separated by a hair.

Mr Rattigan's garden room had been turned into a ballroom; everyone stood at the side (waiting, as usual, for Marilyn to arrive). Music was piped out to the lantern-lit gardens and floated softly back into the room. Conversation was at a minimum. A full, fat moon hung over the trees outside, so perfect it was ignored as a prop. Guests ranged from Louella Parsons of Hollywood, to the wife of a Cabinet Minister and press agents and publishers. Everyone there was quite used to personalities, yet none was prepared for the fabulous Monroe timing and staging. Marilyn was (of course) an hour late. She couldn't dance; the dress was too tight. She was content to be the centre of attention. This was her one and only social occasion.

During the filming of *The Sleeping Princess*, she was constantly guarded; the studio police and all other employees treated her as someone both sacred and frightening. Could she really like this, I wondered? Nobody dared take even modest decisions for her. Rumours of tension on the set broke through the wall created around her, especially over 'differences' between her and Olivier over her bouts of (neurotic?) illness. It was no secret to anyone near the centre of the stage that work didn't come easy to Marilyn.

It appealed to many women that she had chosen an egg-head to marry. Just before, without kindness to Joe di Maggio, her previous husband (who rescued her body and buried her lovingly after her death), she announced she hoped to 'find a man who was a man ... tall or short, and whether or not he can dance'.

Her marriage to the intellectual playwright took out of circulation a man many sophisticated New York women coveted – if only to give him maternal protection; that grave crag of a man had a strange appeal. English women particularly liked the way his lined face creased into smiles when he turned towards Marilyn.

Marilyn (like her brunette counterpart, Elizabeth Taylor, for Mike Todd) turned Jewess to marry Mr Miller. The idea of Marilyn struggling over serious studies of Judaism added lustre:

the little girl taking her third marriage vows seriously. And for naught. It didn't keep this marriage from breaking up.

I felt a great lump of sadness when she finally succeeded in dying – by as yet undisclosed means. I never suspected such a fate when the three of us charmed one another in Connecticut. Even Mrs Vester is dead.

Only Marilyn's cult still lives. Films she made are being re-issued (*All About Eve* especially popular). Marilyn Monroe products appeared after her death, including jig-saw puzzles of her nude photographs, wall posters, two books (one by Norman Mailer). A Marilyn doll is available, wiggling and whispering, with bleached blonde wig and 'wearing Chanel No. 5'; there is a travelling photography exhibition, and rhinestone-studded T-shirts.

One person (who claims he probably knew Marilyn best), Dr Ralph Greenson, spoke out for the first time after being appalled by the commercialization. 'She was a good human being. She was a sad and lonely woman who never got over being a waif.'

Conchita Cintron: first lady of the bull-ring

I have been fascinated by beautiful Conchita Cintron since I was very young, when I saw her perform as the world's only woman bull-fighter in the ring in Mexico City, my first bull-fight. Getting to know her has not changed my attitude.

In the ring she was tiny, beautiful and elegant, always dressed in sober brown and black, scorning the famous, brilliantly embroidered 'suit of lights' which the male peacocks wear. And brave: she literally flew around the ring on her remarkable horse, teasing a raging bull. When she dismounted for the kill, after having planted her own banderillas in the bull's nape, she stood unafraid in the sand on her toes, ready to plunge a sword into the back of the skull of the bull.

She is surely the only great bull-fighter of all time to be a woman;[1] she has remained feminine after fighting bulls for seventeen years. Before she retired (aged thirty-one, old by matador standards), she had killed her 600th bull, as masculine a record as any great bull-fighter can match.

Yet she left this career for the most ordinary female reasons, she fell in love and married. She has since brought up four sons and a daughter with the same skill and panache she brought to the bull-ring. She is still beautiful, very.

Conchita Cintron was born in Peru, her nationality like a delightful cocktail — one-half Spanish, one-quarter Irish, one-quarter American. Even her childhood was unusual: at the age of seven, so keen on every sort of animal, she had collected her own little zoo, taking one animal at a time to school. Above all, she

[1] In April, 1970, sixteen-year-old Ana Maria became Portugal's first professional woman bull-fighter when the National Bull-Fighters' Union accepted her as a full member.

loved horses. It was therefore not surprising that she learned to ride so skilfully that she was able to fight her first bull on a horse, *a la rejoneador*, at the age of *eleven*.

Her riding instructor, Guy de Camara, happened to be an ex-bullfighter who had retired in Peru. His stories of the bull-ring were too much for Conchita so she persuaded Camara to coach her in the bull-ring as well.

The thought of one's eleven-year-old daughter fighting a bull on a horse would send most parents to the asylum. Her American army-officer father (who had trained at America's famous Military Academy, West Point) was adamant that 'Conchita will never fight', but her mother (more Latin, or had she less imagination, or was she more philosophical?) gave her consent. 'Why not let her fight bulls? She might choose to be a pilot. That would be much worse!' her mother reasoned.

One concession was made: Guy de Camara's conservative Catholic wife had to go on the circuits as Conchita's duenna. The threesome were inseparable for seventeen years, until, in 1952, Conchita married Camara's nephew, Francesco de Castello Branco. They now live outside Lisbon.

Before retiring, she was the first woman bull-fighter in our time. She fought with all the great men: 'Armillita' Gaona, Balderas (killed by a bull), Carnicerito (killed by a bull), Manoleto (killed by a bull), Solorzano, Pepe Luis, Antonio Ordonez, Luis Miguel Dominguin, Lorenzo Garza, Procuna, Silverio, Belmonte, El Soldado, Manola Vazquez.

On one weekend she spent with us in Sussex, I had a chance to discuss her past. After years of following the bulls myself, I had collected many questions.

A lone woman in any man's world is in a difficult situation; was *she* in the intensely masculine world of bull-fighting which by tradition excludes women? No, she didn't have any trouble when she fought alongside bull-fighters confident in their *own* capacity.

What happened when she entered the bull-ring? Did she have to change herself in any way, to *think* like a man, *act* like a man, *switch* her mentality or personality in any way?

'Not at all, I do not believe that a woman can ever think or act or proceed as a man. If she does so, she ceases to be a woman and becomes a freak of nature, no matter whether it is bull-fighting or housework. Narrowing down your question to the arts,' she continued, 'and more specifically to bull-fighting, we have proof through ancient drawings that in the festivals of Crete it was the women who were the stars in the arenas. Modern bull-fighting takes no physical effort that cannot be endured by a frail woman.'

Incredible amounts of money have been earned by bull-fighters like Dominguin and Ordonez. How much had Conchita earned as a fighter? In Bogota, over thirty years ago, it was the first time anyone had earned twelve thousand dollars for killing two bulls, she recalled.

We were talking in a country where the attitude to bull-fighting is contemptuous and angry. How did this woman, who'd risked her life and made history by it, react to the English view of it as a cruel and inhuman sport?

'Nonsense! Every bull is born to be killed by man. The difference between a domestic bull born in England and one on a fighting-bull farm is that one is born only to be meat and the other goes into the ring to show how well he can die.

'If you're going to put human sensitivity into the argument,' she continued, 'men in England betray their own domesticated animals, which are generally emasculated and killed at the age of two for beef. The fighting bull (who wears his master's colours) is reared under the most idyllic conditions in the open fields.[1] He has a wonderful life for four or five years. When he comes into the ring and puts up a good fight, he is applauded. He's drawn round the ring in triumph. Flowers are flung at him (the fighter could have been booed off the stage for a poor show). The bull has had his doomsday but he never knows it.'

In point of fact, there *is* a real difference between the fighting bull and a domestic one; the fighting bull's first instinct (he's born with it) is to fight *whatever* is moving, no matter what. Conchita described this difference.

'The mother of a bull always hides her baby in the tall field grasses when he's born until she feels he is able to fight for himself. Even when he is tiny and his legs are too spindly to hold him up

[1] *Bulls of Iberia* by Robert Vavra (printed privately) is an astonishing photographic essay, a new book on the life of the fighting bull.

on his feet, he charges at horses. I was on one of three horses who were charged when we came along to see a new-born calf. The mother also charged us, a very different animal from the ordinary farm animal most people visualize. I can recall seeing young bulls destroy themselves by charging the first trains they saw moving across Andalusia.'

Did she fear the brave bull or the cowardly bull most, I asked her. 'In animals, as in men, the cowardly ones are most dangerous. Brave men, and animals, are generous, confident in their strength. They fight in the open. Example: many a dog will bite out of fear, when you least expect it ...'

The part of the fight Conchita Cintron loved most was the cape work, when the fight really begins. 'It was incredibly thrilling to be able to pass the bull after he'd turned back at me – proof of the bull's own bravery. He came out, straight from darkness into the sun in the ring, saw someone disappear behind high wooden barriers and he tried to go right through it to kill him.'

Even people who like bull-fighting deplore the fact that, in fighting bulls from a horse, Conchita Cintron not only risked her life but her horse's. How could this be justified? I asked.

'I don't need to. The horse is placed on earth to serve us; to go to war, to jump in competitions, to pull carts, to be a child's companion. I lost the best horse I ever had to a bull. We both fell in the ring, with the bull on top of us. He chose the horse to kill. It could have been me. Yet you can't imagine how sad it made me – how much I felt that loss of a horse who'd shared my best moments in the ring.'

The noise of the crowd (the boos as well as olé's) affects a bull-fighter, but the only thing that really shakes a fighter, Conchita claimed, is indifference. If the public is interested, that is enough. Even a nasty public makes every action worthwhile; you have at least converted them to you. If thirty thousand people are shouting that it cannot be done, the fighter reasons he'll have to prove it can be.

If you've ever watched a bull-fight, you must have asked yourself how far the matador can be aware of what is going on during a fight. Conchita was specific: 'When you fight, your consciousness is so acute, so perfect, so delicately strong, you are aware of everything. When I face a bull, I know precisely what goes on behind me. If a bandarilla falls, I know how far I must move, and in what direction, to avoid it. Eyes and ears develop everywhere in your head.'

She has twice been gored (a fairly innocuous record for so many years of fighting), once just a scar. The other time, the wound required two and a half hours of surgery. On this occasion, she had dismounted and was making her last pass on foot when the bull suddenly tripped. As he fell, he took his eyes off the cape she was holding and suddenly looked at her standing there underneath. All he had to do was to hook round, which he did, making a clean gore right into her leg – the full length of his horn.

'Did it frighten you to go back into the ring after that?' I asked her.

'No, a wound doesn't affect a matador at all unless he's already frightened. You don't need a wound to be frightened.'

'What about those waiting moments before it is *your* turn in the ring? Aren't you always frightened beforehand?'

'Yes, I was always frightened of the uncertainty of the outcome; how well would I do? Also, vaguely, would I come out ...?'

I wondered what she'd say if one of her four sons or her daughter chose to fight the bulls today. 'First of all, I know what a load in itself my name would be to carry. Still, if a son or even my only daughter wanted to fight the bulls – and had a good teacher – *why not?* If I became a good fighter (not only in the ring but in life itself) it was because I had such a great *maestro*. I don't believe in the self-made artist.'

'What about today's bull-fighting? Has it changed since you left the ring?' I asked her.

'Yes, there is TV now. And now one finds the paid critics among the honest ones (money has altered the whole of the bull-fighting world). Also, in my time, the fighter was judged by far fewer people but they were better qualified. Now it is the tourist who judges (and so few know how). Wasn't it Charles I of England who said that democracy is the power of equal votes for unequal minds?'

Her greatest fight, she claims, took place in Bogota, before an audience exclusively of children. 'Youngsters could never get in to see me fight, so I went to the authorities and said I'd like to donate an afternoon to them. The Government sponsored the event and closed the schools for all students under twelve. For one hour before the corrida began, all transportation was free to the bull-ring. There was no entrance fee. Trucks and ambulances brought the crippled children. Not one grown-up tried to get in amid the children. It was a beautiful, sunny day.

'Thirty thousand kids squeezed into the arena's twenty thousand seats. They cheered, they were happy. I made it a clean fight, not allowing the sight of even a drop of blood to be shed – I felt it was worth while having been a bull-fighter all those years just for that one very moving afternoon.'

When I asked her to rate El Cordobes, Spain's young god of the bull-fighting world, she replied, 'Cordobes is a phenomenon. He is not technically good. He kills badly. His cape-work is bad. But he has made a cult of everything he does. And he puts so strong a personal emotion into it the emotion is directly communicated to the audience. The one great TRUTH about him is that he's *truly* risking his life each time he fights – yet without the effortless-ness so great a bull-fighter usually displays. He *should* be like a great concert player or singer ... no effort ... only skill ... He's lucky not to be killed. He's lucky in the things that turn out right for him. He's even lucky in being gored in the arenas which bring him glory. It could happen in some lonely bull-ring without the right crowd.'

Everyone either likes or hates bull-fighting, there just is no half-way reaction. I asked Conchita for her own personal definition of it: 'To me, bull-fighting is not a sport but a form of art, or simply an expression between the bull and the fighter. If I had to do it all over again, I wouldn't change a thing. If anything would have been worth changing, I would have done so at the time.'

Would she rather have been an opera-singer or a ballet-dancer, I wondered. No, she wouldn't. 'I don't believe that there are, in any other profession, such great memories or so great an experience.'

She went on: 'In no other art do life and death go by the hand united. Many of our arenas are half sun and half shadow. It is a

world where men, at the peak of their triumph, may be killed –
yet men, who fail terribly, may live.

'I do not know which is the preferable ending, but this is only
one of the million meditations that may be brought up around the
world of the fiesta. One may like or abhor the bull-fight, but it
could never be considered a banal way of life.'

Baroness Blixen: Isaak Dinesen, teller of tales

When I first met Baroness Blixen, I could only regret that I didn't know her when she lived in the blue Ngong hills of Nairobi, which she immortalized in her book *Out of Africa*. I determined to bone up on her life – and did – before seeing her again when we entertained her in London a few years later.

She was born in 1885, named Karen (which she ultimately exchanged for the strange Isaak). She lived to be nearly eighty, but looked more like a hundred when she died. Her life had been one of extremes, of drama, of elaboration, of aristocratic and eccentric behaviour. Her gaunt face, etched by tragedy, told it all.

The first blow was the suicide of her idolized father when she was very young. Her marriage at the age of twenty-eight to a Danish cousin, Baron Bror Blixen, was yet another disaster. For whatever reason they wed (and romance was not the main factor) the nobleman deserted her soon after, leaving her lonely and unhappy in Africa.

The one great passion in her life was an Englishman, Denys Finch-Hatton. They met in Africa, a place he had fled to for its solitude and beauty, to become a white hunter, swooping about in the tiny plane in which he was ultimately killed. When that happened, Karen Blixen was once again left alone, grief-stricken.

She immortalized the farm she loved in *Out of Africa*. Everything she knew and loved about the continent and its people was written, though she left out most of her own painful experiences which followed on the heels of her honeymoon in 1913. Soon after the First World War began, Bror Blixen drifted out of her life.

She had to take on 10,000 acres of farmland single-handed,

trying to defend her coffee-plantation against constant plagues of locusts and drought on an estate which was basically too high up for the coffee it tried to grow. Even that beloved home was lost in the end; she had to sell the farmlands in 1931 for very little money. She left behind a part of herself.

She loved the native servants and they in turn worshipped her like some strange white goddess. She learned Kikuyu and Swahili, probed into everything possible about the people, the animals, her few friends—and particularly the servants she left behind so sorrowfully.

After returning to Denmark, illness pursued her relentlessly. Ultimately she couldn't move. Worst of all, she almost entirely lost the desire to eat and became so downright skinny she seemed an incongruously elegant concentration-camp inmate. She hardly ate at all, in fact she seemed to dislike food. When she did eat, it was in a bird-like way—mainly oysters and grapes (and when these were out of season, she reluctantly made do on artichokes and asparagus).

Years of such aristocratic fasting aged her quickly. She became so delicate, one wondered how she could walk alone; eventually she did need help. Her eyes became sunken like two deep, black caves (which she ringed in black chalk, just as the Egyptian women used to do with their kohl). Her lashes hung thick and heavy with mascara. Overall, there was an eerie quality to her face, accentuated by eyes literally on fire.

At one time, she needed several spinal operations and for quite a while couldn't even sit up to talk or write or type. Undaunted, she elected to stay flat on the floor. Day after day, she dictated to Clara Svendsen, her secretary (dictating for the first time in her life). It was this way that she produced *The Last Tales*. Though the title of this book seemed to imply prophetically that it would be her last work, she somehow managed a year later to write five more stories, called *Anecdotes of Destiny*.

In 1959, she went to New York, which she won completely, taxing herself to the limit. Our mutual friend, Ruth Ford, wrote to me: 'She rushed and tore around like a sixteen-year-old, giving three readings at the Y.M.H.A., made innumerable TV appearances, went to parties galore. She even managed a week in

Boston. She got down to less than four stone and had to spend a week in hospital.'

Her overall appearance would take pages to describe in detail. If one used the word gaunt too frequently, it would be because it was unavoidable. She was, quite simply, a human needle, topped by a gaunt skull, topped by a cap of hair. Under her transparent face (stretched tightly over bones) she was exactly like an Eastern ancient. The structure of her face was divided by a long thin nose, was dotted by owl-like eyes and decorated sparsely with sable hair, every strand of which was meticulously tended and carefully glued in precise curls over her forehead. When she sat, she seemed like a dying queen placed on a throne. Her gaze was royal. She also claimed immortality! 'I am really 3,000 years old and have dined with Socrates,' she once announced.

If her make-up was eccentric, her clothes were more so. And just as exotic as her language. Because she looked so like a Gothic statue herself, an image was forced upon her, late in life, which I doubt she enjoyed. I longed to ask how she took the comparison of her style and eccentricity with Edith Sitwell's but Isaak Dinesen died before I could find out.

Similarities did exist, whether or not the two women cared for them: both Baroness Blixen and Dame Edith Sitwell toured the United States triumphantly; both gave public readings, both were photographed with Marilyn Monroe ('the gaunt with the fleshpot' was obvious camera-fodder); both had liberal doses of charm mixed with literary gifts; both became legends (in which fame for their work became confused with fame for the way they looked); both displayed a sometimes amusing, sometimes annoying arrogance, both were openly vain; both loved the company of young people (Karen Blixen's last years were dotted with young male disciples attached impermanently and stormily to her). And both were romantic conservatives, living in a strange amalgam of the past and present. Except for the modern setting of her farm in Kenya, Karen Blixen seemed to love best the eighteenth and nineteenth centuries.

Even choosing a signature for her writings was a complex matter. What name to use? There is a collection of somewhat bewildering pseudonyms: her two best known names appeared on two different books, 'Isaak Dinesen' on *Seven Gothic Tales* and 'Karen Blixen' on *Out of Africa*. Other books were signed variously: once 'Pierre Audrezel' (again, a man's name) and another, 'Osceola'.

Her friends ignored all those and simply called her Tania. Even her biographer, Parmenia Migel, calls her Tanne and Titania. (Why not Titanic, I must ask?)

Writing must have given her great pleasure. She did it with such extravagance, some sort of musical drama must have been playing in her veins. The richness of her life and all her tragedies were poured into words with an incomparable mastery of English, which she learned to think in and to speak as a child in Switzerland and in England.

It wasn't until 1934, when she was forty-nine years old, that her first book was written. After that her average output was one book every ten years. She loved, in between, to 'speak' her tales, to think out loud what she would write. The atmospheric *Seven Gothic Tales*, couched in her luminous language, every detail embroidered, is surely one of the finest books of our time.

When she was young she painted – and this explains why her writing is really so visual and pictorial. The books were the final perfect expression of her favourite occupation – which was telling tales to her friends.

Winter's Tales, written in 1942, had to be smuggled to the United States for publication, to avoid the eyes of the Germans occupying Denmark. She wrote to a friend to explain (and with such a measure of courage!) that, 'Jews were in her kitchen and Nazis in the garden ... the hair-raising problem was to keep them from meeting.'

Out of Africa is, of course, everybody's book. It simply must be read, and for so many reasons (and millions have done). Only recently, I bought my umpteenth paperback copy to read on a plane going to Brazil and though I'd done it so many times before, I was sad to reach the last page.

To read it today is particularly significant, almost an obligation, like a dose of racial medicine. Few have understood the changing Africa or come to terms with it so uncomplicatedly. Isaak Dinesen saw the blacks very clearly, understood their tribal customs and

their killings and, best of all, themselves. There was no condescension in her views.

Apart from her timeless ability to see the blacks as they were,
she used that artist's eye of hers relentlessly; she saw everything
and brought all the sights on to the pages of this entrancing book.
As I am a painter of wild animals, I will never forget her descriptions: 'The giraffes, looking like long-stemmed speckles of
gigantic flowers ...'; 'the lion, face red up to the ears with blood
from a dawn feast ...'; 'the elephant, lumbering along as if it had
an appointment at the end of the world ...' These are but a few.

Her prestige was never confined to a private or exclusive club,
although it was other writers who most appreciated her art. When
Ernest Hemingway received his Nobel Prize, he was moved to
announce on that occasion that, 'Karen Blixen deserved it instead.
Why had she never won it?' It was a fair question.

Her personal motto told a lot about her: 'To set sail somewhere
is more important than life itself.'

Before I met her, I had a mental picture of an intrepid woman of
poetic vision – based on the person whose image was created by
reading *Out of Africa*.

When I saw her the first time in Copenhagen, I was not ready for
the apparition which appeared. My husband and I were visiting
Denmark. A mutual friend, who thought we should know each
other, arranged for us to meet. In incredibly bad typecasting, I
imagined she might appear in jodhpurs and habit. How wrong I
was to equate mental and physical courage and a proud sense of
honour with an athletic body ...

As she slowly walked across the room to say 'Hello!' I was
quite overcome. She seemed like a wraith; I was absolutely
hypnotized. She seemed plainly dressed, but it was merely the
drab colour of her clothes. She was entirely covered up (even on
her head she wore a skull-cap of sorts). A huge coat (or a cape
perhaps?) hung to the floor over her wasted body.

We talked for hours: when we left, I realized I had hardly said
a word.

She was then living in Rungstedland in what was originally an eighteenth-century inn, on the road to Elsinore. I never went back, but a few years later I was able to offer hospitality to her in return. She had become a devotee of Ruth Scott when she played Ophelia in the courtyard of the Danish Kronberg Castle in Elsinore (which is steeped in the tale of Hamlet). They soon became friends. When Ruth and husband, Zachary Scott, came to London to appear in a William Faulkner play, Isaak Dinesen came to see their performances and I arranged to give a party in her honour.

I tried to pick guests who would know and appreciate her gifts. Particularly, I wanted her to meet noted women. Clemence Dane was still alive at that time and that rather eccentric woman, heavy of body and beautiful of mind, delighted the Baroness, who knew her books. So did women like Rebecca West and G. B. Stern and Margaret Leighton and some of the most prominent ladies in Parliament. I chose interesting men to balance the famous women, from publishing, the theatre and from among painters. At noon of the party day, I had an opportunity to add to the guest list unexpectedly when the indomitable Helena Rubinstein telephoned to say she was in town. I asked her to join us.

If, indeed, Karen Blixen was a bird out of a nest, the Helena Rubinstein who arrived was like a Mayan princess out of some ancient kingdom dressed in a heavily-beaded Balenciaga dress, a royal robe of painted stones. Overlaid on her chest were her famous ropes of huge grey and white baroque pearls and uncut emeralds. Her fingers were hidden by vast rings; on her head she wore the tiny fedora she loved in those days, her tight black bun of hair sitting on her neck below it. Her face, as usual, was heavily painted and mask-like. If you knew her very well, as I certainly did, you knew that it concealed tremendous mental activity; much went on behind that silent façade. In fact, there was as much humour as there was scheming and nothing missed her penetrating eye. Lavish as she was, her outfit couldn't compete with the appearance of Karen Blixen who arrived late enough to make an awesome entrance, which I doubt any guest will ever forget.

Every eyelash was heavy, eyelids outlined; every wrinkle was set with layers of white powder. A beauty mark gleamed like a beacon on a cheekbone. Every curl was in place. And below that head was an outfit worthy of a Camille laid on her couch before death, incredibly romantic.

Her pale, coffee-coloured chiffon dress hung to the floor, tailored and neat to the waist and gathered full below. It clung to her tiny arms, to her tiny chest, to her tiny waist, where it was circled and tied in black velvet, hanging in streamers to the ground, ruffles at her wrists and neck. A fat, black silk rose was pinned at her throat.

She moved into the room very, very slowly; soon no one else seemed to count. A few hours later, having cast a spell over most of the guests, she slowly floated out again on my husband's arm to go back to her hotel.

The others left promptly after, only the tiny Helena Rubinstein staying behind. She had sat the whole time without saying a word to anyone, perched on the couch where I had placed her (feet dangling above the floor). Everything had been observed and heard but she hadn't participated by as much as a word. She didn't intend to go until she'd had a word with me so I came back to her from the door to the emptied room. She beckoned me to sit down beside her.

'Didn't you find Baroness Blixen incredible?' I asked. 'You know, she's well over seventy,' I reminded her. She was, in fact, much younger than the beauty queen who was well over eighty then. 'Everyone was fascinated to meet her. I am so sorry you didn't even talk to her.'

Without so much as a word to indicate she'd heard me, Mme Rubinstein looked me straight in the eye, took my hand in hers, and blurted out:

'Fleur darlink, all my life I've been trying to get *you* to use eye make-up!'

With that reprimand off her chest, she struggled to her feet and left.

Camera
Collection

BECAUSE I realize that pictures can and do speak as loudly as words, the following chapter consists mainly of photographs, including some of people not otherwise mentioned in this book.

Very often, when words fail to suggest the mood of even a fully-described situation, the candid camera says it in one impulsively-snatched shot – such as the time when President Nasser leant over to grab my wrist to emphasize a point.

Vanity chiefly inspires the picture of me as I was in 1944 along-side my first aeroplane. I weighed a mere seven stone and had a slim agility. Adlai Stevenson's claim that travel is fascinating, fatiguing and fattening has been proven by my own irrepressible travel since then.

The camera does tell its own tale, but I have tried to add to the initial interest of the photographs by filling in their background in the captions.

Here I am in 1944, alongside the beautiful little Ercoupe plane in which I first flew. It was a delight. Since it was almost totally stall-proof, it dispelled my fear that any 'iron-machine' could drop out of the skies. My own problem was very different; I had to overcome the idea that (like 'The Flying Yorkshireman') I could just fly by 'taking-off' from the ground myself. I soon learned to zoom about and feel like a bird in the Ercoupe.

*To Fleur Cowles
with best wishes
Dwight D Eisenhower*

The still relaxed General Eisenhower had just begun his campaign for the Presidency; we were in Campaign Headquarters in Denver, Colorado. Those early political days must have been his happiest; they were coloured by his disarming amateurism, a great asset at the starting gate for the campaign. He had not yet made his unforgettable appearance ('for the sake of the party') with his arm around Joseph McCarthy, after the rabble-rousing Senator had insulted Eisenhower's friend and mentor, General Marshall. Nor had the political pros yet moved in to direct Eisenhower along conventional Party lines.

Bernie — We can't deny it now!! Love Fleur

I don't want to
Bernie

A bear-hug from Bernard M. Baruch (as the portrait of Winston
Churchill glares disapprovingly down). 'He doesn't look happy!' I
chided Mr Baruch. 'I don't mind,' he growled back. We were in the
beautiful drawing-room of Mr Baruch's New York house, where I had
seen Churchill himself on his last American visit. His portrait dominated
the room – despite competition from other paintings and masses of
photographs of Baruch's friends among the world's leaders. Near by
hung one of Mr Churchill's own paintings – one of the first (and one of
the few) the great Englishman had ever given away.

When Stafford Cripps was head of the Board of Trade, he and his wife were our house guests in the U.S.A. Later, as Chancellor of the Exchequer, on a more melancholy journey, he came to Washington to devalue the pound, making a detour from Washington through New York City on his way home so we could meet.

The photograph shows us visiting the exhibition of Paintings by Famous Amateurs, which I helped organize to benefit New York's Urban League and for which, in fact, I persuaded Dwight Eisenhower to paint a picture. The President didn't like the first picture he made so he turned the board over and painted a second one on the other side. The two-faced painting fetched $27,500 in the auction, the highest figure reached. On the framed side, the President copied the head of the American Indian which appears on all American 'nickels'.

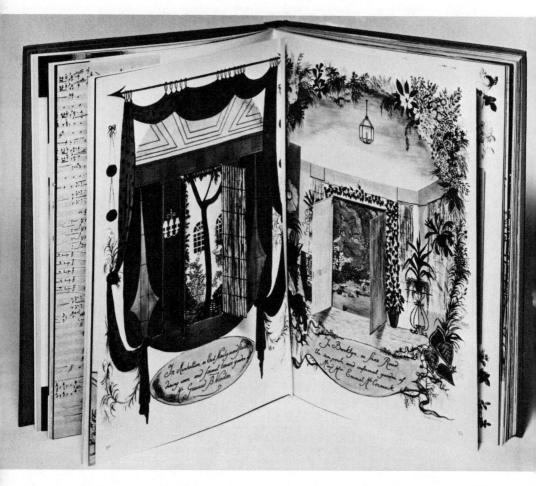

Flair Magazine, with its 'hole in the cover', stimulated *New Yorker Magazine* cartoonists to immediate action; two of their drawings are reproduced below. Their good-natured attention was a great help in publicizing the new magazine.

In 1949, before *Flair* magazine was born, I went through printing plants and paper mills in Europe, where most of the finest hand-work was then being done. Here I am, in northern Italy, quietly studying paper samples in a fine paper plant (apparently of great interest to a friendly cat). I brought back to the U.S.A. some of the talented people I discovered on the voyage to creative Italian circles, including that then stateless genius, Count Federico Pallavacini whom I describe in the chapter on publishing.

I was on a visit to the office of the President of Brazil, Getulio Vargas, with my friend Oswaldo Aranha, who was then Minister of Finance, discussing the financial practices of American businessmen in Brazil. We began to talk about Washington. When I heard that the current popular Brazilian Ambassador was retiring, I impulsively suggested his successor! To my surprise and delight, the banker was actually named to the post.

When he arrived in the United States, he immediately called on me. 'President Vargas told me to present my credentials first to you,' he admitted with a broad grin and a low bow.

President Magsaysay of the Philippines visited me at *Look* soon after I met him in the Philippines. Not long before, he had routed the dangerous Communist Huks out of the hills outside Manila, from which they had been terrorizing the country for years.

While in Manila, I coaxed him to come to the United States. I wanted to expose other Americans to him – to quell the rumours of corruption and misuse of American aid. 'I can't come to your country without being asked officially,' he reminded me.

After returning home, I wrote to him to suggest that 'poor health' could require his examination by American doctors. It worked. Giving his health as his reason, he flew to the United States. Once there informally, it was easy to have talks in the right places.

To the dismay of his admirers, Magsaysay was killed soon after his return; his plane mysteriously crashed on one of his regular flights into the interior of the Philippines, sabotage suspected.

Cary Grant was best man at my wedding to Tom Montagne Meyer in California. When he was making the film *The Gun* in Spain, we went to stay with him in Madrid for a few days. The picnic we planned to take one Sunday to the hills overlooking Toledo was cancelled by a sudden wild thunder storm – with the result that we returned to the hotel to have it there instead. Astonished waiters supplied tablecloth and cups and saucers, and we sat on the floor of his posh suite at the Palace, enjoying the food without benefit of ants, bugs or raindrops.

Perle Mesta, after her famous stint as the 'Call Me Madam' American Ambassador to Luxemburg, was anxious to write about her experiences. We were discussing the possibility on this visit to *Look*'s offices. We were photographed in the lovely room I created, using the eighteenth-century *boiserie* sent me from Paris by Margaret Biddle. I used it as a sitting-room from which to escape my crowded, busy office next door, where the real work of editing was done.

In the wings, America's great poet, Carl Sandburg, and I await our
cues. We were about to appear on a C.B.S. Television Spectacular,
organized by the Overseas Press Club in the 'fifties to raise funds for a
new building (in a campaign for which I was treasurer for a short time).
Columbia Broadcasting Company donated the air-time for this money-
raising event, which produced a two-hour parade of intrepid reporters,
famous writers, great musicians and great performers, who gave their
time and talents free. For me, the hours of rehearsal spent with the
distinguished poet were magical.

Opposite
Mr Wiseman was a Dane who collected dog-barks. He made a fortune
by putting them together and recording them as songs. We met in
Copenhagen when he was analysing bird songs.

As he talked, President Nasser would lean over to grab my wrist to make a point. This meeting took place in his villa which was inside an army camp near Cairo. The room was bare except for the four-piece suite of brilliantly brocaded, gilt furniture so beloved by Egyptians.

In the garden, after our discussion was over, Nasser's wife and children were sent for, Mme Nasser joining us in timid conversation, the children unconcerned and noisy. Loudest of all was the youngest son, nicknamed 'Jimmy Cagney' by Nasser.

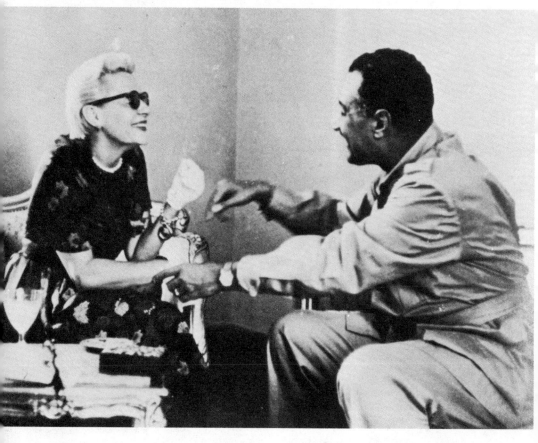

Opposite
One woman in a sea of male faces! I was escorted by the man who is now Adviser to President Sadat, Colonel Hatem. We are 'lost' amid six thousand members of Egypt's entire Officer Corps, during the feast which traditionally honours the country's Head of State (Nasser was the first civilian leader after thousands of years of Kings). Dinner by torchlight was followed by the spectacular firework display which marked all Egyptian military and political celebrations. Another tradition was broken that evening by my presence – probably the first woman ever to be included. Later, I was invited to the top table by Nasser.

I was fascinated to learn who were the heroes of the Shah of Iran when I visited him in 1952. On the mantelpiece is a collection of photographs including Emperor Haile Selassie; King George VI; the Reza Shah, whose throne he inherited; Presidents Truman and Roosevelt.

Soon after this visit to Teheran, I accompanied the Shah and Empress Saroya on much of an informal tour of the United States.

This is the tiny, enchanting son of Prince Abdorreza, the brother of the Shah of Iran. The child took an instant fancy to me when I was visiting the family at their palace in Teheran. The little prince took his good looks from a beautiful mother and a father who was described in advance to me as the 'Tyrone Power' of Iran.

King Paul of Greece playing Bach for me on one of my many visits to the family's private palace, Tatoi, outside Athens. The two serious little girls watching are Princess Irene and Princess Sophie. One is now a concert pianist, the other a Queen.

I recall the marriage of Princess Sophie to Juan Carlos (now King and Queen of Spain) as a dream-like pageant. We non-royals were intrigued by how strictly the protocol was observed in the procession into the Palace Gardens by much of the world's remaining royalty: the most important were first, the lesser ones followed behind. Gina Bachauer (left) and I were photographed talking to the King.

Marilyn Monroe in one of her rare, happy encounters with a stranger – the 'First Lady of Jerusalem', the late Bertha Stafford Vester. Both were guests in my home, each was absolutely fascinated by the other – each found the other incredible.

I knew Lily Mendès-France, the beautiful wife of Pierre Mendès-France, when she lived alone (discreetly and under an alias) in New York City during the Second World War. She eventually returned to France, but kept out of her husband's limelight, preferring to paint. Before she died, I joined them both on a holiday for this skiing weekend in Megève. I still remember holding his skis while he took an incredibly important call (in French) from Winston Churchill – in a public call-box!

How I paint: on a favourite couch, paints alongside, the board on my lap (if very large, it is propped on a table alongside), friends close by, conversation unabated. One, for James Stewart, is shown below.

The
Birth of a Hospital

My interest in helping people who have suffered facial mutila-
tion came through an appeal by the wonderful woman whose
own vision created America's eye-bank (eyes from the dead to
give sight to the living), whose energy and persistence made the
establishment work as an important adjunct to eye surgery in the
U.S.A. Ouida da Costa Breckenridge was already too old and too
preoccupied with her own mission to take on another – but she
knew there was one in the wings, and she honoured me by thinking
I was the person to take it on. I had never met her before she came
to me at *LOOK* with her proposal.

She knew of a dedicated doctor, she explained; he needed help.
He longed to start work on the vast army of mutilated people
hiding in despair all over America. The doctor, she continued, had
operated on mutilated soldiers and pilots in the Morocco theatre in
the last war. He dreamt of continuing to use his skills with civilians,
children having priority.

In the United States in the late 'forties, there was no centre for
such surgery. Reconstructive plastic surgery wasn't even being
taught in any school in the land. The young doctor, who was considered a saint by so many of his patients, wanted to build such a
hospital – and to teach the art to post-graduate students as well.

After a series of near misses I finally met John Marquis Converse,
and the story of how his hospital was built (today a distinguished
and moving success story) follows in this chapter.

My motivation, like Dr Converse's, was mainly the terribly
mutilated children – some of whom were born without mouths,
some without ears or noses, some with cleft palates. Others had
faces which were destroyed by accident or fire (and those were the
most horrendous).

I am grateful for the chance I was given to help save many of
them (as well as countless tragic adults) from isolation and from a
living hell.

John Converse: how reconstructive facial surgery got its chance

How is a hospital born?

I participated in the birth of one in New York City, the Institute for the Facially Disfigured, and the story is worth telling. The plot had been laid by Mrs Breckenridge to arrange a meeting between me and Dr Converse – in which, it was hoped, he would enlist my help. Nothing came of it. The doctor described his work very modestly. He didn't ask for help.

When I was again put before him, he still failed to take up the bait. The evening, which I remember so clearly, was staged at my own house in New York City. I sat the doctor on a stool in the middle of the drawing-room after dinner, and asked him to explain to the other guests what it meant to be a 'reconstructive plastic surgeon'. He did this with simple sincerity, but asked nothing. My chance came later – and today there is a fine institute in a teaching medical centre (which will always be a memorial to his idea) of which I am a trustee.[1]

There is only one way to understand Jack Converse's persistent dedication. One must go back to the pre-war beginnings of his career. He never even wanted to go into medicine. He had always hoped to be a sculptor, and would undoubtedly have been a good one. The decision to 'sculpt human faces' instead of clay wasn't taken entirely by design, but by accident. An actual accident pushed him into this career.

His father, a San Francisco doctor in general practice, had gone

[1] The Institute of Reconstructive Plastic Surgery at New York University Medical Centre.

236

to Paris as head of the United States Public Health Service in Europe and then remained as director of the American Hospital. John was barely nine years old. He entered medical school in Paris simply to please his mother – who died just before her wish was realized – facing a future as a surgeon when what he really wanted was to finish at the art school in which he had already registered.

The accident which changed his life also changed his inspirations. When he was in his first year at medical school, a beautiful girl-friend was in a car accident. He saw her face badly smashed up and took her to someone capable of repairing it. When he did this, he met the gifted French surgeon, Dr Thierry de Martel, who drew him to reconstructive surgery. He had a tremendous influence on him then, and still does, though he is long since dead.

Dr Thierry de Martel was one of the three illustrious men in the world who introduced neuro-surgery to medical science, but during the war he turned to plastic surgery. Plastic surgery was a fascinating art which seemed to have fallen into some disrepute since its origins in the First World War, and then underwent a renaissance after the Second World War.

John Converse took the girl with the smashed nose and damaged cheekbone to de Martel. He watched him at work: the emotional impact of seeing a beautiful girl disfigured – and then repaired – was a genuine inspiration.

'This is tremendously interesting surgery. If I were to begin my own career again, reconstructive surgery is the only thing I'd do. Only quacks and guess-work are involved now,' de Martel explained. Later, Converse was able to work with him and learn the elements of surgery.

Since Converse had never been inspired by the work of his father, and realized that reconstructive surgery was in itself a form of sculpture, he decided to become a plastic surgeon. As well as training with de Martel he eventually went to work with the great Dr V. H. Karanjian at the Massachusetts General Hospital in Boston. But before going any further he returned to Europe to help the French, joining ambulance volunteers organized by the Red Cross. The group went to Bordeaux where

Anthony Drexel Biddle, then acting-Ambassador from the U.S.A. to the Free French, warned them that the Germans were on the ambulance's heels. When they had eventually crossed the river in Bordeaux, Converse fled in an embassy car to the frontier —first to Spain, then to Lisbon, and finally aboard the S.S. *Manhattan* which safely took him to New York.

War mutilations were beginning to mount up; Jack Converse wished to continue his work with them. So he sailed to England (the boat was sunk on its return voyage) to join the staff of the American Hospital there. Together with Archibald McIndoe and his famous uncle, Sir Harold Gillies, the New Zealander who became wartime father of reconstructive surgery, Dr Converse worked on burned airmen whose faces and hands had been destroyed by fire in the Battle of Britain.[1]

In France, 'Les Gueules Cassées' (the broken mugs) still exist as a French counterpart to McIndoe's 'Guinea Pigs', but with a difference: they have multiple membership, including 15,000 men *from the end of the First World War*. They have done much to highlight the misery of the mutilated in a world which places such importance on physical perfection. They also give their help to the expansion of surgery which prevents the isolation inflicted on anyone with a hideously deformed face. No one knew how to help them at the time of the First World War. Their ranks were swelled by the 2,000 Second World War casualties, though membership is now limited to victims of enemy action or concentration camps.

These French survivors, by the way, live in a huge château given them in 1924 by an American woman whose husband was connected with the Eastman Kodak camera company. It is worth a slight detour in my story to describe it. The château sits on a 200-acre piece of land, 45 miles north of Paris, with hotel facilities and a summer camp for children. There is also a house in Paris for meetings (and a place in southern France is being discussed). The organization benefits from France's National Lottery; one-fifth of all the money (about $100,000 a year) goes to 'Les Gueules Cassées.'

[1] The 'Guinea Pigs', as McIndoe named them, still meet regularly to enjoy each other's company and to compare notes on progress in their lives.

Converse never had an easy time of it. Once, when he was assisting in an operation, de Martel turned to him in irritation. 'Young man, a concert pianist doesn't learn to play at a concert. You are at a concert and you don't play well enough to be here. Go home. Use these,' he ordered, handing him a batch of surgical instruments. 'Learn to tie 160 knots a minute. Get nimble. Be precise. Learn to use both hands and *not* just your right – anyone can do that!'

Converse went around for months tying string on door knobs and backs of chairs, trying out both hands. He was insulted into becoming ambidextrous – and fast – and ended up working deftly with both hands.

An amusing aside comes to my mind: when I moved abroad, I became close friends (through Converse) with that great plastic surgeon (and hero to war victims) Archibald McIndoe and his wife, Constance. I often had an unusual glimpse of his great dexterity in my own home. He used to carve the joints whenever he came to dine, a privilege he claimed as a matter of station. First of all, his slices were as thin as skin grafts! Secondly, we all used to watch goggle-eyed as he used his left and his right hand to get at the object. 'Very useful in my work,' he used to murmur gleefully.

Converse's great French hero is now dead. Confused by fear of Communism, de Martel either joined or sympathized with France's semi-Fascist organization called the Croix de Feu. He worked day and night on wartime casualties who came into his neurology surgery, but when the Germans arrived to take over France's capital, this was too much for the exhausted man. Discouraged by the defeat of France, he shot himself the day the Germans entered Paris in 1940.

While working in England during the war, the tragedy of facial disfigurement and its psychological repercussions made a deep impression on Converse. Men were ordered to bring planes back at whatever cost, so they could be repaired and sent into the air again. Often the men were burned beyond recognition.

Converse longed to establish a unit for the facially disfigured in the U.S.A. He could never get rid of the memory of the airmen of the Battle of Britain. One of them had said to him, 'Here I am, a healthy man, but with a burned face and burned hands. I know how a girl shudders at a kiss.' Converse tried to help him. Nothing could be worse than such senseless disfigurement.

When he got back to the U.S.A., he dedicated himself to the facially mutilated. Cancer left gaping holes in faces; burns left children without skin, without necks, without head-movement; babies were born with unspeakable malformations; men and women involved in motor-car mishaps often led a life of seclusion, not daring again to be seen.

All needed his sort of help. No hospital existed. There were few teaching services for plastic surgery and few hospital beds available for this type of patient. Special facilities had to be established and the public made aware of the needs.

Converse began by pushing his way into hospital wards. He started on the original decrepit Bellevue Hospital, whose wards and corridors filled with patients he would raid, offering his services with a team of dedicated pioneers: a dental surgeon, a sculptress (for new ears from cartilage) and a photographer.

That project went on from a crawl to a run. His call for help finally came to me; 'Were you serious when you said you were interested?' he asked me one day, out of the blue. I was. My earliest contribution was film supplies to begin the documentation.

The first step was a pilot unit at Manhattan Eye and Ear Hospital – he soon outgrew that. Years of fund-raising followed (crowned by a gift of a one-million-dollar conditional grant from the Avalon Foundation, started by the late, generous Ailsa Mellon, as the single biggest feather in our tattered caps). This led to the now distinguished Institute of Reconstructive Plastic Surgery of the New York University Medical Centre. Since that great start, we've watched the project grow: the million was matched and the Institute was set up; with it, the first endowed chair of plastic surgery was also established for Dr Converse.

Three million dollars was raised in 1970 alone, one million dollars from the De Witt Wallaces, proprietors of *Reader's Digest* magazine, and another two million from the Billy Rose Foundation.

Billy Rose's two million dollars came after a most unlikely start. He called on Converse in 1960 saying he had thirty-five million dollars as the largest single stockholder invested in American Telephone and Telegraph shares, and wanted to use some of the money to start a Foundation for the rehabilitation of old actors.

'What have you in mind?' Converse asked. 'Well, when actors are too old', Billy Rose explained, 'they can't get work. If they could have their faces lifted, they could go back to acting ...'

'There's nothing much I can do about that. My activities are devoted to badly disfigured people. The Foundation you describe wouldn't fit into our programme,' Dr Converse sighed.

Nevertheless, many years later, the Institute found itself the fortunate beneficiary of two million dollars from the late Billy Rose's estate. It was earmarked for the establishment of a Centre for Craniofacial Anomalies. A fervent supporter, Charles Wohlstetter, had been made President of the Billy Rose Foundation. 'I want you to do for others what you did for my son,' was his deeply moving and simple explanation.

President Kennedy's father, Joseph, was involved at an early stage on behalf of an old lady of eighty who lived in New York at the Savoy Plaza Hotel with her maid. She had received a letter describing an accident in which a man in France had a bomb explode in his face. 'He needs a mask to be seen. He must retire to a monastery as his face is so out of joint; he is an object of complete horror. Can you help us?' the letter asked. Mrs McKay went to Mr Kennedy, who spoke to Dr Converse.

Three benefactors went to his rescue: Joseph Kennedy, Cardinal Spellman and a family named Burke (of the B. Altman department store), and an operation by Dr Converse was arranged. It was not known in advance that the man was a bleeder, suffering from a rare condition known as 'fibrinolysis', a condition connected with fear of death. Jack Converse so tranquillized the patient that he removed this fear; the man was cured of bleeding and a new face was made.

Fund-raising was a fairly grim experience in our early days. We used shock techniques to force people to see how hideously wounded their unseen compatriots could be. We began by giving demonstrations in a room attached to wards where our patients sometimes lay for years at a time. They might have to endure as many as twenty or thirty bouts of surgery, and were often doubled up uncomfortably for months to enable skin-grafts to be made. Arms or legs had to be attached to faces and heads for grafts to be made of their own skin.

We would begin our demonstration by showing large, blown-up photographs of a mutilated child or adult. Eventually, a door would open and a healed patient walked in – showing the face that had been created. To have someone fall over in a faint was quite normal for the course. In fact, the bigger the man, the harder his fall as he dropped off his chair, unable to stand the horrific sights.

Dr Converse, always calm, cool, kind, patient, was there to carry on the discussion after my introductory remarks. To the victims he was a saint. Children trusted and loved him instinctively.

For years the struggle was up-hill. Apart from all these problems, there were those from within the medical ranks of jealousy caused by the attention given to Dr Converse. And it was terribly hard to make potential money-givers realize the size of the population which needed their help. Sixty thousand mutilated people were hiding in the darkness and only publicity could bring the facts to the public's attention. Cynicism was another hurdle. 'If this is such necessary surgical knowledge, why isn't it being taught in every university?' we were often asked.

A typical example of the difficulty in arousing interest in those days was provided by a man attending a demonstration, the president of a giant air-line. He announced: 'I'm interested in more serious things than this. Converse is interested in fenders. I'm interested in making the engine work!' He eventually became a supporter.

Not only the face but the hands, the upper and lower extremities, the genito-urinary system and the breast are involved in major accidents. All must be repaired – and men must be taught how. Hand surgery is under constant research and improvement. Many research programmes are going on, particularly to help the severely burned. There are now banks for such spare parts as bones, limbs, skin ...

Such plastic surgery requires several personal qualities in the surgeon – and is therefore not to be confused with simple cosmetic surgery such as lifting chins and sorting out nose-profiles. In remaking a mutilated face each of three skills must be involved, and in equal parts; first, surgical expertise and dexterity; second, the ability to visualize form and shape (which deals with functional as well as aesthetic problems), and, last of all, a tender concern for human suffering.

John Marquis Converse demonstrably possesses all three skills. He is a man whose dream has been realized.

Jacqueline Auriol:
a new face for a brave woman

The two greatest women pilots are both Jacquelines: one a Cochran, the other an Auriol. I've known them both. For years, the Harmon trophy swung like a pendulum from one woman to the other for achieving records in the air. But Mme Auriol's personal story is the more dramatic and I once had a connection with it.

In 1950 Dr Converse was in Paris and was invited to the Elysée Palace to examine Jacqueline Auriol's face. She had already undergone extensive plastic surgery following a serious plane accident, and his help (as the foremost American in reconstructive plastic surgery) was solicited in a last attempt to give her back a human face.

After twenty-two operations, during which an attempt had been made to rebuild the structure of her face, she was still severely disfigured. She felt so monstrous and was so distraught over her own appearance that her two sons, at her insistence, were kept from seeing her. She was then just over thirty, famous for her style and chic as well as for her flying prowess. She lived in the Elysée Palace. Her father-in-law was President of the French Republic.

Undaunted by her terrible accident, she insisted that she must live a normal life and must fly again. A miracle was needed to make her face acceptable. The crash had occurred as she had been co-piloting a new hydroplane which suddenly nose-dived into the Seine. She was thrust against the instrument panel.

She was barely alive when pulled from the wreckage, a ravaged international beauty. The bone structure of her face had been

244

horribly broken and pushed forward, there were two hundred fractures; her mouth and nose were smashed out of shape. Miraculously, her eyes escaped injury, but her face was gone.

At thirty-one, she joined the dark ranks of the facially mutilated. There are tens of thousands of these unhappy people in the U.S.A. alone. They tend to appear only at night, work only in the dark and spend their time hiding their faces. Jacqueline Auriol once said, 'A broken face is the face of a child without playmates, a man without a job, a woman who locks herself away from all her family and shuns mirrors.'

Could Dr Converse make a new face after so many attempts? Could Mme Auriol ever again live a normal life? He agreed to try, on one condition. She would have to be moved to his own operating theatre in New York, where he had a trusted and remarkable team at hand. The decision was made and she was taken, heavily bandaged, to the hospital which was the first clinic for the Facially Disfigured, the tiny precursor of the important hospital which now exists.

Jacqueline Auriol arrived bearing a false name; only Mme Bonnet, wife of the French Ambassador to the U.S.A., and I were told. Although I had never met her, the fact that I was a close friend of the doctor and on the board of the Institute where she was taken for surgery (and living close by) made me an obvious collaborator. It was my good fortune to be able to offer friendship, the occasional visit and to bring her out in public when it was felt she was ready to face that ordeal.

Dr Converse's incredible skills were soon demonstrated. After one day of interminable surgery, a new face was designed, built and stitched into place. Whether or not it resembled the old one (it did not) was immaterial. It was a round, even gay face. The only drawback at any time was that her nose seemed to be constantly 'dropping', which plagued her.

'My nose melts,' she used to say. 'It drops to my lips.' When the tissue which had been used to rebuild her nose was removed and replaced by a bone graft from her own hips the nose grew straight and permanent. Complaints stopped.

Not only a new face but a new personality emerged. Mme Auriol made a remarkable mental post-surgery recovery, and when she did, the aviator in her was re-awakened. She insisted on flying again.

Between scar-tissue removals, she was able to go (still incognito) to the Bell Aircraft Corporation, makers of helicopters, in Buffalo, New York. There the late Laurence Bell, also one of our Trustees, put a helicopter and an instructor at her disposal. 'There's a French dame coming up here for lessons, just keep her happy — she's a born pilot,' were his terse instructions.

I believe she was the first woman in the U.S.A. to get a helicopter licence. And later, when everyone felt she was psychologically set for the experience, I arranged for her to meet, incognito, General Vandenberg (on whose staff I served as Adviser on Women's Air Force, recommended to him for the post, by the way, by Jacqueline Cochran, the other great woman pilot). She was able at last to get back into a jet again, to try out her nerves as well as her skill. Courage won. She returned to France and to the air again. But not before a touching emotional experience which nearly destroyed her capacity to be among people.

I took her out to dine in public; it was the first time she felt ready to see and meet people casually again. I chose the Pavillon Restaurant because I had a regular table there and could arrange beforehand for a minimum of attention. The two of us were just about to slide into the seats in my corner banquette when a visiting French general recognized me as we passed his table. He stood up, bowed low over my hand. He hesitated for a moment after looking at Jacqueline Auriol, then merely smiled and sat down. No introductions were exchanged.

Mme Auriol knew this much-decorated war hero far better than I, but obviously he had not recognized her, and, with her new face, she was far from ready to admit her real identity to someone who ought to have jumped to her side. It was an unfortunate and unexpectedly dramatic coincidence for this Frenchman to be sitting four feet away from us in a New York restaurant, unaware of her identity.

The general soon finished his meal and came to my table to say goodbye. Turning from me, he looked at her intently and apologized. 'Do forgive me for smiling at you before. For just a fleeting moment, I had the mistaken idea you were Jacqueline Auriol,' he explained as he turned on his heel and left the restaurant.

She dissolved in tears; I had difficulty in hiding mine. 'I've lost my identity. My own friends don't know me. *Who* am I?' she sobbed.

Eventually she went back to the Elysée Palace, where I saw her again. Since then, she had chosen to live in the air, tempting fate by terribly dangerous flying. She described to me, during my visit to the Palace, how she intended to break her own speed record by flying in a fixed circle; which surely must have been dangerous. Back in 1959, when such figures were dramatic, she flew 1,344 miles an hour in a Mirage.

I haven't kept up with her flying record since then, but one can't be blamed for suspecting that breaking records is part of a death-wish.[1] It's easy to think she went back to test-piloting (often setting her course in near-suicidal challenges which only a dare-devil would attempt) because she only really seems content in the air and prefers to die there too.

Not long ago another accident to her face occurred. A hair-drier, pulled down rashly over her head, hit her nose and broke the laboriously-created bone graft. Once again, Dr Converse was called in to the rescue.

Today she is far from a recluse, recognized and admired wherever she goes. Strangers approach her and congratulate her on her feats. She is so much a personality, I'd like to see her become Honorary Chairman of an Institute for the Facially Disfigured in Paris, similar to the one we've created in New York. She would be a remarkable symbol. She has a tremendous opportunity to help other mutilated people.

It will be wonderful if, in future, someone so attractive (and who was once so terribly disfigured) does something for other French victims, especially mutilated children.

Meanwhile, an aeroplane seems to fill her life completely. Just after France's new fold-back winged jet crashed in 1971, she went off to Istres to fly one – to beat yet another record.

---

[1] She did make the headlines again in September, 1971, as Concorde's First Lady – the first lady to fly it. She flew with it on Latin-American, African and Orient tours as a super lady agent to help sell it.

Anecdotal Carousel

I SPOKE of an anecdotal carousel in the Introduction to this book. Years of journalism have contributed to a large collection of stories. Going places and meeting people has provided countless others. Travel, which first became an integral ingredient in my years in publishing, still continues as a way of life and will remain so until a tourist-crowded world (and hijacking and grenades?) robs it of all joy.

I actually love being in the sky. I am genuinely happy – whether looking down on the beautiful earth below me or being enveloped by cloud. I've written many things in a corner-window seat of a plane, peaceful and content to be in the air.

However, one word of dissent: I'm not eager to fly in space – not after a recent trip to NASA in Texas, where astronauts are trained and prepared for the moon. It had been arranged for me to have what is known as The Head of State Visit; I was even lowered into a real capsule, feeling much too large in there alone, utterly unable to visualize the possibility of two large bodies in their heavily-laden and enlarging space-suits. I was spared from donning such bulk but claustrophobia and instrument-terror were both instantaneous.

One of the clichés about travel is the notion that the jet age has made the world smaller. I disagree. Every time I get to some remote corner, I realize how *far* I am from home, how far we really still are (mentally) from each other, how quickly our differences multiply when on the spot. Asia isn't any nearer simply because a swift plane gets one there quickly.

When an anthropologist like Margaret Mead leaves America for a Samoa, a Russia or a New Guinea, she deliberately leaves behind her the speech, the food, all the familiar patterns of her own way of life – and seeks to understand and live the life of the other people. She deliberately enters a new culture, and takes advantage of it.

251

Yet when we travel back and forth, even just across the Atlantic, we don't seem able to follow her example. We remain the same, tending to see the others as odd fellows.

But changes towards a form of internationalism are always being made, even if slowly. One night recently, after eight days of motoring across six national boundaries in Europe, I realized how much a sign of the times it was that I never had to get out of my car at a border nor fill in a single form (until I met the British authorities). Boundaries were blurring. As I am an internationalist by nature, I liked that.

In politics, in sport, in trade, in the arts (and in travel) internationalism is on the march even if there are still people who shun it; nationalism bends with the times. The cannibal of yesterday is today's medical student; the lion was once (momentarily) replaced by the Beatle as the British symbol, the Olympic games are seen and heard simultaneously all over the globe – with the help of the most international little gadget of all, Telstar. And the man landing on the moon had 600 million viewers watching him from all over the civilized world at the same moment.

Some of us (not I) actually eat fried grass-hoppers without blinking an eye, forgetting how primitive an act it was. Our young generation no longer uses 'Wogs' to describe Arabs, 'Dagos' for Latins or 'Niggers' for black people (and no longer feels the universal contempt which prompted these terms in the 'thirties).

Among the anecdotes I've recalled here are those which do suggest the variety that I've been trying to describe as my life. They include stories about a man and his singing dogs, a despotic ruler in Muscat, meeting a Pope, a paranoic painter, a royal dinner that nearly went wrong, an unexpected Surrealist welcome at an English university – and the time I persuaded a giant airliner to turn back.

Salvador Dali: the hazards of visiting him

I knew that Port Lligat was an integral part of Salvador Dali's existence, so while writing my book about him, I had to go to his home to observe his life-style.

Incidentally, it took me three years of research in Spain and France to check up on Dali's terrible tales: some were maniacal, some perverted, some ridiculous – and all were beyond belief. To my horror, they were all true – and Dali loved having them confirmed. Nobody ridicules Dali better than he does himself.

Once while I was in Madrid, I wanted to talk to people who knew him as a fellow student. I quite unexpectedly found Dali in the foyer of my hotel. After a greeting so lavish that the splendidly elegant Ritz shuddered, he insisted I come up to see him at his Costa Brava home.

'How do I get there?' I asked him. Geography has never been a strong point of mine.

'Very simple. Fly Barcelona, then catch train to Figueros. Putch information telegram. My secretary meet,' he ordered. Translated, it meant his secretary would meet me if I'd telegraph details, which I did. Two days later, the concierge at the hotel fixed up the plane and train and I left.

Of course Dali gave the wrong advice. He should either have sent a car to meet me in Barcelona or suggested I hire one. The lag between the plane's arrival and the departure of the train was *hours*.

My troubles hadn't really begun. Every confrontation with the man has its hazards but visiting him by land was really an adventure. Dali prefers you to arrive by sea and by yacht, the larger the better.

It was bad luck to have come on the slow, crowded and hot

Costa Brava local train. Following that, a journey from Cadagues to Port Lligat had a surrealist quality. The route in those years was harsh and unmanageable.

His secretary would meet me in Cadagues, a telegram promised —in reply to mine. I had carefully specified both the plane and train I would take. At Cadagues, already feeling regretful, I wandered around, looking for a mysterious person who might belong to Dali.

'Secretaria de Señor Dali?' I kept asking shopkeepers and pedestrians in the little square of the town. Shrugs greeted me everywhere. I vacillated between taking the next train back to Barcelona and ordering a car to drive me to Dali's home. I chose Dali's home.

The next hurdle was to find anyone willing to take me there. The local taxi, run by an octogenarian even older than his car, simply refused. The road was too bad for his tired old vehicle. The lure of money, combined with persistence, eventually won; I finally stepped into the battered wreck for the next journey.

As soon as we left the village behind, I understood his unwillingness. I too began to worry.

It was obvious the car couldn't cope with the non-road to Port Lligat (complicated by potholes and crevices and rocks and constantly up-and-down steep hills). Would the car break down? Would I be responsible if it did (morally, if not technically)? Would I ever get there?

The questions were soon resolved. A particularly high and rocky hill loomed before us. The old engine struggled and struggled, then turned over and died. We kept slipping backwards down the hill, a few yards each time, not without a lost heartbeat or two.

In those few moments new decisions had to be made. Wearing high heels, I was not properly dressed for a hike over rock-strewn hills. I had luggage to carry. And how could I leave the poor old man alone, muttering in despair over his motor car?

Suddenly, an incongruous figure appeared over the top of the hill —a man, on a Vespa, shouting with excitement.

'Mais vous êtes très vite! Je suis le secretaire de Monsieur Dali. Bien venue!'

If I was early, it was only because the male secretary was about two hours late. His beaming welcome waving my telegram was irritatingly fulsome.

After a few loud screams by driver and secretary at each other, when I assumed (and later hoped and prayed) that the taxi driver was being offered money and assistance, I was 'invited' to join the secretary on his vehicle.

I had never been on the back seat of a motor-bike before and I was scarcely prepared this time. Somehow (with my dress pulled high, my black silk Dior coat floating behind me, a suitcase in one hand and my handbag in another) I prayed for my life – having no hand free to cling to either bike or driver.

We sailed up the hill. Only osmosis held me on that seat. We navigated each hill only to face a new low valley; up and down we jostled (for what to me seemed like miles), often missing one large rock only to jolt close to another.

Finally, over one high hill, I saw the exquisite little port of Lligat, then almost an empty cove. A tiny hostel and Dali's home (of several connected fishermen's cottages) and an incredible harbour lay before me. The great man himself, his Dalinian moustache twittering in delight, stood there, dressed in odd clothes for some strange tableau.

The motorcycle skidded to a halt. I fell off. I landed on a pile of jagged stones, everything I owned scattered before us. When I was helped to my feet again, one leg was bleeding profusely, my skirt was torn, my clothes a mess.

Dali was hysterical with delight. Looking at the bleeding leg and the pile of rubbish which represented my belongings, he cried out in glee:

'Wonderful! Wonderful! Very Dalinian arrival!'

Why I Wrote my Book about Juan and Evita Perón

Elsewhere, I describe the time I spent with Evita, the dead woman whose influence still rocks the Argentine political scene.[1]

I wrote the book in 1950 after returning from her country to the United States. The reasons for doing so are just as dramatic as the details of the lives of the incredible duumvirate who ruled the country in those days.

The drama began in the residence of the American ambassador, where I was staying in 1950. It was the 4th of July, which Ambassador Stanton Griffis was celebrating with an open house at the residence. I was late, having miscalculated the time needed to get to and from a secret rendezvous outside the city to meet an Argentine friend.

We had gone to a place we were quite sure hadn't been bugged, the home of an American widow who couldn't possibly have had enough political significance to be watched or 'tapped'. The little weekend cottage was much farther away than estimated and I returned to the Embassy late, breathless, apologetic.

The man I'd gone to meet was an open enemy of the Peróns (his anonymity is still important to protect today). Several members of his family had already been intimidated and arrested; his oldest son was still in jail. He was also being constantly threatened, though he continued to criticize. Meeting a prominent American lady editor openly was imprudent, hence the cloak-and-dagger arrangements.

We discussed the government's persistent harassment of the women and men of the family, he quietly assuring me that any

[1] pp. 176–80.

256

well-intended intervention would only worsen matters. More or less to change the unhappy subject, I turned and asked, 'What's the "hottest news" in Buenos Aires today?'

'Well, of course, it's the famous White Paper,' he blurted out, assuming I knew of it.

'*What* White Paper?' I demanded. And then he explained. An opposition Congressman (whose 'token' election had been allowed if merely to prove there were 'free elections') had been arrested and locked up in an undisclosed jail. Many months before, he had written a seemingly routine legislative document on suggested educational reforms. It had been printed, distributed to Peronistas (highly disinterested), passed on to the Education Committee – and promptly 'buried'.

Those who had bothered even to scan the first pages found a proposal to reform the educational system, anyone reading further was in for a shock; the document dived into a detailed account of Juan and Evita's juggling of the law, the finances and the politics of the Argentine.

Unexpectedly, one man *did* read it. All copies of the Paper were immediately confiscated and, in the totalitarian tradition, burned. A few copies, it was rumoured, were saved from the fire.

'So that's the White Paper. I assume you have one of those copies,' I announced to my Argentinian friend.

'Yes, but I am absolutely certain that someone knows I have; I simply don't know who on either our household or business staffs may be a government informer. My copy cannot disappear from my files or my family will pay even more heavily for my actions. Don't ask me to pass it on to you,' he concluded.

'No, I won't do that – nor can I help feeling sad for the poor senator. He'll obviously disappear – without the world knowing what he risked his life to write.'

'I, too, am sad – but don't ask me to do anything about it,' he insisted.

I returned to the Embassy, too late even to dress for the reception. No sooner had I been swallowed up by the crowd than a hysterical woman grabbed me, handing me her card. 'You must come with me, *immediately*! I've been waiting for hours for you!'

'Who are you – and where do you want me to go?' I demanded of a perfect stranger.

'Come with me to the jail, to see the senator. Only you can help him!'

'What senator?' I asked, though suddenly well aware whom she could have meant.

'I'm sure you know who – but even if not, you must come with me. Everyone knows you know Evita Perón and if *she* finds out you are interested in this man, you may save his life,' she whispered frantically.

I took her to a corner in an outer hall to try to calm her down. 'Listen to reason,' I begged. 'To focus attention on a political prisoner through a well-known foreigner is probably to sentence him to death. Don't you realize that if I take an interest in him, he'll certainly disappear?' I pleaded.

I was too dismayed to be entirely coherent myself. 'What a dreadful position you've put me in. I'm living in the American Embassy. You are asking me to involve the Embassy and Ambassador,' I explained.

'In fact, I'd be willing to do something as rash as you ask if I thought it would save the man. But I have just been advised by a close friend here (whose life is also endangered) that it would be harmful to anyone for whom I intervened. Please go away,' I pleaded with her. 'If you do, I promise to think over what might be done.'

I returned to the others in a state of numbness, after literally pushing her out of the door. Who could I safely consult, I wondered?

Before the guests drifted away, Ambassador Griffis had a word with me. 'Here in Buenos Aires, it is safe, it seems, to talk openly in nightclubs – the noise makes bugging useless. Would you like to dine in one tonight with a few other ambassadors?

'Fleur, everyone knows you've spent a lot of time with Evita. Everyone wants to ask questions. What about it?' the Ambassador asked.

I was absolutely exhausted; it was already ten o'clock and dinner would be served at midnight but, of course, I agreed.

Amid the noise and the music, we talked freely about my

experiences in and outside the Casa Rosada, Perón's residence, now occupied by Evita's pale successor, Isabelita. Although I summoned up all the required answers and details, I was really thinking about the imprisoned senator. Noise, added to emotional fatigue, made me a bag of nerves. Had I really done the right thing not to go and see the man in jail?

Sir Jock Balfour, then U.K. Ambassador to the Argentine, was seated on my right. We talked of Britain's sensitive position in the Argentine – of the insurmountable problems over beef and wheat. My mind wandered.

Later that evening, realizing how overwrought I was about the Peróns, he whispered to me: 'If you think the Peróns are terrible, you should examine the history of their predecessors. Have you ever heard about Manuel and Encarnación de Rosas? If you haven't, you should.

'They're the pair who tried everything *first*,' Ambassador Balfour continued. 'The Peróns are poor copies; their predecessors really wrote the manual. Get out your history books and you'll see where the Peróns get all their ideas!'

Suddenly I asked another ambassador across the table (entirely out of context):

'By the way, have *you* got a copy of the famous White Paper?'

'Yes, I have – how could you possibly know?'

'I'd like to read it – will you let me have it?'

'No! Don't ask me for it; I cannot implicate my Government in the Argentine's internal politics.'

I pointed out that the man would probably die in anonymity.

'What a tragedy for him,' were my last words to the ambassador.

I left the Argentine the next morning, never more pleased to see the back of a country. There was a last taste of 'Peronism' at the airport, however: a crowd was there to see us off. A giant basket of orchids from Evita (taller than I) was placed at the foot of the steps of the Pan American plane, accompanied by photographs, farewell speeches. The lot.

Suddenly, I saw a lean, erect figure swiftly crossing the tarmac in our direction. It was the ambassador who'd refused the night before to give me his copy of the White Paper. Under his arm was a small thin package. '*Here.* You have a long trip ahead of you and

I've brought you something interesting to read,' he hastily explained as he tucked it under my arm and nudged me up the stairs.

In mid-air, the door safely locked, I opened the package. It was the copy of the White Paper, and inside the first page, a note in the ambassador's own hand, explaining why he had to bring it himself.

'My chauffeur is an Argentinian,' he explained, 'I can't trust him. *Who knows?*'

To do the right thing about the White Paper became an obsession. To expose the man behind Juan's grin and the woman behind Evita's glittering blonde showmanship was equally essential after exposure to them. Thanks to Jock Balfour, the idea for a book had practically been put in my lap. I wrote it in the next few months, setting the Perón story against their forgotten predecessors (whose stories were identical).

History books on the Rosas period had been rewritten in the Argentine but uncensored research about that pair existed in England – to which Rosas fled after his wife Encarnación died of cancer (*just as Evita eventually did* – to complete the parallel).

I reproduced the entire White Paper as the epilogue of my book; a copy went to every member of the American Congress, to Allen Dulles at the C.I.A. and to every influential person I knew. The senator did die, but he did not die anonymously, although I can claim little else for his martyrdom. Interest in Latin America in the United States in the early 'fifties was very slight indeed.

There are three interesting sidelines on this tale: the man prevented by Russia's veto from replacing U Thant as Director General of the United Nations at their last election was Ambassador Carlos de Rosas, a descendant of the same Manuel de Rosas about whom I wrote. The contemporary de Rosas is a remarkable person, very much on the right side of all moral issues, and a very different politician from his famous forebear. He has become a close friend.

Secondly, when the manuscript of the book on the Peróns had been put into my American publisher's hands, two major situations developed. First of all, threats to my life stepped up. 'Don't insist on publishing the book,' I was repeatedly warned. The F.B.I. eventually uncovered and arrested the black sheep son of a Buenos Aires newspaper proprietor who had been sent as a Perón agent to intimidate and frighten me in New York.

The third situation was much more significant. Until my book appeared, interest in the Peróns was superficial – mainly in his virility and her jewellery, and mainly in magazines and tabloids. In those days the Press treated Evita more as they would a film star or a pop singer today; her political skills and their effect on Argentina's history were basically overlooked, even ignored.

In the absence of any others, I became the only known foreign ally of the anti-Perón underground movement as soon as my book was published. Endless data began to pour into my office at *Look* by post, usually sent under dramatic circumstances.

Editorials in Buenos Aires newspapers, extolling what the Peróns were doing, were the daily diet of the Argentine's controlled press. The articles whose claims were the most glaringly inaccurate were cut out, coded in red ink and sent to me – after having been given to a very brave man or woman to swim with it across the River Plata to Montevideo in the dark of night. From Montevideo they were mailed to me with a coded explanation attached; first of all, the lies and then the real story. I sent this correspondence to Allen Dulles, knowing no better use to make of it.

Most moving of all was the reaction to my book in the Argentine. I found this out entirely by chance sitting next to a stranger on a plane in 1952. I was getting off in Brazil but the gentleman alongside was going to Buenos Aires. When he heard my name mentioned by the stewardess he was almost speechless with excitement.

This was his story to me: when the Rosas regime of a century before was at its peak of cruelty, a movement to unseat the pair was begun by a group of intellectuals. I had written about them in my book – and he knew it – but he had a new point to make: the plot to hatch a revolt against the Rosas tyranny had been drawn up in the basement of a bookshop in Buenos Aires. *The anti-Peronist plot was hatched in the very same cellar.* The same bookshop, owned by a woman who'd fled from the Nazis, had become the meeting place of anti-Peronistas. In that same basement, secret meetings were held – and they always included discussions of my book, studying one *page* at a time to avoid the crime of being found with the book itself.

'Each page was passed around secretly until thousands of us knew your book,' the elegant solicitor explained to me. He gave me his card, hoping one day I would use it in the Argentine.

A less revolutionary type couldn't be found. Nor a more grateful man. 'No one else seems to show any serious interest in our difficulties. Come and let us repay you one day.'

Just twenty years later, late in 1972, I sat next to a fascinating man at a dinner given for me, an Argentine Cabinet Minister who had come to address the U.N. in New York City. When he heard my name, he roared with laughter.

'I'm glad to meet you here,' he exclaimed. 'But don't come to the Argentine. I couldn't guarantee your safety!'

The Peróns were not the first dictators to use the lure of democracy in order to deny it to their people. But the pair of Peróns got away with the fiction while they were in power, and the myth remained long after Evita died. The legend continued for sixteen years while Juan Perón himself languished in luxury in his chosen exile in Madrid after fleeing the Argentine.

A charge of treason followed him, also charges of fraud over the misuse of public funds and the acceptance of bribes. Sixteen years later, as part of his 1972 pre-election bid, most charges were dropped.

Life had been good to the fiercely nationalistic army colonel with a gift of oratory. In 1943, he had already put into practice the lessons he learned from watching Mussolini in Rome, where he had been sent as Military Attaché. He married Eva, the right girl, as his second wife. Together, they ruled a country as big as India.

Under them the world's largest beef and wheat exporter became a country so destroyed it had to import beef and wheat to feed itself. The oil and mineral wealth of the Andes was wasted. The peso, which was 58 to the dollar in 1947, went down to 1,100 to the dollar in early 1972.

Life for the Argentinians in 1973 continued to be a trial of endurance. Prices rose so sharply that men needed to moonlight with at least a second job and there were those who held down as many as three. Money was spent as soon as it was earned – before its value could decrease (with gambling getting a lion's share even amongst the working classes). Guerrillas were in full cry.

In the years since Perón fled (with the support of one-third of the nation), Peronism has bedevilled Argentina. In 1962, President Frondizi even allowed Peronistas to put forward candidates in the elections again; when he did, the armed forces ousted Frondizi instead.

But even the Army had to change its tactics during seven years of troubled power, ending with the election of Perón's personal 'stand-in', Hector Campora, in 1973. The new government was short-lived; Campora resigned after a few months in office to make way for Perón himself; it had all simply been preparation for his return.

Very soon after, the same old man who had originally led his country to economic and political chaos, became President of the Argentine for the second time. Perón died on July 1st, 1974, nineteen years from the day when he was deposed in a *coup d'état*. He had fled like that mid-nineteenth-century predecessor, Manuel de Rosas, who died in London.

Perón lived less than a year after his election; he was an ailing man of seventy-eight. Even in this short time, his tarnished reputation was repolished, his popularity chanted again from the streets; many of his people were heady with unfounded hopes in him.

Once, he had been agitator and fomenter of class hatreds; this time he tried to be peacemaker, offering moderation and peaceful methods instead of guns. Once a sarcastic rabble-rouser, chasing hotly after enemies, he acted more like an elder statesman – using broad smiles and conciliatory rhetoric in an attempt to prevent war between the left and right in his own Peronista party.

Perón himself chose the right, disillusioning his followers on the left by this historic right-about-face. No longer calling to the *descamisados* ('shirtless ones') to overthrow the rich, he pleaded instead for young radicals and guerrillas to move to the centre.

He died of a heart attack before his illusions could be totally shattered, and left behind another woman whom he had elevated to the top. His third wife — Isabel Martinez de Perón — became President of the Argentine.

Isabelita shares the humble origins of her predecessor, Evita; both had been entertainers when they met Juan Perón. After Evita's death, Perón discovered Maria Estella Martinez in Panama; she was then a cabaret dancer and waitress, best known by the nickname Isabel.

At Perón's death, Isabelita made the short, white-haired Lopez Rega, pale-faced clairvoyant of fifty-seven, her closest adviser. Although little is really known of Mr Rega's background, his enemies claimed he formerly managed the café where Isabel met Perón. Rega became the most influential figure in the life of both Peróns (and with typical nepotism, brought in his daughter Norma and her husband Raul Lastiri, a closely-knit group of five soon known as 'the family').

When Mrs Perón became the first woman to be Head of State in South America, her future was unpredictable but one thing seemed certain: she didn't have the political 'savvy' of Evita nor the great allure with which Evita's oratory set fire to the masses. Life ahead looked ominous.

The future? Perhaps only Lopez Rega's crystal ball could tell.[1]

[1] It is said he has had a giant crystal ball installed as a monument in the square outside the Casa Rosada.

Mr Wiseman and his Singing Dogs

Driving with one's radio on can be hazardous. For my husband and me, once listening to a B.B.C. musical programme, it proved expensive, time-consuming and hilarious. We heard 'O Suzanna' being barked out, in perfect tune, by dogs!

We stopped and I called the B.B.C.: it was an American record we'd heard; the dogs were Danish; the producer (or conductor) lived in Copenhagen; the record was near the top of the American Hit Parade.

I'd only just arrived in England; life was less hectic so we flew off to Copenhagen the next weekend to find the man and his singing dogs. I went to the editor of a top Copenhagen newspaper, introducing myself as a fellow journalist. Fortunately, knowing me by name, and completely intrigued by the request, he lent me an English-speaking reporter.

We soon found Mr Carl Wiseman, an ornithologist who never questioned the difference between a bird's chirp and a dog's bark. He quickly dispelled all mental visions of a dog-choir: they were not a superbly trained group of big and little dogs lined up in a row, responding to his baton. His system was simpler:

'You take five dogs. Make a couple of grimaces. Make the dogs bark. Let your tape-recorder run. Cut the tape in precisely the right places. Glue the pieces together again. Make music accompaniment. And then you wait.'

Mr Wiseman waited long enough to become almost an instant millionaire. And in searching him out I met one of the most delightful of eccentrics; he was thin and small, wore a worn old coat and a beret, had a great twinkle in his eye.

An ornithologist, he had been a radio and TV contributor,

mainly making bird-broadcasts.[1] Assigned to make a schools broadcast, 'Letters about Dogs', he set out as usual, in a borrowed radio-car with borrowed equipment, to hunt dogs' voices. In deadly seriousness, he recorded the barks of nearly twenty dogs. He wondered, playing them back, if he could make a melody of them. 'O Suzanna', whose theme repeats and repeats itself, seemed the easiest to copy. A prominent Danish pianist was persuaded to accompany the dogs.

People tried unsuccessfully to buy the incredible dog-song but Wiseman had gone back to the job of recording birds. For weeks he lay in forests – watching birds, listening to them and taping their sounds, ending up 4,000 kroner (£250) in debt.

In 1948 he spent another 1,000 kroner going to England to try to sell both his earlier bird-sounds and his 'O Suzanna' record. Though turned down then, not many years later he earned all the money back ('with compound interest!' he boasted).

In 1954 he finally placed one record in English schools; it was of some children's songs, including 'Pat-a-cake', 'Three Blind Mice', and 'Jingle Bells'. In ten days 400,000 records were sold!

Suddenly, things began to happen for him; from the United States *Life* magazine wired its Danish correspondent: 'Get everything about the Danish dog-man.' Huge sales in Germany, the Netherlands, Sweden and Norway followed.

He was already theoretically a very rich man when we met him in 1956, but he was still dog-hunting. The day before, he managed to get 'some handsome basses and a few beautiful baritones (from St Bernards), a perfect Rottweiter-tenor from some Alsatians and a couple of sopranos from poodles'.

The science of taping dogs' barks was not to be slighted, he insisted. 'The barks are worthless unless loud and clear. And it is useless to take a bark when a dog is in an attacking position. When it calms down, you get the single, powerful "Vou" you need. Only then do I press the button.'

Wiseman's big problem was to prevent dogs from getting soppy over him. All dogs liked him, wagged their tails, rubbed

[1] I took away his catalogue of gramophone records: thirteen dealt with seventy types of bird records; one dealt with deer, foxes and boars and squirrels and one recorded such leaping amphibians as fire-bellied toad, tree frog, edible frog and several other varieties.

against his legs and whimpered little sweet noises. 'Only when I put on a strict face and make ugly signs do they react properly.' And the dogs, he added, had to be under three years of age (when their voices are finest).

Dog-lovers in England were both incensed and pleased to hear 'O Suzanna' and the other record. A letter in the *Daily Mirror* pointed out: 'While I'm writing this, I listen on my radio to some poor, dumb [!] animals—five dogs which are trained to sing different melodies. This is simply horrible cruelty to animals.' The editor of the *Mirror* replied that the B.B.C. had assured him the dogs weren't harmed.

Wiseman was busy recording other animal voices while we were in Copenhagen; we went with him to the Zoo where he was after growling bears, roaring lions and laughing hyenas for TV.

Sadly, when we left Copenhagen, he was still waiting for some cash—so badly off that in the Danish Broadcasting system he was known as the 'poor millionaire'. He looked poor. He was poor (he had only a few kroner in his pockets) although he was a paper millionaire.

'What are you going to do with all your money when you do get it?' I asked.

The money would buy the most lavish portable recording caravan with sound equipment one could order—'just like the big one the television people use. It will go with me to New Zealand!' New Zealand was his main target; there he intended to prove a scientific theory.

Apparently, towards the end of the last century, a sentimental Englishman had brought thirty-four types of English songbird to New Zealand. Their singing, he hoped, would keep the real England alive in his mind.

'Descendants of 26 of those 34 kinds of birds are still alive. Ornithologists all over the world are much interested in whether or not these birds sing with a New Zealand accent—or have the birds of New Zealand now learned to sing with an *English accent*?

'This is my secret dream. I will prove to the world *which* is which. I want to prove this very important scientific fact before I die!'

There is ample scientific and other background for his claim. I still recall an interview in *The Times* with writer Laurie Lee. It appeared after he'd purchased an eighteenth-century cottage in Slad, the tiny Cotswolds village he'd put on the map when he wrote *Cider With Rosie*. One reason he gave for liking Slad was 'because the birds sing with a distinctive Gloucestershire accent.' ...

Muscat: a sultan's decision

In January 1962, when the heat lay low and the sands were smooth and unblowing, I journeyed across the Hadhramaut, that vast, unseen, little-known, incense- and slave-route which cuts like a harsh narrow band across the heart of the Southern Arabian peninsula.

I was in a twin-engined plane, an American Aero-Commander, which I sometimes co-piloted (especially when heat draughts required four hands to hold us in the air). We were unarmed with the electronic miracles on jet planes — all we had were topographical maps with which to study the lunar hieroglyphics below.

I had followed in the footsteps of that intrepid and distinguished writer, Freya Stark, who had made the same trip, over the exact route, twenty years before. I, in the jet age, by plane; she, by primitive dhow from the port of Aden to Mukalla and then plodding on with a donkey into the harsh Hadhramaut.

I've written at length about that journey elsewhere. But what I couldn't write then, and am free to do now, is of my unexpected visit to Muscat. I had been refused a visa, but it eventually arrived.

Flying down the Hadhramaut, the logical last stop would normally have been Muscat, at the end of the road — where desert land meets the sea, facing Bombay across the Indian Ocean.

Getting to Muscat was not easy; not only was it inaccessible but in those days there was a despotic sultan who refused access. Visitors were unwelcome although half a dozen got there each year. Americans were then lowest on the popularity list and women the most unwanted of all. The chances of my getting into the walled town in 1962 were remote.

Notwithstanding all this, my friend Antonin Besse, who knew him, made a persuasive but polite request to the Sultan, through Britain's William Clark, then the ruler's adviser. I had flown off into the Hadhramaut without the final royal assent, hopeful that the approval would be radioed to us there.

No communication came, so we returned to Aden from Tarim. On the journey back, Christiane Besse suggested that we refuel in Aden, load up with more food and go to Addis Ababa instead, where we'd meet the Emperor, Haile Selassie. Naturally, I didn't find going there an unexciting substitute for Muscat.

We never got to Ethiopia. Instead, we went back over the Hadhramaut, this time to the end of the trail. We had been, in fact, getting ready to take off in Aden for Addis Ababa, when a man came running across the Aden airfield. 'Mrs Cow-less, Mrs Cow-less,' he shouted, waving his arms wildly. Since no person in an Arab country has ever pronounced Cowles otherwise, it was not difficult to decide who the man was after.

Although the Sultan had relented, it was on two strict terms; one, that I would agree never to write about Muscat; two, that I would remain inside the walled city, never going into the desert outside.[1] A council was quickly held, and I accepted the terms promptly, since the 'Royal O.K.' was indeed a rare gift. The plane turned its nose to the east instead of the west, and we started on our journey in the beautiful Aero-Commander plane.

Once again we bumped through hot air pockets over those same terrifying johls, with the same casual navigation assistance, and stopped for fuel at the same British Air Force base at Mukalla.

Reaching Muscat took ten hours of flying – and the landing was precarious. The port and town are like a deep inverted plate; there are steep mountains on three sides and the sea on the fourth. Circling and dropping altitude from nearly 12,000 feet, very suddenly, was hazardous enough, but our landing was further complicated by dusk. Day turned into night with a sudden sweep of darkness; if we'd arrived five minutes later, we would never have made it (and I shudder to think about the alternatives). The

[1] I kept the first commitment (not to write) until the Sultan was deposed in 1970. More importantly, when the British troops and Governor departed from Aden, Antonin Besse moved most of his interests and all of his family from the area.

light dropped away so suddenly we could hardly see the small landing area which had been flattened for civil and Sultanate Air Force use.

We stepped out of the plane, sighing with relief, to be met by the Sultan's Minister of Defence, the tall, handsome English mercenary, Brigadier Waterfield, M.B.E., a native of Devon, typical of the best of the British professional soldiering in the Arab world.[1] Later, when inside the town, we were received in William Clark's home. The grey-haired aristocrat, who was the Sultan's adviser, was a close friend not only of the Besses but of my own husband's family.

Brigadier Waterfield was obviously delighted. Visitors were rare and ours was an exceptional invasion. After handshakes were over in the little airport hut, I discovered over a drink why the Royal consent had been delayed.

'I wouldn't like you to misunderstand the Sultan's motives,' the Brigadier announced with a wry smile. 'Bill Clark kept at him for days and days, pleading with him to reconsider. He was obdurate until yesterday, when he relented.'

'I'm deeply grateful to His Majesty, and please convey this to him,' I commented, 'but I'm longing to know what was so worrying about me that he refused to let me come.'

'It is very simple,' he replied. 'I tried to persuade the Sultan to give his permission but he was absolutely adamant.[2] When I pushed him for an explanation, I got a very weary reply. "That terrible American lady must not come here. She's going to get killed!"'

I turned pale. 'How am I going to get killed?'

'Well, there's guerrilla warfare going on here now, and as you may know the desert is mined. It is dangerous outside the walls. It's more or less like Vietnam ...

'The potential oil under Muscat and Oman's sand is the prize for which the neighbouring kingdoms jostle, especially those

[1] Brigadier Waterfield retired to England at his own request early in 1970, to assist the old Sultan, Said bin Taimur, who came to England after being ousted by his son. The old man died in exile in 1972, but the present sultan had the good grace and gallantry to invite the Brigadier and his wife back to Muscat to thank them for their care of his father whilst in exile.

[2] Another lady reporter, whose name was easy to confuse with mine, had written a piece after a visit, which irritated him.

from the north. British officers, seconded to train and lead little groups of Arabs in the Sultan's private army, are ensconced throughout the desert.'

Attempting casualness, I begged Brigadier Waterfield to go on. The Sultan assumed I would be killed and simply didn't want the bother of it. 'After she's been killed', the Sultan pointed out to the Brigadier, 'trouble really begins for us. As she's an outsider, we'll have to find the assassin – to satisfy the American Government. I'll have to take hostages from each of my sheikhdoms. I'll have to put them in the dungeon. Feed them. Not too much, but a little – until someone confesses. Since she is an American, we'll have to worry about justice – a trial, all that nonsense.[1] And put the man to death painlessly. The Americans will be watching. It will be a long and costly affair – and *what for?*[2]

'She doesn't even offer to pay me!' the Sultan concluded.

After that story, I realized I had given rise to one of the better examples of the cold-blooded middle-eastern mind.

'Of course,' Pat Waterfield said, 'now that you are here, you'll be safe. I'll see to that – and what's more, you'll see everything, go everywhere and do whatever you want outside the walls.'

And he made good that promise.

The same journey to the newly-named Sultanate of Oman ought to be less difficult today. Change came when Sultan Said bin Taimur, the despotic old ruler, was ousted in the summer of 1970. The Sultan who was once called by *The Times* 'the most consciously reactionary ruler in the Arab World' was deposed by his twenty-eight-year-old Sandhurst-educated son, who began by instantly changing his father's policies as well.

The former Sultan had preserved a stern and sterile little empire

[1] The former Sultan, educated in England, had one great preoccupation when he came to London; he loved to go to the Old Bailey, where he watched with fascination. Justice (according to Islamic law) was different back home. Death sentences were invariably carried out in public by shooting in the presence of properly appointed judges. If sentenced by this court, not even the Sultan could set it aside. Such public executions, although abhorrent to Westerners, prevent an autocratic ruler from putting an enemy to death secretly.
[2] In Shara Law (Islamic) there is no crime against the State. Thus, if I had actually been killed in Muscat, my relatives or the United States Government (and not the Sultan) would have had to seek justice in the Muscat Court. A very tiresome business for the ruler to contemplate.

in splendid isolation from any other world, savagely punishing any attempts to modernize his kingdom in any way. He intended to keep progress out and his subjects in, and he succeeded. A curious example of this, when I was there, was a relative of the Sultan. Of uncertain but youthful age, he had been educated abroad in a military academy before returning to Muscat and Oman. He was never again allowed outside the country, except for one guarded trip to India for medical treatment.

Though he and I could not communicate in any known language, he never left my side. Most of all, he wanted copies of our photographs; countless were taken of us together. He was like a shadow and as harmless.

Everywhere, while we were in Muscat, we heard tales of the old Sultan's mania against progress. He feared all economic developments, especially in oil. Anyone daring even to repair the walls of his mud-hut in the town was severely punished by flogging, fines, prison or death (but with hands intact, unlike the renowned practice in Saudi Arabia). For building without permission, destruction of the new building could follow. A man might repair a *barusti* or palm house but if he increased the standard of the house by using cement or stone, he would be in trouble with the law. Or if he was found using a torch instead of the old lanterns, he ended up in jail for the night, to be released after paying a fine.[1]

One soon understood the sight of photographs of that promised emancipator, Nasser, on walls inside those huts (it will be impossible for any other Arab figure to build such a following in remote places).

Under the old Sultan's rule, the gates to the city closed to vehicles every day three hours after sundown – although pedestrians could always pass. No one knew when that could occur since the huge gate swung shut at different hours depending on the changing time of sunset. The signal to the populace was the firing of a gun at Merani Fort (in response to a nod from the Sultan), in the harbour overlooking the town.

With Brigadier Waterfield's protection, I felt quite safe from

[1] Even Brigadier Waterfield was arrested one night by his own police, which was regarded as a great joke by all concerned.

mines and snipers when we travelled outside, but life was hard for mere subjects of the realm.

I left with a certain amount of jingoistic pride after seeing the work of the American Mission doctors there, two fully-qualified surgeons who had opted for the fly-plagued world of the poor desert.

Wells Thoms and his dedicated wife were working then in a primitive hospital (painful to see by our standards but a godsend in the desert). They had been out there since 1930. With them was also a fully-qualified Indian surgeon. Somehow, without recourse to research or modern developments, they performed all ordinary surgery quickly and efficiently.[1] To me, they seemed saints. They retired in 1969.

His father founded the hospital on Muthrah and, in fact, died there after falling from a telegraph pole while repairing the line between Muthrah and Muscat.

The present young Sultan, Qabus bin Said, has changed all. Exiles were invited to return. He has instituted a whole list of reforms, has permitted the importation of agricultural machinery (outlawed by his father), listened to development ideas, and even appointed an American to be his petroleum adviser, so oil has now started to gush (a mere 300,000 barrels a day compared with the Arabs' nine million, but supplying most of the revenue for modernization).

Sultan Qabus has so far built a hundred primary schools and a large number of hospitals, thus creating an unprecedented construction boom. Workers and technicians from abroad are in demand; even diplomats, and all have established homes there. With effort, the building of a modern world has been accomplished in a few years. They even have colour television, though there are few television sets.

---

[1] Mostly eyes; when I was there, at least 80 per cent of the people suffered from glaucoma. Ultimately one got used to the sight of children with sore eyes thick with flies, but I'll never forget it. An enormous percentage of the people are sightless in at least one eye.

There is also an Army hospital for the military (with five British and Indian doctors).

Royal Dinners: feasting a king and queen

I've known the Greek royal family since 1950; in fact, I've been present (by accident or invitation) during some of their most happy and serious moments since then. I've probably kept this friendship through trust; they knew I would never tell or write about these incidents, some of them happy, some of them tragic. I certainly don't intend to break this habit now. However, there is an anecdote (involving being entertained in my home), sufficiently amusing yet totally unpolitical, that I like to tell.

It occurred when the late King Paul and Queen Frederika, on their 1953 state visit to the United States, made an informal stay in New York City. They came to us for cocktails before going to the theatre to see *South Pacific* that evening. To get them there before curtain time, we settled for drinks at a very early hour, five-thirty in the afternoon.

I asked about twenty friends. Among them were Marlene Dietrich and Noel Coward; so was Elsa Maxwell, who invited herself. While in the line being presented to Queen Frederika, she blurted out that a 'Celebrity Cruise' to the Greek Islands ought to be a great help to Greek tourism – to which the Queen readily responded, 'What a good idea!' The Queen's remark was soon repeated as a 'royal command' – and a trip was actually organized.

When I thought the hour approached for the royals to leave, I hid them away in another room and once out of sight, announced to the others that the King and Queen had gone. It took a bit of doing to get the other guests not to linger to chatter about the well-informed and highly amusing guests of honour. I could only push them out by admitting the royals were, in fact, still with us and that I needed to have the others out of the way.

I returned to our library, ready for farewells. To my surprise the King and Queen seemed to have settled in for the evening. Finally, I murmured to King Paul about curtain time and asked, 'You must have a meal waiting for you somewhere?'

'Oh no – nothing of the sort!' he replied.

'Then where will you eat before going to the theatre?' I blurted out.

'With you! That is, if we can take pot luck,' he announced with his renowned, devastating smile.

Although overcome by the implied flattery, I realized we hadn't even made any plans for our own meal. Excusing myself, I fled into the kitchen, clutching Andrée Lartigan (the miraculous friend-housekeeper who kept my life together in those days) to ask if she could rustle up a meal in half an hour. 'The King and Queen have decided to stay!'

'Don't worry. Go back to your guests. Leave it to me,' the remarkable woman replied without a hint of concern. Not a hair turned. I did so, trying hard to keep my mind on conversation and off the meal. What would be served? How would it look on such short notice?

Shortly after seven, dinner was announced. We sat down to a beautiful table, including a glorious flower centrepiece which Andrée had managed. The food was superb. Never have little *poussins* tasted so good. The French cheeses which went with the salad were in perfect condition. Wines had been decanted. The linen was beautiful. The light, pre-theatre meal, if planned for months, couldn't have been more perfect.

Getting the royals to leave began to look like a problem. Only by reminding the King and Queen that the curtain wouldn't *rise* for *South Pacific* until they were actually in their seats were we able to see the two to their car. Very, very anxious royal attendants were waiting for them on the street.

Pope John: a surprise meeting

While in Rome during an exhibition of my paintings at the Obelisco Galleries, a very kind gentleman arranged for me to visit the Vatican. An invitation arrived, looking to me like a card printed by the thousand for special visitors who throng the private rooms of the Vatican daily.

I borrowed a well-worn lace mantilla, put on the regulation long black dress which, fortunately, is always in my wardrobe, and drove off in style in the friend's car. I soon found myself being directed through a maze of halls and corridors, ending in a vast room; hundreds of others were already waiting there.

My card, it seems, was not the conventional one; as soon as it was spotted, courteous and very special attention was bestowed. I kept being sped on my way from one room to the next, each time I found fewer persons in each.

The process continued; the card led me through elaborate areas until I found myself in the elegantly panelled room in which ambassadors presented their guests. But it was not to be my final destination. A handsome Roman prince came forward to whisper frigidly (a style which little befitted the Pope he represented) that I was going to have a private audience, that I'd be seen in a very few moments and would I follow him to the Pope's library? My heart stopped. A private audience, without preparation?

In fact, I'd been expecting for years to meet Pope John one day (he had been a close friend to the uncle of Enrico Donati, my best friend). Both men had been in Paris together when Pope John was Nuncio there.

The little Paris apartment I always used at the Hotel Lancaster whenever I was there, called 'Le Cottage', faced my friend's

277

uncle's flat across Rue de Berri. I was so near to both men opposite on that narrow little street that I felt like shouting over to them whenever I saw them. When he was elected as Pope I felt I already knew the wonderful man.

It was, nevertheless, a jolt to be told I'd be seeing him alone in a few seconds. What could I say? I hadn't an idea as I fully expected to be with a large group; I'd been told he usually walked through, blessing the throng in one grand gesture.

'In what language does one address His Holiness?' I finally blurted out to the Prince.

'I speak every language,' the snob replied; he made one almost feel as if there was no point to the Pope's private audience.

Before I could collect my wits, Pope John was in the room, beside me, beaming in friendliness. While I stood there tongue-tied, trying to compose the suitable opening remark, he made it himself. I nearly fainted with delight.

'And how is your exhibition going?' he asked, making it seem that nothing could be more important to discuss!

The ice broken, we chattered away (in English by the way!) absolutely informally, as if we were two old friends catching up. Before we were parted by the infuriated aide (who quite rightly wanted to get the Pope on his way to larger audiences) we covered incredible ground.

I explained about 'Le Cottage' in Paris and how often I'd seen him from across the way. In turn, he was pleased to know more about the tiny, flower-laden hotel penthouse which he'd often looked into from his friend's apartment. The fact that it had originally been decorated for the opera singer Mary Garden (and never altered) absolutely delighted him.

Then we actually began to talk about 'his job'; he explained how sad he was that he had that very day been stopped from going to the jails to visit prisoners. And also from going to his favourite *trattorias*. Too dangerous, it was decided, to let the Holy Man go into such public places ...

'Tell me your most favourite places,' I pleaded. 'We'll eat in one this evening and drink to your great good health! And we'll visit them all, one by one ... '

He described the places carefully, then – after blessing a few

278

coins I brought to give to Catholic friends in London — he swept out of the room. But not before I succumbed to a temptation to hug him goodbye. The impulsive act was almost too much for the royal aide to bear (and, in retrospect, I can understand why).

That evening we ate at the Pope's favourite little restaurant to which he was now barred from ever going again. And did so for four nights in a row. His choices were superb. We ate marvellously.

A Surrealist Welcome at Durham University

In November 1968, I was happily moving about Brazil after a successful exhibition of my paintings in Rio, longing to stay on in order to explore Bahia. Instead, I had to return to England to make a speech at Durham University, in one of England's loveliest northern towns.

The plane I took back arrived in England on a Saturday, giving me time to go to Sussex for half my usual weekend – to rest, catch up with mail and try to refocus again from Brazil to think of something to say in opening the Surrealist Exhibition at Durham University on the following Monday. The invitation had been extended many, many months before – and there the date was, upon me.

One can normally fly from London to Durham in an hour, on a plane which leaves at eleven each morning. Sadly, I had to take the train (at ten o'clock for a four-hour journey) because of the risk of fog.

Writing the speech had been worrying after returning from hot Brazil to cold England in a state of exhaustion. I had very little sleep before I boarded the train for Durham. Being tired, the train's lack of heat was infuriating. Just as we were about to depart, my chauffeur rushed back with the travel-rug he snatched from the car! 'You'll need this,' he warned prophetically as he leapt off.

He was right; the train was absolutely frigid. Not once, during the four winter hours, had a speck of heat been pumped into our carriage. The guard was oblivious to both entreaty and insult. I found myself doing what thousands of train travellers do – cursing British public transport.

A Surrealist Welcome at Durham University

The carriage got so cold I eventually was embarrassed to be the only one with a rug; in an impulsive gesture of camaraderie I removed my own woollen stockings and offered them to the blue-faced lady sitting opposite me. She took them with gratitude (putting them on over her own) and I rewrapped my feet tightly in the rug, feeling less guilty, but certain that a little Charlie Chaplin man must have arranged it all.

The point in repeating this unimportant but sordid little vignette is to describe the condition in which I reached Durham for what turned out to be a thankless job. I was tired, the trip was uncomfortable. It was a distinct personal sacrifice to come from Brazil to keep the appointment. It didn't take long for me to question my judgment.

I was met by a good friend, Louis Allen, one of the university's most influential dons. Through his eyes, I saw the fabled beauty of the ancient city, which has one of the earliest and most beautiful cathedrals in Europe. The river, flowing low between the sides of an immense deep gash in the earth, cut the university from the cathedral. It was spanned by a spectacular bridge, crowded with students. What met the eye was good and I am happy I've seen it.

I had been asked to open the exhibition because, when I'd written a biography of Salvador Dali I had come to know Professor Allen, himself a great authority on the painter. One of my own paintings was hung amid the paintings in a Surrealist exhibition that rated the best walls anywhere.[1] The students had acquired a loan exhibition which was so remarkable most museums would proudly have claimed it.

Having said all this in praise, I'll now get down to the unpleasant details. When the hour arrived, I was led by Professor Allen and Ian Barker, the students' Exhibit Chairman, to the dais in the hall next to the one in which the exhibit hung. There, after a few kind words of introduction by Vice-Chancellor Christopherson, I was on my own.

I should have been prepared, but I wasn't. After all, it had been my fate to spend years of my life investigating the eccentricity of surrealists, orienting myself to the vicissitudes and nonsense of working with a self-styled genius like Salvador Dali.

[1] From the collection of Sir James and Lady Carreras.

I knew surrealists enjoy making trouble; many of them equate it with genius.

Here, the students had planned a riotous bit of trouble-making to celebrate the occasion. As soon as I started to speak, a gun was shot off. Continuous loud bangs were followed by students dancing in the aisles. The music? About fifty men were seated just outside the hall, each playing an instrument he'd never seen before. The noise was deafening.

My inclination was to stop, to thank them for their welcome and to leave. My next instinct was to ignore the nonsense, to go through with the whole speech, saying all I had prepared – which I did. Fortunately, it was written in a light-hearted mood.

At the end, I asked for a moment of silence. 'You've made a great mistake in asking me instead of Salvador Dali. *He* would have enjoyed this nonsense.

'And may I make an extra point,' I continued. 'Some students think that drugs are a short cut to surrealism. I don't. I think it's cheating.'

I then went straight to the home of Louis Allen, where I was to spend an evening in the warm atmosphere of their home, with other college friends – mostly professors, all experts in their fields. Talk was lively, civilized, intriguing.

In the middle of it all, the front door bell began ringing loudly. A large delegation of students were outside, 'to apologize to Fleur Cowles'. With my acquiescence, Professor Allen agreed to welcome a delegation of any three of them – in his tiny, book-crowded study. Two boys and a girl arrived, asking if they might also do an interview.

The two boys appeared to be holding up a very pale and rigid girl. As they started asking questions, I noticed the girl's colour. Her face changed from white to yellowish-green and at that moment she fell forward, flat on her face.

'*Send* me your questions,' I begged, as I accepted Professor Allen's plea to return to the other guests.

I got into bed at midnight (gallantly given the Allens' own great bed, I feel sure) with a feather quilt over me and two hot-water bottles tucked inside. I was no further than twenty feet from Durham Cathedral's walls and the famous great bell. The constant peal, announcing each hour, seemed to break inside that room — marking the passage of time. At seven in the morning I had to get up to catch the 8 a.m. train for London.

Why do I always say 'yes' I kept asking myself as I returned to London to the tune of the clicking wheels of the same ice-cold train.

Rio de Janeiro: a pilot answers my plea

In 1965, I flew to Brazil to attend the opening of the VIII Biennale in São Paulo, where nine of my paintings hung in the special section called 'Surrealismo e Arte Fantastica'. My journey can only be described by the same adjective.

The flight left England at dusk, arriving in Rio de Janeiro at seven-thirty the next morning. I didn't realize the last leg to São Paulo had to be made on a connecting plane. I never intended leaving my seat until São Paulo, so it was in a most unprepared fashion that I was unceremoniously disembarked in Rio.

I had taken a pill to sleep, and was still groggy. My hair was tied inside a head-scarf, my dress rumpled. I was almost the last to stagger down the steps – with arms full of quickly-gathered belongings.

I couldn't imagine for whom on board the plane the large group of photographers and ladies holding bouquets were gathered at the foot of the plane. To my horror, I soon realized from the roar of welcome and the flashing cameras that they were there to welcome bedraggled me.

Two dear Brazilian friends, ex-Ambassador and Mme Raul Boppe, whom I'd known for years while he was *en poste* for Brazil abroad, had gathered together this welcoming group. To meet the plane at seven-thirty (and they'd arrived nearly an hour before) they'd all had to leave their homes no later than six o'clock – and had got up even earlier to do so. Blinking before the flashlights, hugging some and shaking hands with all the others, I began to realize this awesome thought.

We marched into the V.I.P. lounge – to be handed drinks and canapes (what an hour! I thought). Many were newspaper-writers, and questions were popped like firecrackers. My mind simply wouldn't turn over, but I tried to do justice to the sacrifice all had made in order to greet me so fulsomely. Suddenly, I remembered my plane to São Paulo – and my baggage. When was the first leaving, and where was the second? No one seemed to know.

The airport was lifeless. Breath hadn't yet poured into its structures when my London plane had roared in – the only incoming traffic. 'São Paulo? The plane to São Paulo?' Everyone looked vague.

I started to rush out, begging to be forgiven as I ran from the building towards the tarmac. There was no sign of movement anywhere near. Nevertheless (all following), I ran towards the other end of the field because there seemed to be some activity there. We were a screaming crowd!

A man started running towards me. 'Miss Cowles? Miss Cowles?' he shouted.

'Yes! I'm Miss Cowles – is that the plane to São Paulo?' I shouted back. The plane had revved up and was slowly turning on to the runway with a spurt of deafening noise from the engine.

'Yes! You've just missed it!' he screamed back in rage. 'I've been looking everywhere for you and the plane is already twenty minutes late. You've missed it!'

'No! It mustn't go without me!' I exclaimed – and started running after the plane. I waved hysterically to the pilot, 'Come back! Come back!'

The big bird moved slowly away from us – and everyone began to crowd around me in consolation. In the V.I.P. lounge we had obviously been hidden away from the other passengers, and all attempts to find me had finally been given up.

I was terribly distressed because I knew that much had been done to ensure that my plane was met in São Paulo and I knew that if I missed that plane, I'd soon be lost in the ensuing confusion of arrivals from all over the world. What hotel was I to go to? What about the paintings I'd sent down? What was I expected to do? How would I ever be found again? Many nervous questions flew through my mind in torment as the plane lumbered down the air-strip.

Suddenly (and all turned pale with delight) the plane turned round and slowly headed back to me. When it got near enough, it stopped and its front steps astonishingly folded down. I was beckoned by a disbelieving stewardess.

I dashed up the stairs — to face a cabin-load of irate, disgruntled passengers. All were angry to have been held up while the search went on for 'the lady from London'. Tempers were short and I was greeted by glares of disgust and grunts of rage from men and women around me.

One long, hot, stormy hour later, the pilot announced to the passengers that, *thanks to me and my delay*, the plane had just missed a terrible tropical storm. All other planes had been sent to other airports — we were the first to land because the storm had subsided. People shook my hand in gratitude as we disembarked.

It had been a sensationally funny episode, and a good omen. The Biennale was a fascinating experience — and very important to my record as a painter.

Interesting
Talk

FOR fleeting moments and only rarely and only before tape-recorder became a dirty term, one did long to capture conversations for posterity (such as when a Jack Benny or a Peter Ustinov held forth, or when a political raconteur filled the room with great stories).

Since my guests flatter me by their trust, I don't repeat their conversations and don't even own one of those battery-operated devices. However, there are always a few stories which break no confidences, nor do any harm to recall.

One, for instance, told many years ago by the late President of the United States, Herbert Hoover, only came to mind recently at the time of ex-President Nixon's resignation drama.

Another time, at a luncheon in Sussex, Harold Macmillan announced with a wry smile (he later repeated it on television); 'The trouble with de Gaulle is that he never forgave the British for defeating the Germans.' Other Macmillan anecdotes about de Gaulle (whom the ex-Prime Minister personally liked and admired despite his intransigence) need no repeating – most have been told by him in public – but there's a special one, an amusing incident told to our guests and ourselves with relish about the visit of the French leader to Mr Macmillan's home in Sussex.

One illustrious occasion Mr Macmillan dined with us when John Alex McCone, once head of the C.I.A. and former Chairman of the United States Atomic Energy Commission, and his wife were weekend guests. Ignoring the rest of the guests rather absent-mindedly (which no one minded), the two men sat across the table, discussing significant events which had occurred during the terms of four American Presidents: Roosevelt, Truman, Eisenhower, Kennedy. In these years, both Mr Macmillan and Mr McCone were in the Cabinet or other high positions of Governments in both the United States and Great Britain.

289

We were all quite speechless, fascinated by the trigger-sharp total recall of the two distinguished gentlemen reminiscing over dramatic episodes; they were, in fact, dealing with modern history. When we got up from the table, I turned to Mr Macmillan and thanked him for his confidence.

Quite recently, in London, what a man didn't say to me at a small dinner-party turned into a story which might well be a classic in financial circles. His identity, for his sake, must remain secret.

A very different sort of conversation occurred whenever the late Sam Goldwyn was on hand. Though he made some of Hollywood's truly great films, he achieved a second kind of immortality by inventing the Sam Goldwyn language (in which he not only fractured English but generally got things *right* by saying them wrongly). For many years we used to tell each other stories and (to my eternal wonderment) I could even make *him* laugh.

Once, in order to return to serious conversation, I suddenly asked him if *he'd* ever consider writing his autobiography. Without a pause, he exclaimed: 'Certainly not! I can't do that until long after I'm dead!'

Nixon and Alger Hiss

The ordinarily tight-lipped Herbert Hoover discussed Richard Nixon with pleasure and pride one evening when I dined at his Waldorf Towers suite in New York City. Mr Hoover not only admired Nixon as a fellow-Republican, but applauded his vigilance on the Committee for Un-American Activities and for the way in which he trapped Alger Hiss – and so rode to fame. In spite of this admiration, the accounts of two American Presidents of an episode in American political history seem to me to differ widely – and I'd like to repeat Mr Hoover's version.

This generation probably never heard of the Un-American Committee, but the emotional controversies it unleashed in its search for Communists operating against America's interests in the Government and elsewhere rocked the United States during its tenure. Hence this account by an ex-President of one of its celebrated incidents is of interest. Mr Hoover particularly wanted to tell Mike Cowles and me the story of how Nixon got Alger Hiss safely inside his investigatory net.[1]

The Hiss affair began in the summer of 1948 on a sultry August day when Jay Vivian Chambers testified before Nixon's Committee and not only admitted he had been a Communist but that Alger Hiss had also been one – between 1935 and 1937. Hiss was a former New Dealer and highly-placed State Department official (and head of the Secretariat at the San Francisco Conference which established the United Nations organization). He was a mild man, whose hobby (and his wife's) was bird-watching.

He was soon embroiled in the sticky web of questioning which

[1] Ex-President Nixon himself describes the Hiss case as the first major crisis in his political life in his own book, *Six Crises* (published by W. H. Allen).

followed Chambers's testimony. 'Never before in the stormy history of the Committee was a more sensational investigation started by a less impressive witness,' Mr Nixon wrote in his book. When Chambers casually mentioned Alger Hiss, it was the first time Nixon gave the man a thought.

Mr Hiss demanded, by telegram, that the Committee give him an opportunity in public session to deny these allegations – and he was given the chance to do so the next day. After what Nixon describes as a virtuoso performance, Hiss left behind a clear impression of innocence; this was either a terrible case of mistaken identity or perhaps even a fantastic vendetta. But Hiss didn't completely overcome Nixon's aroused suspicions.

The Committee was in trouble with 90 per cent of the Press.[1] Even most of the Committee members thought a terrible mistake had been made and that an apology was owed to Hiss. Thus began a ground-swell: 'This case is going to kill the Committee unless it can prove Chambers's story,' was the common cry. Who had told the truth – the unsavoury-looking Chambers or the honest-looking Hiss?

The Committee re-convened in a virtual state of shock, berated for not checking Chambers's veracity before releasing his testimony.

Only Nixon disagreed – and his arguments prevailed. He was appointed to head a Sub-Committee to question Chambers again (this time in executive but *closed* session). Nixon not only wanted to trap Hiss, but to keep the Committee alive to serve a necessary and vital purpose.

On August 7th, the Committee met again to question Chambers. For three hours, Nixon bombarded the man with questions to prove in intimate detail whether he and Hiss had, in fact, been the friends Chambers claimed. This involved questions on the personal details of the Hiss family life, their possessions, their habits – and Communist activities. For nine days after, the

[1] There were other targets during the Committee's life: Nixon reached out to such big fry as President Truman and his Secretary of State, Dean Acheson, both of whom he accused of treason. He called Adlai Stevenson 'the arch-traitor of our generation', to which Mr Stevenson replied, more prophetically than anyone realized in 1952: 'Nixonland is a land of slander and scare, of sly innuendo, of a poison pen and anonymous telephone calls, and hustling, pushing and shoving – the land of smash and grab and anything to win.' Mr Stevenson didn't live to see Watergate.

Committee's staff worked round the clock to check Chambers's testimony. According to Nixon, Foster Dulles read the testimony and backed his decision to proceed with the case.

First, Nixon went to see Chambers alone. In dilapidated rocking chairs on the front porch of the farmhouse, both men discussed Hiss's involvement. Hiss was called to testify again in executive session on August 16th — a very different man. According to Nixon: 'now he was twisting, turning, evading, and changing his story to meet the evidence he knew we had.'

Mr Hoover's account which follows does not fit with Mr Nixon's own detailed version of the next steps, but Mr Hoover must certainly have believed it to be true to have passed it on: 'Nixon was convinced of Hiss's guilt. He studied all the testimony in minute detail and concluded that Hiss had to be brought back to testify yet again (after doing so for so many times — with increasing antagonism). Hiss had denounced Chambers's testimony and disavowed Communist connections — first in icy coolness and condescension and then in anger.

'This time,' Mr Hoover continued, 'Hiss declined to testify again. "I've done all the testifying I intend. You know all I know — and I'm a very busy person. I'd like to accommodate the Committee, but it happens that I must leave for New York tomorrow morning and proceed from there to Maine — where my wife is looking after a very sick son. Sorry. No more!" he announced.'[1]

Mr Hoover continued: 'Mr Nixon offered his sympathy but stood firm. "We understand your situation. If you can't spend the time in Washington, we'll come up to New York City and see you for an hour or so in the Commodore Hotel before you take your train. We don't want to inconvenience you in any way."[2]

'Reluctantly, Hiss had to give in. Reluctantly, he agreed to see them for one half hour. Reluctantly, he reminded them that his wife expected him to take the train and arrive on time that evening — that though he thought the whole exercise was expensive, time-consuming and unwarranted, he would, for the last

---

[1] In Nixon's account, Hiss pleaded that he was somewhat indisposed after just reading of the death of a friend.

[2] The Committee usually met in the Federal Courthouse in Foley Square (where in fact they had listened to hours of testimony by Whittaker Chambers).

time, agree to see the Committee members for a short discussion.

'The Commodore Hotel is built directly over New York City's Grand Central Station, from which all trains to the North depart. Meeting there would allow the maximum time with Mr Hiss, as well as the least inconvenience to him. A suite was reserved for the private special session, which began promptly at 3 p.m. on the Friday afternoon. Mr Hoover continued:

'Nixon carefully prepared his new interrogation, with questions designed to evade loopholes, too searching for facile replies. Apparently Hiss got more and more irritated. The half hour to which the interview was supposed to be limited stretched on and on. Although Hiss never committed himself, he lost his cool and became irritable. Suddenly, after half an hour had elapsed (and presumably long after the train he was to take had departed) the telephone rang.

'Who on earth could possibly know they were there (*in secret session*)? Nixon took the telephone call in the bedroom beyond closed doors. It was Hiss's wife, *in a white heat*, Mr Hoover explained.

' "Tell my husband I'm sick and tired of waiting around for him downstairs," she announced, "I'm going home for dinner. He can join me whenever he is ready!"

'The fictitious story about his wife tending a sick son four hours away from New York clinched Nixon's suspicions. Quite significantly, when the phone rang, the Committee was discussing Mrs Hiss's own reputed membership of the Communist Party. Mr Hiss's patience broke. So did the Committee's,' Mr Hoover concluded.

Hiss and Chambers finally had to confront each other and their past was linked. The inexplicable chain of events which sent Alger Hiss to prison had been set in motion.

Harold Macmillan and Charles de Gaulle

Harold Macmillan's anecdote about Charles de Gaulle was both amusing and revealing. No one can ever paraphrase him properly but one can try:

He and de Gaulle were privately great friends despite the French leader's well-known reserve about the British. De Gaulle wanted to see and speak to the Prime Minister, but he wanted at all costs to avoid the pomp and ceremony of a state visit. So he arranged an informal weekend when the British monarch was abroad. He also made it clear he would rather meet Mr Macmillan at his home in Sussex than at Chequers. This was, naturally, an inconvenience, but the Prime Minister agreed.

Preparations took weeks; security was a priority problem because, shortly before, one of the most dramatic assassination attempts had been made on de Gaulle's life. The official French aeroplane, when it landed at Gatwick Airport, carried a host of protectors; when the motorcade of cars left the airport for Chelwood Gate, it included de Gaulle's personal physician, French security men and detectives – and the requisite complement of British security staff.

Describing the occasion, Mr Macmillan went on: 'Conversation started that evening in earnest. Perhaps conversation is the wrong word. De Gaulle held the stage and pontificated. After about forty minutes, a junior male secretary, with fear and trepidation, passed a small note over my shoulder. The note read: "Mac wishes to see you".' Mac was his Scottish gamekeeper.

'I ignored it, of course,' Mr Macmillan told us. 'But within an hour, another note arrived, written in a different hand. It just said I was needed at once.

'I rose at this urgent summons. De Gaulle scowled: he was still in full sail.'

Outside the door, Macmillan (expecting a crisis of State) was astonished to see only his gamekeeper standing there. The fellow-Scot, who had served the Macmillans for many years, was a blunt and definite man, and he was plainly enraged.

'Either he goes – or I go,' he announced. 'All those French detectives are ruining the pheasant covers and we're meant to be shooting on Monday!'

Highly amused but not revealing it, the Prime Minister assured his irate gamekeeper that de Gaulle and retinue were leaving in a day.

Chuckling himself, he thought the story would really amuse Monsieur le Président: so on returning to the library, he retold the incident.

'It was greeted with icy silence and disapproval, I'm afraid,' Mr Macmillan commented enigmatically.

A London Banker: a classic in banking tales

At times, conversations can be dangerous, especially between strangers — as the following story suggests. It was not very long ago that a London banker and I crossed swords, at a most uncomfortable dinner-party. Introductions beforehand had been so inaudible, I never heard the name of the man I found on my right at table. If that fact worried me, it was of no importance to him.

He practically climbed into the plate of soup before him; head bent, working at it as if it was his first meal in weeks, never looking to the left or right, never speaking. Everywhere else chatter was lively; What have I done to be so strangely treated, I wondered? Did my being an American (a fact which no one ever actually brings up) call for unpleasant treatment?

Finally, I turned to him, explaining that I hadn't heard his name. Without looking up, he muttered it, but in his soup. I still didn't know it.

'What do you do?' I pursued.

'I'm a banker,' he responded, head still down.

'Well, talk banking to me then,' I demanded, my anger rising. 'I'm used to the subject.'

Silence followed. In a cold rage by then, I asked sharply: 'What bank?'

His own temper flared. Looking at me with impatience, he literally tossed the name of his bank at me. And there he met his unexpected Waterloo.

That same afternoon, a Wall Street banker, trying, I suppose, to impress me into changing my brokerage account to his firm in the U.S.A., telephoned me from New York City. Was I interested in making a fast and possibly big profit?

'What's the rub?' I asked suspiciously. My instinct was right.

'Oh, it's a fiddle, of course—but there's a lot of money in it. Such-and-such a bank in London' (and he named it), 'with whom we work, is going to unload a certain stock' —*and he named that too*. 'When the price has dropped quite a bit, you should buy. We're going to pick it up and buy heavily in the U.S.A. and then divide the loot.'

'But you must be mad! I don't go in for dishonest deals—and this one is particularly revolting,' I replied as I hung up.

The weapon in my hand was devastating: the rude person next to me had named his bank and it was the one the New York broker had identified in his rash telephone call a few hours earlier!

This time, in control, I turned on him with a broad smile and announced:

'Oh! Now I realize why you don't wish to talk to me; you're *ashamed* to do so because I know that you and your bank are involved in an illegal and revolting swindle over such-and-such shares!'

The man turned grey; he dropped his spoon in astonishment.

'How do *you* know?' he pleaded.

'If you weren't so insufferably rude, I'd tell you,' I announced quietly as I turned to the man on my left. The next course had arrived and I spent the rest of the meal in pleasant conversation.

The banker has tried since in every way conceivable to see me, talk to me, apologize. When last approached, I told a mutual friend who'd been sent to appeal to me, that there were no circumstances which would suggest my ever speaking to him again.

The Duke of Windsor: a luncheon in the Bois

One comment, which I think will delight readers, took place a
year or two before the Duke of Windsor died. I flew to Paris for a
luncheon with the Duchess and him in their home on the Bois. It
was a late October day; snow had fallen suddenly. The high green
gates and laurels and yews were smothered in frozen, glistening
icing. Inside, burning logs and immense bouquets of forced spring
blossoms and tulips and arum lilies dispelled the chill outside.

A tiny table for three was set by a garden window and the Duke,
though frail, came down to join us. His conversation covered a
wide range of subjects, which he explored knowledgeably but
still with curiosity. We even talked of fashion, since this was quite
natural with the Duchess. I asked the Duke if he was interested
in the subject. 'Not at all!' he responded.

'He isn't really interested in fashion; he only notices a thing
when it is terrible!' observed the Duchess.

But the Duke suddenly thought of Queen Mary and the way
she had dressed. 'My mother', he pointed out, 'never once
changed her style during the whole of her lifetime!'

It was the first time in over twenty years I'd heard him mention
his mother.

Last Word

This book is essentially a book about friends and what they mean to me. My life has always revolved around a pivotal threesome: expectation, achievement and friendship. I've built a highly personal existence on this trio, but as I grow older, friendship becomes the key ingredient. I've been able to make unusual friends (and some of them through most unusual circumstances) but what has been of the keenest importance to me is that most of them remain in my life. They are of enduring value to me. In some cases, I to them.

All are essential to the way I live, to my search for knowledge, my interest in ideas and politics, my connection with the arts and all things creative, and to my pleasure in being with and entertaining people I love and admire.

It isn't difficult to help a friend in need when one's own circle is so wide and so varied. I am intrigued that, so often, by tapping one friend to help out another, two favours are frequently done. I hope this makes me the right sort of catalyst.

A sense of timing and a dollop of luck are essential to anyone's success. If anything, this book (though only partial evidence) should suggest to the reader that I have much good fortune.

Index

Acheson, Dean, 24, 168–9, 292n
Adenauer, Dr Conrad, 148
Allen, Louis, 281–2
Ana Maria, 197n
Anderson, Clinton, 20
Aranha, Oswaldo, 19, 156–61, 161n, 162–4, 166
Arden, Elizabeth, 114
Argentina, 173–4, 176–80, 256–64
Arnold, Eve, 91n
Aronson, Boris, 98
Auriol, Jacqueline, 244–6, 247n

Bachauer, Gina, 174
Bacon, Francis, 74
Balderas, 198
Balfour, Sir Jock, 259–60
Barker, Ian, 281
Baruch, Belle, 143n ·
Baruch, Bernard, 80, 88, 143, 143n, 144–6, 146n, 147–55
Baruch, Bernard M, Jr, 143n
Baruch, Renee, 143n
Beauregard, General, 125
Beaverbrook, Lord, 87, 164
Bell, Laurence, 246
Belmonte, 198
Ben Gurion, David, 137
Benny, Jack, 289
Berlin airlift, 130–31, 131n
Bernal, Professor John, 95
Bernhard, Prince of Netherlands, 116
Bessborough, Lady, 32
Bessborough, Lord, 32
Besse, Antonin, 270, 270n
Besse, Christiane, 270
Biddle, Anthony J. Drexel, 181, 238

Biddle, Margaret Thompson, 181–3
Blixen, Baron Bror, 204
Blixen, Baroness Karen (Isaak Dinesen), 204–10
    Out of Africa, 204, 207–8; The Last Tales, 205; Anecdotes of Destiny, 205; Seven Gothic Tales, 207; Winter's Tales, 207
Bloody Precedent, 174, 176n, 178
Bolivar, Simon, 159
Bombois, Camille, 69, 71, 89–91, 91n
Bombois, Mme, 89–91
Bonnet, Mme, 245
Boppe, Raul, 284
Boppe, Mme Raul, 284
Bradley, General Omar, 115
Branco, Francesco de Castello, 198
Braque, Georges, 69, 77–9, 89, 99, 102
Breckenridge, Ouida da Costa, 235–6
Briand, Aristide, 159
Brook, Peter, 127
Buchwald, Art, 115
Burchett, Wilfred, 64
Bustorff-Silva, Dr Antonio Judice, 135–6
Byroade, Henry, 138
Byroade, Mrs, 138

Cairo, 137–40
Campora, Hector, 263
Carnicerito, 198
Carras, John, 174
Carreras, Sir James, 281n
Carreras, Lady, 281n
Case of Salvador Dali, The, 70n
Chagall, Marc, 74

303

Chambers, Jay Vivian, 291–4; Whittaker, 293n
Chandor, 149
Chaplin, Charlie, 189
Chase, Gertrude, 28
Chateaubriand, Assis de, 156, 164–9
Chiang Kai-shek, 184n
Chiang Kai-shek, Mme, 184, 184n, 185–7
Chirico, Giorgio de', 74
Christopherson, Vice-Chancellor, 281
Churchill, Lady (Baroness Spencer-Churchill), 81–2, 84, 86, 88, 91n, 151
Churchill, Randolph, 84, 86, 153–4
Churchill, Sir Winston, 24, 80–88, 91n, 115, 135, 149–55, 155n
Cintron, Conchita, 197–203
Clark, William, 270–71
Clifford, Clark, 38
Cochran, Jacqueline, 244, 246
Cohen, Mr, 57
Coit, Margaret L., 143–4
  Mr Baruch, the Man, the Myth, the Eighty Years, 143n
Converse, Dr John Marquis, 235–45, 247
Coronation of Queen Elizabeth II, 45, 111, 113–21, 165
Costa, Sergio Correa, 162
Courbet, Gustave, 102
Coward, Noel, 194, 275
Cowles, Gardner ('Mike'), 13, 43–4, 47–53, 55, 57, 59, 61–2, 141, 147, 154, 185, 291
Cuevas, Marquis de, 97–8
Cushing, Harvey, 237

Daily Mirror, 192, 267
Daily News (New York), 43
Daily Worker, 64
Dali, Salvador, 69–70, 74, 98, 105–6, 106n, 107, 253–5, 281–2
Dane, Clemence, 209

Dart, Jane, 185
Dart, Justin, 185
Davis, George, 54
Debuffet, 99
de Camara, Guy, 198
de Duarta, Juana Ibarguren, 180n
de Gaulle, General Charles, 135–6, 289, 295–6
Delvaux, Paul, 74
de Martel, Dr Thierry, 237, 239
Denman, Gilbert, 39
de Rosas, Carlos, 238
de Rosas, Encarnación, 178, 259–60
de Rosas, Manuel, 178–9, 259–60, 263
Des Moines Register, 47, 59
Des Moines Tribune, 47, 59
Dewey, Thomas E., 146, 146n
Dietrich, Marlene, 275
di Maggio, Joe, 195
Dominguin, Luis Miguel, 198–9
Donati, Enrico, 69, 97–8, 277
Dostoevsky, Fyodor Mikhailovich, 194
Doughty, Sir Charles, 80
Downey, Margaret, 181n
Downey, Morton, 181n
Dudley, Drew, 20, 21
Dufau, Michel, 100–101, 103
Dufau, Paul, 69, 99, 100–104
Dufau, Renée, 100–103
Dulles, Allen, 260–61
Dulles, John Foster, 114, 130, 293
Duncan, Isadora, 193

Eden, Sir Anthony, 119
Eisenhower, General Dwight D., 12, 18–19, 36, 59, 61, 113, 138, 147, 150, 157–8, 166, 189, 289
Eisenhower, Milton, 158
El Cordobes, 202
Elizabeth I, Queen, 116
Elizabeth II, Queen, 19, 37, 45, 111–14, 116–18, 120–21, 123–4, 165

Ellyn, Martha, 21
El Soldado, 198
Ernst, Max, 74
Erwin, Sam, 60
Esquire magazine, 53
Evening Star, 45

Fantin-Latour, Henri, 128
Farouk, King of Egypt, 140–42
Faulkner, William, 209
Finch-Hatton, Denys, 204
Flair magazine, 13, 27, 44, 51–2, 52n, 53–5, 69, 73, 147, 182–3
Fonteyn, Dame Margot, 128
Ford, Ruth, 205
Foreign Affairs magazine, 139
Foyle, Christina, 13
Frederika, Queen of Greece, 119, 121, 275–6
Frondizi, President, 263

Gaona, 'Armillita', 198
Garbo, Greta, 135
Garden, Mary, 278
Garland, Judy, 126
Garza, Lorenzo, 198
Gauthier, Simonne, 77–8, 89–90
George, Colonel, 120–21
Gillies, Sir Harold, 238
Gingrich, Arnold, 53
Gnoli, Dominico, 72–4
Goebbels Diaries, The, 161n
Goldwater, Barry, 25n
Goldwyn, Sam, 290
Graca, Annibal, 162
Grace, Princess of Monaco, 33
Graham, Kay, 20
Grant, General, 125
Greene, Amy, 188
Greene, Milton, 188, 190
Greenhill, Denis, 119, 119n, 120
Greenson, Dr Ralph, 196
Griffis, Stanton, 256, 258
Guggenheim, Alicia, 145
Guggenheim, Harry, 145

Gunther, John, 46, 61
   Inside Europe, 46n; *Inside USA*, 46n; *Inside Africa*, 46n; *Inside South America*, 46n

Haile Selassie, Emperor, 270
Hatem, Dr Mohammed, 138–9
Hearst, William Randolph, 164
Hemingway, Ernest, 208
Herald Tribune (Paris), 193
Herbert, Sir Alan P., 130–32
Hickenlooper, Senator, 147
Himmler, Heinrich, 179
Hiroshima, 25, 146n
Hiss, Alger, 291, 291n, 292–3, 293n, 294
Hitler, Adolf, 177, 179
Hogarth, William, 111
Hollis, General Sir Leslie, 119–21
Hoover, Herbert, 17–18, 20–21, 27, 27n, 28, 150, 279, 291, 293–4
Hopper, Hedda, 143
Horsley, Sir Victor, 237
Howe, Louis McHenry, 30
Humphrey, Hubert, 38

Ingelfingen, Prince Hohenlohe, 181n

Jackson, Charles, 21
Jaipur, Ayesha, 174–5
Janusse, President, 179
Jeffress, Arthur, 72
John XXIII, Pope, 277–9
Johnson, Claudia (Lady Bird), 22–3, 32–6, 36n, 37–9, 173
   White House Story, 32n
Johnson, Luci, 32–3, 35
Johnson, Lynda Bird, 32, 34–5
Johnson, Lyndon Baines, 18, 23, 32–8
   The Vantage Point, 38
Jones Siriol, 193
Juin, General, 116

Karanjian Dr V. H., 237

Kennedy, John F., 36, 37, 241, 289
Kennedy, Joseph, 241
Kennedy, Robert, 57, 58n
Kissinger, Dr Henry, 18, 36
Klee, Paul, 74, 99
Koestler, Arthur, 58
  Darkness at Noon, 58
Korean War, 24, 26, 61–5
Kubitschek, President, 167
Labisse, 74
Labouisse, Eve, 23–4
Labouisse, Henry, 23–4
Lago, Antonio Correa do, 162
Lambert, Baron, 76
Lartigan, Andrée, 276
Lastiri, Norma, 264
Lastiri, Raul, 264
Lee, Laurie, 268
  Cider with Rosie, 268
Lehman, Robert, 105–7
Leigh, Vivien, 194
Leighton, Margaret, 209
Lenya, Lotte, 54
Levin, Bernard, 73
Life magazine, 266
Lincoln, Abraham, 19
Lippmann, Walter, 31
Look magazine, 12, 27, 43, 47–50,
  52–3, 61, 69, 77, 90, 176, 188, 235,
  261
Loos, Anita, 173
  Gentlemen Prefer Blondes, 173
Luce, Clare Booth, 113, 143
Luce, Henry, 159
  The Ideas of Henry Luce, 159
Luis, Pepe, 198
Luiz, Washington, 157

MacArthur, General Douglas, 26,
  61
McCarthy, Joseph, 57–8, 58n, 59–60,
  121
McCone, John Alex, 60, 289
McDermott, Eugene, 33
MacDonald, Ken, 59

McIndoe, Sir Archibald, 238, 238n,
  239
McIndoe, Lady (Constance), 239
McKay, Mrs, 241
Macmillan, Harold, 128, 289–90,
  295–6
Magritte, René, 74
Mailer, Norman, 188, 196
Malechek, Mrs Dale, 35
Manoleto, 198
Marietta, 77, 79
Marshall, George Catlett, 113,
  115–16, 119–21
Marshall, Mrs, 119–21
Mary, Queen, 299
Maugham, W. Somerset, 84, 86, 148
Maxwell, Elsa, 275
Mead, Margaret, 251
Meir, Golda, 173
Melbourne, Lord, 111, 122
Mellon, Ailsa, 240
Menuhin, Yehudi, 75
Meyer, Eugene, 20
Meyer, Tom Montague, 12, 70, 94,
  127–8, 136, 149
Migel, Parmenia, 207
Miller, Arthur, 191, 193, 195
Miller, Merle, 58n
  Plain Thinking, 58n
Miró, Joan, 74, 99
Modigliani, Amedeo, 71
Molyneux, Captain Edward, 76
Monroe, Marilyn, 188–96, 206
Monteiro, Joes, 157
Morrison, William Shepherd, 132
Morse, A. Reynolds, 106n
Murrow, Ed, 151
Murrow, Janet, 151
Mussolini, Benito, 262

Nagasaki, 25
Naguib, General, 140–41
Nasser, Colonel Gamal Abdel, 19,
  57, 59, 137–42, 273
Nasser, Mrs, 139

Navarro, Elizabeth, 147–50
Neatta, 74
New York Times, 76, 174
Nguyen Cao Ky, 36
Nichols, Beverly, 75
   The Art of Flower Arrangements, 75
Niehans, Dr, 148
Nijinska, Mme, 98
Nixon, Richard M., 27, 289, 291, 291n, 292, 292n, 293, 293n, 294
   Six Crises, 291n

Observer, 191
Offergeld, Robert, 55
Olivier, Laurence (Lord Olivier), 190, 194–5
Onassis, Aristotle, 86
Ordonez, Antonio, 198–9
Oursler, Fulton, 187

Pace, Frank, 65
Pagliacci, 152
Pallavacini de Berzeviczy, Count Federico, 54–5
Panmunjon Truce Conference, 61, 63–5
Parsons, Louella, 195
Paul, King of Greece, 22, 275–6
Pearson, Drew, 114
Pedroza, Sylvio, 167
Penrose, Roland, 95
Perón, Eva, 159, 173–4, 176–7, 177n, 178–80, 180n, 256–62, 264
Perón, Isabel, 259, 264
Perón, Juan, 173–4, 176–7, 177n, 178–80, 257, 259–64
Picabia, 74
Picasso, Jacqueline, 95
Picasso, Pablo, 69, 74, 79, 95–6, 102
Pius XII, Pope, 148
Power, Tyrone, 167
Procuna, 198
Pryce-Jones, Alan, 13

Qabus bin Said, Sultan, 274

Rainier, Prince of Monaco, 33
Ramie, Hugette, 96
Ramie, Jean, 96
Ramie, Suzanne, 96
Rattigan, Terence, 194–5
Ravel, Maurice, 98
Rayburn, Sam, 20
Realités, 182–3
Rega, Lopez, 264
Ridgeway, General Matthew, 62–3
Roe, Mrs Frederick, 123
Roosevelt, Eleanor, 18, 29–31
   On My Own, 31
Roosevelt, Franklin D., 18, 24–5, 27, 29–31, 145, 158–9, 161n, 185, 289
Roosevelt, Theodore, 30
Rosa, Jana Guimares, 70
   Stones, 70
Rose, Billy, 144, 240–41
Rostow, Walt, 33
Rousseau, Henri, 71, 89
Rousseau, Ted, 107
Ruark, Robert, 144
Rubinstein, Helena, 209–10
Ruby, Jack, 60

Sadat, President, 139
Said bin Taimur, Sultan, 271n, 272–3
Schine, Mr, 57
Schuman, Henri, 116
Scott, Ruth, 209
Scott, Zachary, 209
Shakespeare, William, 132
Shaw, George Bernard, 193
Sickert, Walter, 81–2
Sidey, Hugh, 38
Silverio, 198
Sinyavsky, 73
Sitwell, Dame Edith, 206
Soames, Sir Christopher, 81
Soames, Lady (Mary), 81, 88
Sola, Ugo, 161
Solorzano, 198
Spellman, Cardinal, 241
Spry, Constance, 117

Stark, Freya, 269
Stern, G. B., 209
Stevenson, Adlai, 292n
Stevenson, Sir Ralph, 141
Steves, Marshall, 39
Steves, Mrs Marshall, 39
Stone, William, 122–5
Strasberg, Lee, 193
Sunday Times, 193
Sutherland, Graham, 69, 80–88
Svendsen, Clara, 205
Symington, Stuart, 57, 60

Taft, Senator, 27
Tamayo, Olga, 92–4
Tamayo, Rufino, 69, 92–4
Tanguy, 74
Taylor, Elizabeth, 195
Thant, U, 260
Thompson, Colonel William Boyce, 184
Thoms, Wells, 274
Thomson, Lord, 164
Time magazine, 38
Time-Life, 159
Times, The, 25, 73n, 192, 268, 272
Tito, President, 26
Todd, Mike, 195
Townsend, Aina, 28
Truman, Bess, 22
Truman, Harry S., 17, 19, 20, 22–5, 25n, 26, 27n, 58n, 146n, 150, 289, 292n
Truman, Martha, 25
Turner, J. M. W., 129–30

Ustinov, Peter, 289
Utrillo, Maurice, 71

Vandenberg, General, 246

Van Ess, Blanche, 148
Vanity Fair, 143
Van Meergeven, 106n
Vargas, Getulio, 19, 157–8, 160–61, 161n
Vavra, Robert, 75, 199n
    Tiger Flower, 75, 75n; *Lion and Blue*, 75; *Bulls of Iberia*, 199n
Vazquez, Manola, 198
Vermeer, Jan, 105–6, 106n, 107
Vertes, Marcel, 98
Vester, Bertha Stafford, 189–90, 196
    Our Jerusalem — An American Family In The Holy City, 190n
Victoria, Queen, 114

Wallace, De Witt, 240
Wallace, Mike, 49–50
Warren, Chief Justice Earl, 37, 115–16
Washington Post, 20–21
Waterfield, Brigadier Pat, 271, 271n, 272–3, 273n
Watergate, 57, 60
Welch, Joseph Nye, 58
Welles, Sumner, 161
West, Rebecca, 209
Weybright, Helen, 22
Weybright, Victor, 22
Widgery, Lady, 136
Widgery, Lord Chief Justice, 136
Willkie, Wendell L., 47, 159
Wilson, Woodrow, 145, 150
Windsor, Duchess of, 299
Windsor, Duke of, 148, 299
Winnington, Alan, 64
Wiseman, Carl, 265–7
Wohlstetter, Charles, 241
Wood, Alan, 69–70
Wood, Daniel, 69–70
Wylie, Philip, 30

Publisher's
Note

Since so many chapters in this book reflect Fleur Cowles' past experiences, you may wonder about her life today. One simple word describes it completely: *crowded*.

She still roams the world, whether to launch a book or open another exhibition of paintings, to satisfy a newly aroused curiosity, or to go somewhere on behalf of the World Wildlife Fund, or just to visit friends—distance being no barrier, particularly since the advent of the Concorde. Last year she took a Concorde flight to Venezuela, to visit the then governor of Caracas (now the Minister of Tourism and Communications and, as she points out, inevitably the President of his country). She first met Diego and Tiqui Arria at a World Wildlife Congress, and the instant friendship which bound them together soon required exchange visits. Venezuela is now another country on her itinerary. In recent years the LBJ Ranch in Texas has become a regular destination. Fleur Cowles continues to think of Lady Bird Johnson as "First Lady." They spend much time together in exploring places— whether Texas, Mexico, Sussex, or Spain. Each journey brings new stories and new friends.

Recently she was honored by Spain, given the Order de la Dama de Isabela Católica, an unusual tribute to a person from another country. Previously Fleur Cowles had received decorations from France, Greece, England, and Brazil. The medal from Spain expresses official appreciation for her restoration of a historic castle in the depths of untraveled Estremadura in Spain.

The castle, which she bought in ruins eight years ago, has been expertly reconstructed according to old drawings. Once used as an *alcázar* (fortress), the original site dates back to the fifth century; Romans, Visigoths, Moors, and Spaniards all left their imprint there. Other than a view from its towers of miles of countryside, only crenellations of ancient buildings can be seen. Pizarro, and some eighteen other Spanish conquistadors of Latin America from Mexico to Peru, left the hard Estremadura countryside to find a better life elsewhere. With the history of the Spanish explorers of Latin America in mind, it pleases Fleur Cowles to think of the restoration of the castle by an American.

When she is in residence in Spain, enjoying the Moorish garden she created behind the ancient walls, the past is always with her. There she leads a peaceful life working on new books, or painting for a coming exhibition. Her most recent show was in the Singer Museum in Holland, the fifth museum to exhibit her work. She has often been identified as "the lady who paints jungle animals and flowers," but there is nothing so naïve in her work as this description might imply. Exhibitions include tapestries, enameled boxes, and limited edition prints, as well as paintings on wooden panels. Her work is in a number of important public collections including those in the Seattle Art Museum, the A. Reynolds Morse Museum in Cleveland, the A. Block Museum in Rio de Janeiro, at Loyola-Marymount College in California, and at the Fisher Foundation in Iowa, as well as a number of others.

As an International Trustee of the World Wildlife Fund, she has organized the first exhibition in art history in which nearly thirty of the world's most prestigious artists have almost simultaneously presented works on a single theme, "The Animal in Art." Involved are such diverse museums as the Smithsonian in Washington, the British Museum in London, Topkapi in Turkey, and the Los Angeles County Museum in California.

An important companion to these museum activities is the book Fleur Cowles invited the distinguished art historian Kenneth Clark, author of *Civilisation,* to write. Lord Clark's book, *Animals and Men,* explores man's attitudes toward animals throughout history as reflected in Western art. It was published in October,

1977, by William Morrow & Company, and all sales benefit the World Wildlife Fund.

The European-based Louis E. B. Leakey Foundation was recently launched in England with a conference of distinguished international scientists in the spheres of anthropology, paleontology, and human history. Fleur Cowles is chairman of this Foundation and a trustee in the United States.

Her homes in London and Sussex are meeting places for people from all over the world who share her special interest in wildlife and the arts. The general concern on most occasions is for the future of all mankind, and often certain subjects implying an uncommon trust in her discretion are openly discussed at her table. That is perhaps the greatest honor that has been paid to her, and she treasures it.